Dover Memorial Library
Gardner-Webb University
P.O. Box 836
Boiling Springs, N.C. 28017

D1226812

FOR REFERENCE
Not to be taken from library
GARDNER-WEBB UNIVERSITY LIBRARY

WOMEN AND RELIGION IN BRITAIN AND IRELAND

An Annotated Bibliography from the Reformation to 1993

DALE A. JOHNSON

ATLA Bibliography Series, No. 39

The Scarecrow Press, Inc.
Lanham, Md., & London

R◦F,
HQ
1394
.J64
1995

SCARECROW PRESS, INC.

Published in the United States of America
by Scarecrow Press, Inc.
4720 Boston Way
Lanham, Maryland 20706

4 Pleydell Gardens, Folkestone
Kent CT20 2DN, England

Copyright © 1995 by Dale Johnson

British Cataloguing-in-Publication Information Available

Library of Congress Cataloging-in-Publication Data
Johnson, Dale A., 1936-
Women and religion in Britain and Ireland : an annotated bibliography from
the Reformation to 1993 / by Dale A. Johnson
p.   cm. — (ATLA bibliography series: no. 29)
Includes bibliographical references and index.
1. Women and religion—England—History—Bibliography. 2. Women
and religion–Ireland–History–Bibliography. I. Title. II. Series.
Z7963.R45J64   1995   [HQ1394]   016.2'0082–dc20   95-33428 CIP
ISBN 0-8108-3063-9 (cloth : alk. paper)

♾™ The paper used in this publication meets the minimum requirements of
American National Standard for Information Sciences—Permanence of
Paper for Printed Library Materials, ANSI Z39.48–1984.
Manufactured in the United States of America.

To the earliest groups of students

who worked with me

in this subject —

for their interest and encouragement

CONTENTS

3 1640-1740: Civil War and Restoration; Women in the Quaker Movement and the Larger Culture

4 1740-1850: The Evangelical Revival and the Ideal of Womanhood

5 1850-1914: The Women's Movement, Social Reform, and Suffrage

6 1914 to the Present: Retrenchment, Secularization, and Women's Ministries

Contents

ABBREVIATIONS

AEH	*Anglican and Episcopal History*
AHR	*American Historical Review*
BIHR	*Bulletin of the Institute of Historical Research*
BJRL	*Bulletin of the John Rylands Library*
BRH	*Bulletin of Research in the Humanities*
EHR	*English Historical Review*
ELR	*English Literary Renaissance*
HMPEC	*Historical Magazine of the Protestant Episcopal Church*
IJWS	*International Journal of Women's Studies*
IRM	*International Review of Missions*
IRSH	*International Review of Social History*
JBS	*Journal of British Studies*
JEH	*Journal of Ecclesiastical History*
JFHS	*Journal of the Friends Historical Society*
JHI	*Journal of the History of Ideas*
JPHS	*Journal of the Presbyterian History Society*
JRH	*Journal of Religious History*
JSH	*Journal of Social History*
JURCHS	*Journal of the United Reformed Church History Society*
PMLA	*Publications of the Modern Language Association*
PWHS	*Proceedings of the Wesley Historical Society*
RSCHS	*Records of the Scottish Church History Society*
SCH	*Studies in Church History*
SCJ	*Sixteenth Century Journal*
TBHS	*Transactions of the Baptist Historical Society*
TCHS	*Transactions of the Congregational Historical Society*
TJHSE	*Transactions of the Jewish Historical Society of England*
TSWL	*Tulsa Studies in Women's Literature*
TUHS	*Transactions of the Unitarian Historical Society*
UMPWS	*University of Michigan Papers in Women's Studies*
WSIF	*Women's Studies International Forum*

EDITOR'S FOREWORD

Since 1974 the American Theological Library Association has been publishing this bibliography series with the Scarecrow Press. Guidelines for projects and selections for publication are made by the ATLA Publications Section in consultation with the editor. Our goal is to stimulate and encourage the preparation and publication of reliable bibliographies and guides to the literature of religious studies in all of its scope and variety. Compilers are free to define their field, to make their own selections, and to work out internal organization as the unique demands of the subject indicate. We are pleased to publish Professor Johnson's *Women and Religion in Britain and Ireland*.

Following undergraduate studies at Colgate and Oxford Universities, Dale A. Johnson received the B.D. degree from the Lutheran School of Theology at Chicago and took a doctorate in church history at Union Theological Seminary in New York City. He is the author of several books, including *Women in English Religion, 1700-1925* (1983) and numerous scholarly articles. Since 1969 he has taught church history at Vanderbilt University in Nashville, Tennessee.

Kenneth E. Rowe
Series Editor

Drew University Library
Madison, NJ 07940
USA

PREFACE

The connection between women and religion is certainly no less complex than that between women and fiction discussed by Virginia Woolf in *A Room of One's Own* (1929). It is not simply determined by activity or conviction, however important each of these is; it is also about reflection, perception, image, and ideal; and it is about power, prophecy, resistance, and critique. When taken with an historical focus, the complexity increases. To present some access to that connection and to its complexity in British and Irish history since the sixteenth century is the primary purpose of this bibliography.

In the past two decades, interest in women's history in Britain and Ireland has steadily risen. Within that investigation, the recognition that religion is an important and multivalent part of that history has led to increased attention to that particular dimension. Scholars who have taken up this subject since its emergence in the 1970s occasionally still express surprise at the importance of religion in the lives of women. Perhaps with greater awareness of the research already accomplished, this sense of surprise will be reduced, the connection more appropriately made, and the larger story better told. The connection is engaging not only because there are multiple levels, but because the relationship is significantly ambiguous—religious institutions and convictions have been part of the structures of patriarchy, but they have also been occasions of opportunity and empowerment as well. Interest in the subject has been heightened by several contemporary topics and questions before the public, including a substantial body of feminist scholarship offering multiple perspectives and the question of the ordination of women to the Anglican priesthood (the latter taking a new turn with the first ordinations in England in March, 1994).

At this point in the development of work on the connection between women and religion, it would be difficult to call it a recognized trajectory of historical scholarship, much less a field of study.

The relevant materials are extensive, but they are scattered and of greatly varying quality; of the many perspectives and points of view, some are clearly antiquated and others are strongly contested. Only recently have broader and more synthetic studies begun to appear; more will surely follow, but no comprehensive bibliography exists to guide readers and potential researchers to what is available. This volume makes such an effort. It attempts to comprehend the substantial work that has been produced on both sides of the Atlantic and spread over a range of journals, collections, and networks. It recognizes the significantly interdisciplinary character of the scholarship relevant to the subject by including topics pursued and questions investigated in such fields as literature, social history, and women's studies, thus considerably extending the standard sources used in the study of religious history. Important new issues of interpretation have emerged as topics previously thought to be exhausted have been explored from new, especially feminist, angles, such as the contributions of Renaissance humanism, the distinctiveness of the Puritan perspective on women, Milton's usefulness as a supporter or critic of a patriarchal system, and the roles of women in nineteenth-century moral reform movements. While there is no substitute for engaging original sources, perhaps the greater visibility of scholarship that pursues gender questions will enlarge the sense of the importance of such questions for historical understanding and assist in the enrichment and revision of historical narrative.

There is also some gain in presenting a larger picture of the subject than is usually available to those who work on particular dimensions of it. Scholars who do research on Quakers in the seventeenth century or Methodists in the eighteenth, for example, would at this point be aware of resources that explore the special relationship of each movement to women; yet that awareness seldom extends to themes or issues outside of the individual movement being pursued. And by noting the range of scholarship on a particular topic, it is possible for a discerning reader to identify gaps in those many places that still await more serious attention than they have received to date. In addition, one might hope that the various religious traditions themselves would profit from greater historical perspective and critical assessment of women's engagement with religion as they face contemporary issues relating to women, their ministries, and their future.

The period of coverage in this bibliography is from 1500 to the present, with the latest entries being from 1993. The sixteenth century is an appropriate starting point because the earlier medieval period has its own literature and can more easily be tied to continental developments than the later centuries can be. The chronological divisions marking the chapters are more benchmarks than self-contained units, but I thought they fit the topic better than other standard periodizations. Some unavoidable overlap in the literature occurs especially when an article or monograph pursues a topic over the course of a particular century; where items overlap chronological periods in their scope, they are usually placed in the earliest one. Because of the liveliness of recent issues, the current generation of publications on contemporary issues and topics is also included, so as to provide a guide to those discussions and controversies and to their connection to older questions; but in this case, newspaper and magazine coverage of current events are not represented here.

The bibliography presents secondary materials on the broad subject of women and religion published in the twentieth century, with materials on some related topics as they seem helpful for context or broader understanding. This rather wide net is intended to assist in providing both scope and perspective; the risk with such a wide net is that important items might be missed or items of dubious usefulness included, but that risk seemed worth the potential gain of offering an introduction to writings on the subject. While a few nineteenth-century historical accounts continue to be valuable for certain topics, they are not so numerous as to represent much loss in their exclusion. Except for a small number of anthologies and for a cross-section of twentieth-century, including contemporary, materials, primary sources are not part of this volume; the notes to many of the resources here catalogued will provide substantial guides to primary texts and documents. I have also reviewed but decided not to include a large number of additional potential resources, in order to keep even this focus reasonably clear; different persons might make different decisions, but any gaps in topic selection or the omission of relevant items, together with any errors that may still exist in this presentation, are, of course, my responsibility.

The material is organized by topics in each chapter, in an order that I hope will make the resources accessible to a reader. I have attempted to classify the most helpful material or to provide a sense of the development of scholarship on a particular topic; in contrast to some other similar bibliographies, an alphabetical organization did not often appear particularly useful. To reduce the size of the volume somewhat, the names of publishers have been shortened to a minimum (e.g., "Oxford" when standing in the place of the publisher means Oxford University Press and "Indiana" means Indiana University Press), only one publication location is given for any item (in those cases that could be determined, the primary one is used), and a number of frequently repeated journal titles are abbreviated. Some inconsistencies in names or style reflect the actual variety in the literature itself.

Thanks are due to a number of institutions and individuals associated with them who made library resources and catalog systems available to me, including the Vanderbilt University Library (especially to Anne Womack in the Divinity Library); the Cambridge University Library; the theological libraries and librarians of Westminster College, Wesley House, and Westcott House, Cambridge; the Bodleian Library, Oxford; Fawcett Library, London; the Library of the Society of Friends, London; and St. Andrew's House, London. Among the individuals who responded to requests for assistance, special thanks go to Anne Barstow, Richard Golden, Bonnelyn Young Kunze, Mary Tanner, Charles Wallace, Edwin T. Welch, and Diane Willen. Denise Gyauch and Carol Sumner, graduate students in religion at Vanderbilt, assisted in the research at two different stages of the project; and Arliene Dearing provided valuable secretarial aid as well as answers to my computer questions. I am grateful for financial support from the American Theological Library Association and from Dean Joseph C. Hough, Jr., of the Vanderbilt Divinity School to pursue the project.

CHAPTER 1

GENERAL STUDIES

Biographical Dictionaries

1   Todd, Janet, ed. *Dictionary of British Women Writers*. London:
    Routledge, 1989. Pp. 762.
    Over 450 authors from the Middle Ages to the present.

2   Schlueter, Paul and June, eds. *An Encyclopedia of British Wom-
    en Writers*. New York: Garland, 1988. Pp. 516.
    Nearly 400 entries, from the Middle Ages to the present.

3   Crawford, Anne, et al., eds. *The EUROPA Biographical Dic-
    tionary of British Women*. London: Europa, 1983. Pp. 436.
    Short entries for more than one thousand individuals over the
    course of British history, with a good selection of women in
    religious activities.

4   Parbury, Kathleen. *Women of Grace: A Biographical Dictionary
    of British Women Saints, Martyrs, and Reformers*. Stocksfield:
    Oriel, 1984. Pp. 199.
    The biographical dictionary (Part One) goes up to 1845; but the
    focus is on the early and medieval periods, with only sketchy
    coverage of individuals after 1500.

5   Uglow, Jennifer S., ed. *The Continuum Dictionary of Women's
    Biography*. New York: Continuum, 1989. Pp. 621.
    International; expanded version of 1982 publication, with brief
    entries for some two thousand women.

6   *Dictionary of Literary Biography*.   Detroit: Gale Research Co.,
     1978- .
     A multi volume work, including a substantial number of British
     authors.

Bibliographies and Guides

7   Falk, Joyce Duncan.   "The New Technology for Research in
     European Women's History: 'Online' Bibliographies," *Signs* 9
     (1983): 120-33.
     Discusses the possibilities and limitations of database searching.

8   Kanner, Barbara, ed. *The Women of England from Anglo-Saxon
     Times to the Present: Interpretive Bibliographical Essays*. Hamp-
     den, CT: Archon, 1979. Pp. 429.
     Uses a rather traditional periodization, and only limited help on
     the subject of religion, but this is a good introduction to different
     literatures and topics. The relevant essays include: Barbara Kan-
     ner, "Introduction: Old and New Women's History," pp. 9-31;
     Rosemary Masek, "Women in an Age of Transition: 1485-1714,"
     pp. 138-82; Barbara B. Schnorrenberg with Jean E. Hunter, "The
     Eighteenth-century Englishwoman," pp. 183-228; Karl van den
     Steinen, "The Discovery of Women in Eighteenth-century English
     Political Life," pp. 229-58; Sheila Ryan Johansson, "Demograph-
     ic Contribution to the History of Victorian Women," pp. 259-95;
     Patricia O. Klaus, "Women in the Mirror: Using Novels to Study
     Victorian Women," pp. 296-344; Neal A. Ferguson, "Women in
     Twentieth-century England," pp. 345-87; Jeffrey Weeks, "A
     Survey of Primary Sources and Archives for the History of Early
     Twentieth-century English Women," pp. 388-421.

9   Davis, Gwenn and Joyce, Beverly A., comps. *Personal Writings
     by Women to 1900: A Bibliography of American and British
     Writers*. London: Mansell, 1989. Pp. 294.
     Nearly five thousand annotated entries, mostly from the nine-
     teenth century; a subject index helps to locate religious entries.

10   Frey, Linda, et al., eds. *Women in Western European History: A
     Select Chronological, Geographical, and Topical Bibliography*.

New York: Greenwood, 1982-86.
Chronological divisions, subdivided by country and topic; no annotations. Vol. 1: From Antiquity to the French Revolution, pp. 760; Vol. 2: The Nineteenth and Twentieth Centuries, pp. 1024; Vol. 3: First Supplement, pp. 699.

11 Cline, Cheryl. *Women's Diaries, Journals, and Letters: An Annotated Bibliography*. New York: Garland, 1989. Pp. 716.
Nearly three thousand entries, with a heavy Anglo-American representation.

12 Matthews, William. *British Diaries: An Annotated Bibliography of British Diaries Written Between 1442 and 1942*. Berkeley: California, 1950. Pp. 339.
Organized by year in which the particular diary began.

13 _____, comp. *British Autobiographies: An Annotated Bibliography of British Autobiographies Published or Written Before 1951*. Berkeley: California, 1955. Pp. 376.
Organized by author; a comprehensive index provides help in locating religious materials and autobiographies by women.

14 Ballou, Patricia K. *Women: A Bibliography of Bibliographies*. 2nd ed., Boston: G. K. Hall, 1986. Pp. 268.
Over nine hundred entries; this would be especially helpful if pursuing a subject in the field of religion which has connections with another field or topic.

15 Begos, Jane D. *Annotated Bibliography of Published Women's Diaries*. Pound Ridge, NY: n.p., 1977. Pp. 66.
Eclectic and heavily Anglo-American.

16 Brady, Anna. *Women in Ireland: An Annotated Bibliography*. Westport, CT: Greenwood, 1988. Pp. 478.
Several useful topical sections, including lists of important individuals.

17 Rosenberg, Marie Barovic and Bergstrom, Len B., eds. *Women and Society: A Critical Review of the Literature with a Selected*

Annotated Bibliography. Beverly Hills: Sage, 1975. Pp. 354.
Entries cover several disciplines, but organization by author
makes the sections on history and philosophy and religion less
useful than they might have been.

18   Een, JoAnn D. and Rosenberg-Dishman, Marie B., eds.
      Women and Society: An Annotated Bibliography. Beverly Hills:
      Sage, 1978. Pp. 277.
      Continues the above, with an additional 2400 entries.

19   Gilbert, V. F. and Tatla, D. S. *Women's Studies: A Bibliogra-
      phy of Dissertations, 1870-1982*. Oxford: Blackwell, 1985. Pp.
      496.
      Multi-disciplinary coverage, from Arts to Third World.

20   *Historical Research for Higher Degrees in the United Kingdom*.
      London: Institute of Historical Research, 1933- .
      Annual volumes on theses completed and in progress.

21   Bilboul, Roger, ed. *Retrospective Index to Theses of Great Brit-
      ain and Ireland, 1716-1950*. Vol. 1: Social Sciences and Hu-
      manities. Santa Barbara: ABC-Clio, 1975. Pp. 393.
      Contains subject and author indexes.

22   Beddoe, Deirdre. *Discovering Women's History: A Practical
      Manual*. London: Pandora, 1983. Pp. 232.
      Suggestions and resources for entering the subject, especially at
      a local level.

General Histories

23   Bloch, Ruth H. "Untangling the Roots of Modern Sex Roles: A
      Survey of Four Centuries of Change," *Signs* 4 (1978): 237-52.
      Considers two significant transitions in the definition of sex
      roles, the first occurring in the sixteenth and seventeenth cen-
      turies, and the second in the eighteenth and nineteenth; though
      very broad in scope, it gives considerable attention to England.

24   Offen, Karen, et al., eds. *Writing Women's History: Interna-*

tional Perspectives. Bloomington: Indiana, 1991. Pp. 552.
Essays on recent work and issues, including Jane Rendall, "Uneven Developments: Women's History, Feminist History, and Gender History in Great Britain," pp. 45-57; and Mary Cullen, "Women's History in Ireland," pp. 429-41.

25 Anderson, Bonnie S. and Zinsser, Judith. *A History of Their Own: Women in Europe from Pre-history to the Present*. 2 vols., New York: Harper & Row, 1988. Pp. 591 and 572.
Argues that gender gives a basic commonality to the lives of all European women (xv).

26 Davis, Natalie Z. "Gender and Genre: Women as Historical Writers, 1400-1820," in *Beyond Their Sex: Learned Women of the European Past*, ed. Patricia H. Labalme. New York: NYU, 1980. Pp. 153-82.
While broader than Britain, important for perspective.

27 Phillips, Roderick. *Putting Asunder: The History of Divorce in Western Society*. Cambridge: Cambridge, 1988. Pp. 672.
The English situation is included in this wide-ranging study.

28 Marshall, Rosalind K. *Virgins and Viragos: A History of Women in Scotland from 1080 to 1980*. London: Collins, 1983. Pp. 365.
Much of the focus until the final section is on the domestic sphere; only an occasional glimpse into women's religious interests and activities.

29 Rogers, Katharine M. *The Troublesome Helpmate: A History of Misogyny in Literature*. Seattle: Washington, 1966. Pp. 288.
From the ancient world to the twentieth century, an exploration of male fear, dislike, or contempt of women; plenty of opportunity for illustrations using religious authority as justification.

30 Stenton, Doris M. *The English Woman in History*. London: Allen & Unwin, 1957. Pp. 363.
From Anglo-Saxon England to Mill's *Subjection of Women* (1869), with special attention to contributions of women in

literature and society.

31   Houston, R. A. "Women in Scottish Society, 1500-1800," in
      *Scottish Society, 1500-1800: Comparison, Continuities, and
      Change*, ed. R. A. Houston and I. D. Whyte. Cambridge:
      Cambridge, 1989. Pp. 118-47.
      Points to the interaction of economic, legal, political, and cultur-
      al factors in considering the status of women in this period.

32   Spender, Dale and Todd, Janet, eds. *British Women Writers:
      An Anthology from the Fourteenth Century to the Present*. New
      York: Peter Bedrick, 1989. Pp. 921.
      Excerpts, mostly literary in nature.

Surveys of Women in Church History

33   Tucker, Ruth A. and Liefeld, Walter L. *Daughters of the
      Church: Women and Ministry from New Testament Times to the
      Present*. Grand Rapids: Zondervan, 1987. Pp. 552.
      For materials relating to England, see especially chaps. 5-10; a
      special interest in following evangelical themes, issues, and con-
      tributions.

34   Hammack, Mary L. *A Dictionary of Women in Church History*.
      Chicago: Moody, 1984. Pp. 167.
      Short sketches of several hundred women, with emphasis on
      1800 to the present and a concentration on evangelicals.

35   Hardesty, Nancy. *Great Women of Faith: The Strength and
      Influence of Christian Women*. Grand Rapids: Baker, 1980.
      Pp. 140.
      Includes chapters on early Quaker women and Catherine Booth.

36   Moore, Katherine. *She for God: Aspects of Women and Chris-
      tianity*. London: Allison and Busby, 1978. Pp. 221.
      From the Saxon period to the present, with a focus on the sto-
      ries of British women; broad sweep, but limited sources used.

37   Thomson, D. P. *Women of the Scottish Church*. Perth, 1975.

Pp. 409.
From the Reformation to the present; full of detail, with long citations, but not analytical.

38   Hillyer, Ruth. "The Parson's Wife in History." M.Phil., University of London, 1971. Pp. 596.
      Watt, Margaret H. *The History of the Parson's Wife.* London: Faber & Faber, 1943. Pp. 200.
      Two surveys of the subject. The first focuses on the period after 1560 and provides data from the diocese of Peterborough; the second is sweeping but offers only occasional glimpses beyond particular illustrations.

39   Deen, Edith. *Great Women of the Christian Faith.* New York: Harper, 1959. Pp. 428.
      Some fifty "spiritual biographies," with an Anglo-American concentration in the modern period and a tendency to the heroic and the uncritical.

40   *Dartford Priory: A History of the English Dominicanesses.* Oxford: Blackfriars, 1947. Pp. 65.
      A short history over six hundred years.

41   Clement, A. S., ed. *Great Baptist Women.* London: Carey Kingsgate, 1955. Pp. 116.
      Eleven brief portraits from the English Civil War to the twentieth century; notably, seven (all of the nineteenth-century persons selected) were involved in missionary work.

CHAPTER 2

1500-1640:
WOMEN IN THE ENGLISH
RENAISSANCE AND REFORMATION

Bibliographies, Guides, and Anthologies

42 Bibliographies of the period, covering different genres of writing, include:

Wiesner, Merry E. *Women in the Sixteenth Century: A Bibliography*. St. Louis: Center for Reformation Research, 1983. Pp. 77.

Greco, Norma and Novotny, Ronaele. "Bibliography of Women in the English Renaissance," *UMPWS* 1 (June 1974): 130-57.

Gartenberg, Patricia and Whittemore, Nena T. "A Checklist of English Women in Print, 1475-1640," *Bulletin of Bibliography and Magazine Notes* 34 (1977): 1-13.

Travitsky, Betty S. "The New Mother of the English Renaissance (1489-1659): A Descriptive Catalogue," *BRH* 82 (1979): 63-89.

Hageman, Elizabeth H. "Recent Studies in Women Writers of Tudor England. Part I: Women Writers, 1485-1603," *ELR* 14 (1984): 409-25.

_____. "Recent Studies in Women Writers of the English Seventeenth Century (1604-1674)," *ELR* 18 (1988): 138-67.

43 Biographical information is contained in the following volumes:
Bell, Maureen, et al., eds. *A Biographical Dictionary of English Women Writers 1580-1720*. Sussex: Harvester, 1990. Pp. 298.

Emerson, Kathy Lynn. *Wives and Daughters: The Women of Sixteenth-Century England*. Troy, NY: Whitston, 1984. Pp. 407.

Hoffman, Ann, comp. *Lives of the Tudor Age, 1485-1603*. New York: Barnes and Noble, 1977. Pp. 500.

Spender, Dale. *Mothers of the Novel: 100 Good Women Writers Before Jane Austen*. London: Pandora, 1986. Pp. 357.

44 For relevant collections of works from the period, see:

Klein, Joan Larsen, ed. *Daughters, Wives, and Widows: Writings by Men About Women and Marriage in England, 1500-1640*. Urbana: Illinois, 1992. Pp. 328.

Travitsky, Betty, ed. *The Paradise of Women: Writings by English Women of the Renaissance*. Westport, CT: Greenwood, 1981. Pp. 283.

Otten, Charlotte F., ed. *English Women's Voices, 1540-1700*. Miami: Florida International, 1992. Pp. 421.

Ferguson, Moira, ed. *First Feminists: British Women Writers, 1578-1799*. Bloomington: Indiana, 1985. Pp. 461.

Mahl, Mary R. and Koon, Helene, eds. *The Female Spectator: English Women Writers Before 1800*. Bloomington: Indiana, 1977. Pp. 310.

Irwin, Joyce L., ed. *Womanhood in Radical Protestantism, 1525-1675*. Lewiston, NY: Edwin Mellen, 1979. Pp. 258.

General Historical Studies

45 Crawford, Patricia. *Women and Religion in England, 1500-1720*. London: Routledge, 1993. Pp. 268.
The first broad survey of the subject; Crawford's main theme is the significance of gender in religious faith, and she shows how Christianity in this period provided both a justification for female subordination and an occasion for spiritual power for women.

A. 1500-1558

46 Wilson, Derek. *A Tudor Tapestry: Men, Women, and Society in Reformation England*. Pittsburgh: Pittsburgh, 1973. Pp. 287.

Concentrates on prominent figures; gives extended treatment to Anne Ayscough, tried for heresy in 1545-46.

47   Crawford, Patricia. "From the Woman's View: Pre-Industrial England, 1500-1750," in *Exploring Women's Past*, ed. Patricia Crawford. Sydney: Allen and Unwin, 1984. Pp. 49-85.
      An overview, chiefly focusing on social and economic circumstances; but Crawford also addresses ways in which religious changes affected the subordination of women.

48   Weinstein, Minna F. "Reconstructing Our Past: Reflections on Tudor Women," *IJWS* 1 (1978): 133-40.
      Urges historians to use a new set of questions and new periodizations to achieve a perspective that is uniquely female-defined.

49   Houlbrooke, R. A. "Women's Social Life and Common Action in England from the Fifteenth Century to the Eve of the Civil War," *Continuity & Change* (1986): 171-89.
      A broad survey to show that the capacity of women for independent thought and action should not be underestimated, even in a general context of subordination.

50   Andre, Caroline S. "Some Selected Aspects of the Role of Women in Sixteenth-Century England," *IJWS* 4 (1981): 76-88.
      A general study discussing family and social practices and the impact of religion upon them.

51   Levine, Mortimer. "The Place of Women in Tudor Government," in *Tudor Rule and Revolution*, ed. Delloyd J. Guth and John W. McKenna. Cambridge: Cambridge, 1982. Pp. 109-23.
      Reviews the literature on gynecocracy and examines the influence of women on the conduct of affairs of state in the reign of Henry VIII; concludes that women had no significant place in Tudor government.

52   Hogrefe, Pearl. "Legal Rights of Tudor Women and Their Circumvention," *SCJ* 3 (1972): 92-105.
      _____. *Tudor Women: Commoners and Queens.* Ames:

Iowa State, 1975. Pp. 170.

_____. *Women of Action in Tudor England: Nine Biograph-
ical Sketches*. Ames: Iowa State, 1977. Pp. 263.
Hogrefe is interested in women's contributions in the public
arena and in those ways in which they circumvented limitations
placed upon them.

53   Plowden, Alison. *Tudor Women: Queens and Commoners*.
     London: Weidenfeld & Nicolson, 1979. Pp. 182.
     From Margaret Beaufort, mother of Henry VII, to Elizabeth I;
     background and survey, with no detailed examination.

54   Cahn, Susan. *Industry of Devotion: The Transformation of
     Women's Work in England, 1500-1660*. New York: Columbia,
     1987. Pp. 252.
     Investigates how new economic dependence contributed to the
     subordination of women within their families and in the larger
     society.

55   Tabor, Margaret E. *Four Margarets*. London: Sheldon, 1929.
     Pp. 113.
     Short studies of Margaret Beaufort, Margaret Roper, Margaret
     Fell, and Margaret Godolphin (the latter two of the late seven-
     teenth century).

56   Devereux, E. J. "Elizabeth Barton and Tudor Censorship,"
     BJRL 49 (1966-67): 91-106.
     On Barton's religious activities, including prophecies against
     Henry VIII's intention to divorce Anne Boleyn, and the gov-
     ernment's campaign against her.

B. Elizabethan Era

57   Greaves, Richard L. *Society and Religion in Elizabethan Eng-
     land*. Minneapolis: Minnesota, 1981. Pp. 925.
     A massive study of the thought of Elizabethan clergy and laity
     and its connection with social life; Greaves argues that Puritan
     emphasis on the household as a religious unit was important in
     adding the role of catechist to wives/mothers and helped to

enhance the position of women. Extensive notes and a bibliographical essay.

58   Sharpe, J. A. *Early Modern England: A Social History, 1550-
      1760*. London: Edward Arnold, 1987. Pp. 379.
      Bracketed by chapters on politics and society in each half of this
      period, this work considers family and community life, social
      and economic life, and the spiritual and mental world of the
      people.

59   Henderson, Katherine U. and McManus, Barbara F. *Half
      Humankind: Contexts and Texts of the Controversy About
      Women in England, 1540-1640*. Urbana: Illinois, 1985. Pp.
      390.
      The debate over images, understandings, and stereotypes of
      women in the literature of this period; a lengthy contextual
      introduction establishes a foundation for the ten pamphlets and
      several eulogies and condemnations. Both misogynist attacks
      and defenses of women appeal to religious resources for their
      arguments.

60   Spufford, Margaret. *Contrasting Communities: English Villages
      in the Sixteenth and Seventeenth Centuries*. Cambridge: Cam-
      bridge, 1974. Pp. 374.
      Families, landholding, education, and religion in the county of
      Cambridge, focusing on the villagers; the role of women in
      village life is discussed throughout, and the significance of
      religious dissent in this part of the country is stressed.

61   Camden, Carroll. *The Elizabethan Woman*. Houston: Elsevier,
      1952. Pp. 333.
      A survey that focuses on the domestic situation, with only limit-
      ed attention to religion.

62   Notestein, Wallace. "The English Woman 1580-1650," in *Stud-
      ies in Social History Presented to G. M. Trevelyan*, ed. J. H.
      Plumb. New York: Longmans, Green, 1955. Pp. 69-107.
      Describes attitudes toward women found in the literature of the
      period and surveys the disadvantages that women were under to

explain how these attitudes came about.

63   Bradford, Gamaliel. *Elizabethan Women*, ed. H. O. White.
      Cambridge: Houghton Miffin, 1936. Pp. 238.
      A work typical of an earlier era, in that perspectives on women
      are obtained almost solely from men; no interest in religion.

64   Shapiro, Susan C. "Feminists in Elizabethan England," *History
      Today* 27 (1977): 703-11.
      Women's struggle against their subordinate status, its manifes-
      tations, and the responses of their male contemporaries (includ-
      ing Puritan clergy).

65   Scalingi, Paula Louise. "The Scepter or the Distaff: The Ques-
      tion of Female Sovereignty, 1516-1607," *Historian* 41
      (1978): 59-75.
      Jordan, Constance. "Woman's Rule in Sixteenth-Century Brit-
      ish Political Thought," *Renaissance Quarterly* 40 (1987):
      421-51.
      Two essays on the debate over women's rule, including consid-
      eration of the religious foundations of these views.

66   McMullen, Norma. "The Education of English Gentlewomen,
      1540-1640," *History of Education* 6 (1977): 87-101.
      Against those who opposed education for women, advocates
      stressed the enhancement to virtue and religious faith and the
      preparation for a more advantageous marriage which education
      would bring.

67   King, John. *Tudor Royal Iconography: Literature and Art in an
      Age of Religious Crisis*. Princeton: Princeton, 1989. Pp.
      285.
      _____. "The Godly Woman in Elizabethan Iconography,"
      Renaissance Quarterly 38 (1985): 41-84.
      Considers "images of Protestant women as embodiments of
      pious intellectuality and divine wisdom" (41). Chap. 4 of the
      monograph is on the "godly" queens.

C. The Seventeenth Century

68   Fraser, Antonia. *The Weaker Vessel: Woman's Lot in Seven-
       teenth-Century England*. London: Weidenfeld, 1984. Pp. 554.
       A series of vignettes about women's lives, organized topically
       and chronologically; argues that advances made by women in
       the middle decades were lost by the end of the century.

69   Veevers, Erica. *Images of Love and Religion: Queen Henrietta
       Maria and Court Entertainments*.   Cambridge: Cambridge,
       1989. Pp. 244.
       A study of Charles I's court from the point of view of his
       French queen; Veevers sees a link between the queen's cult of
       Platonic love and her Catholicism.

70   Ezell, Margaret J. *The Patriarch's Wife: Literary Evidence and
       the History of the Family*.   Chapel Hill: North Carolina, 1987.
       Pp. 272.
       Attempts a revision of the prevailing model of domestic patri-
       archy in the seventeenth century through the investigation of the
       writings of literate women of the middle and upper classes. She
       concludes that "the patriarch's wife, both in family and in soci-
       ety, wielded considerable power, . . . but that power was to a
       large extent displayed on a private level, not through the public
       institutions" (163).

71   Glanz, Leonore M.   "The Legal Position of English Women
       under the Early Stuart Kings and the Interregnum, 1603-1660."
       Ph.D., Loyola of Chicago, 1973. Pp. 311.
       Considers the complexity of English law concerning women;
       Glanz argues that as anachronistic and overly protective laws
       were disintegrating, women gained a measure of social and
       economic freedom.

72   Prest, W. R.   "Law and Women's Rights in Early Modern
       England," *Seventeenth Century* 6 (1991): 169-87.
       Through a study of a 1632 work by Thomas Edgar, Prest sug-
       gests that improvements occurred in the law's provision for
       women in this period, contrary to some general views on the

subject.

73   Warnicke, Retha.   "Private and Public: The Boundaries of
     Women's Lives in Early Stuart England," in *Privileging Gender
     in Early Modern England*, ed. Jean R. Brink.   Kirksville, MO:
     Sixteenth Century Journal, 1993.   Pp. 123-40.
     A discussion of social roles, including the importance of the
     religious experience in defining and shaping the boundaries.

74   Pollock, Linda.   "'Teaching her to live under obedience': The
     Making of Women in the Upper Ranks of Early Modern Eng-
     land," *Continuity & Change* 4 (1989): 231-58.
     On the rearing of children and the task of "transforming girls
     into the idea of femininity depicted in the scriptures" (237).

Renaissance and Christian Humanism

75   King, Margaret L.   *Women of the Renaissance*.   Chicago: Chi-
     cago, 1991.   Pp. 333.
     A comprehensive work, both geographically and chronological-
     ly, with chapters on women in the family, church, and high
     culture.   King concludes that despite continuing disabilities and
     prejudices, something changed in this period in women's sense
     of themselves, which had its roots in the spiritual experience of
     women and provided a foundation for a better future.

76   Maclean, Ian.   *The Renaissance Notion of Woman: A Study in
     the Fortunes of Scholasticism and Medical Science in European
     Intellectual Life*.   Cambridge: Cambridge, 1980.   Pp. 119.
     An analysis of texts in theology, science, politics, and law,
     concluding that there is less change in the notion of woman over
     the course of the Renaissance than the general intellectual fer-
     ment might lead one to suspect.

77   Dowling, Maria.   *Humanism in the Age of Henry VIII*.   London:
     Croom Helm, 1986.   Chap. 7, "Women and the New Learn-
     ing."
     _____.   "A Woman's Place? Learning and the Wives of
     Henry VIII," *History Today* 41 (June 1991): 38-42.

Considers education of women for the household and for piety, with attention to the different activities and views of Henry VIII's wives in promoting the new learning and religion at court.

78   Warnicke, Retha M. *Women of the English Renaissance and Reformation*. Westport, CT: Greenwood, 1983. Pp. 228.
_____. "Women and Humanism in England," in *Renaissance Humanism: Foundations, Forms, and Legacy*, ed. Albert A. Rabil, Jr.   Vol. II: Humanism Beyond Italy. Philadelphia: Pennsylvania, 1988. Pp. 39-54.
On the English acceptance of classical training for women, beginning with the program put forth by Thomas More; the contributions of many individuals to translations, devotional literature, etc., are regularly noted. Warnicke concludes that while a number of notable accomplishments occurred, there was no "golden age" for women.

79   Kelso, Ruth. *Doctrine for the Lady of the Renaissance*. Urbana: Illinois, 1956; rept. 1978. Pp. 475.
On the chasm between theory and practice in the case of "the lady."

80   Hood, S. J. R. "The Impact of Protestantism on the Renaissance Ideal of Women in Tudor England." Ph.D., Nebraska, 1977. Pp. 253.
An investigation of the Renaissance ideal of woman as wife and mother as dogmatized by the Protestant concept of the calling.

81   Hannay, Margaret P., ed.   *Silent but for the Word: Tudor Women as Patrons, Translators, and Writers of Religious Works*. Kent, OH: Kent State, 1985. Pp. 304.
Among the literary perspectives covering Renaissance themes are Valerie Wayne, "Some Sad Sentence: Vives' *Instruction of a Christian Woman*," pp. 15-29; Rita Verbrugge, "Margaret More Roper's Personal Expression in the *Devout Treatise Upon the Pater Noster*," pp. 30-42; Jon A. Quitslund, "Spenser and the Patronesses of the *Fowre Hymnes*: 'Ornaments of All True Love and Beautie'," pp. 184-202; and Gary F. Waller, "Struggling

into Discourse: The Emergence of Renaissance Women's Writing," pp. 238-56.

82 Kaufman, Michael W. "Spare Ribs: The Conception of Woman in the Middle Ages and the Renaissance," *Soundings* 56 (1973): 139-63.
Contends that the literary idealizations of woman had little to do with the lives of the vast majority of women.

83 Welch, D'arne. "Sixteenth-Century Humanism and the Education of Women," *Paedagogica Historica* 24 (1984): 241-57.
Argues that the early English humanists made several important breaks with tradition; they saw women as rational beings capable of benefitting from an education, linked virtue and piety to learning, altered the traditional feminine ideal by focusing on the lay woman rather than the nun, and made education an important part of the feminine ideal—all this despite an implicit restriction to upper-class women and the inability to see any role for women outside the home.

84 Yost, John K. "The Value of Married Life for the Social Order in the Early English Renaissance," *Societas* 6 (1976): 25-39.
_____. "Changing Attitudes Toward Married Life in Civic and Christian Humanism," *Occasional Papers of the American Society for Reformation Research* 1 (1977): 151-66.
Studies the shift from previous recommendations of celibacy to a more appreciative view of marriage.

85 Travitsky, Betty S. "The New Mother of the English Renaissance: Her Writings on Motherhood," in *The Lost Tradition: Mothers and Daughters in Literature*, ed. Cathy N. Davidson and E. M. Broner. New York: Ungar, 1980. Pp. 33-43.
Concludes that growth in the influence of the mother represents an advance over medieval thinking; the new mother "was the most liberated female developed in the English Renaissance, in what was still a family-centered, religiously oriented time" (41).

86 Discussions of the More household, women's education, and its implications are found in:

Hogrefe, Pearl. *The Thomas More Circle: A Program of Ideas and Their Impact on Secular Drama*. Urbana: Illinois, 1959. Pp. 350.

Moore, M. J., ed. *Quincentennial Essays on St. Thomas More: Selected Papers from the Thomas More College Conference*. Boone, NC: Dept. of History, Appalachian State College, 1978: especially J. P. Jones and S. S. Seidel, "Thomas More's Feminism: To Reform or Re-form," pp. 67-77; and L. C. Khanna, "Images of Women in Thomas More's Poetry," pp. 77-88.

Khanna, Lee Cullen. "No Less Real Than Ideal: Images of Women in More's Work," *Moreana* 14 (December 1977): 35-51.

Murray, Francis G. "Feminine Spirituality in the More Household," *Moreana* 27-28 (1970): 92-102.

87   Studies of individual women include:

Warnicke, Retha M. "The Making of a Shrew: The Legendary History of Alice More," *Rendezvous* 15 (1980): 25-36.

Reynolds, Ernest E. *Margaret Roper*. London: Burns & Oates, 1960. Pp. 149.

Kaufman, Peter Iver. "Absolute Margaret: Margaret More Roper and 'Well Learned' Men," *SCJ* 20 (1989): 443-56.

Gee, John A. "Margaret Roper's English Version of Erasmus' *Precato Dominica* and the Apprenticeship behind Early Tudor Translation," *Review of English Studies* 13 (1937): 257-71.

Mackenzie, Mary L. *Dame Christian Colet*. Cambridge: Cambridge, 1923. Pp. 116.

88   The work of specific humanists who helped to shape views of women is considered in:

Watson, Foster, ed. *Vives and the Renascence Education of Women*. London: Edward Arnold, 1912. Pp. 259.

Kuschmierz, Ruth L. M. "*The Instruction of a Christian Woman*: A Critical Edition of the Tudor Translation." Ph.D., Pittsburgh, 1961. Pp. 419.

Kaufman, Gloria. "Juan Luis Vives on the Education of Women," *Signs* 3 (1978): 891-96.

Bayne, Diane V. "*The Instruction of a Christian Woman*: Richard Hyrde and the Thomas More Circle," *Moreana* 45 (February, 1975): 5-15.

Jordan, Constance. "Feminism and the Humanists: The Case of Sir Thomas Elyot's *Defence of Good Women*," *Renaissance Quarterly* 36 (1983): 181-201.

Yates, Lyn. "The Uses of Women to a Sixteenth-century Bestseller," *Historical Studies* 18 (1979): 422-34.

Holm, Janis Butler. "The Myth of a Feminist Humanism: Thomas Salter's *The Mirrhor of Modestie*," *Soundings* 67 (1984): 443-52.

Literary Studies

89 Krontiris, Tina. *Oppositional Voices: Women as Writers and Translators of Literature in the English Renaissance*. London: Routledge, 1991. Pp. 182.
    Explores the strategies used by six authors of secular and religious literature (including Elizabeth Cary, a convert to Catholicism, and Aemilia Lanyer) to establish their acceptance as writers and engage in a critique of the prevailing ideology of womanhood.

90 Wilson, Katharina M., ed. *Women Writers of the Renaissance and Reformation*. Athens: Georgia, 1987. Pp. 638.
    Covers European women of the sixteenth and seventeenth centuries; Part VII features biographical narratives and primary sources of five English writers: Margaret Roper, Mary Sidney, Elizabeth I, Mary Sidney Wroth, and Katherine Philips.

91 Beilin, Elaine V. *Redeeming Eve: Women Writers in the English Renaissance*. Princeton: Princeton, 1987. Pp. 346.
    Investigates "how social and literary attitudes toward women influenced women writers in Renaissance England" (xvii) and focuses on the theme of feminine virtue.

92 Hull, Suzanne. *Chaste, Silent, and Obedient: English Books for Women, 1475-1640*. San Marino, CA: Huntington Library, 1982. Pp. 247.
    Studies four types of literature published for a female audience:

practical guides, recreational literature, devotional works, and writings on the nature of woman.

93   Ferguson, Moira. "Feminist Polemic: British Women's Writings in English from the Late Renaissance to the French Revolution," *WSIF* 9 (1986): 451-64.
A comprehensive review and classification of reactive, reasoned, and personal polemics over three centuries; some discussion of the role of religion.

94   Lewalski, Barbara Kiefer. *Writing Women in Jacobean England*. Cambridge: Harvard, 1993. Pp. 431.
Chapters on nine women whose writings represent resistance to the patriarchal construction of women, including Anne Clifford, Rachel Speght, Elizabeth Cary, and Aemilia Lanyer.

95   _____. "Re-writing Patriarchy and Patronage: Margaret Clifford, Anne Clifford, and Aemilia Lanyer," *Yearbook of English Studies* 21 (1991): 87-106.
_____. "Of God and Good Women: The Poems of Aemilia Lanyer," in *Silent but for the Word*, pp. 203-24.
Shorter studies of the revision of fundamental Christian myths, now with women at their center (106, 224).

96   Hutson, Lorna. "Why the Lady's Eyes are Nothing like the Sun," in *Women, Texts, and Histories, 1575-1760*, ed. Clare Brant and Diane Purkiss. London: Routledge, 1992. Pp. 13-38.
On Aemilia Lanyer's critique of Christian humanism.

97   Rowse, A. L., ed. *The Poems of Shakespeare's Dark Lady: Salve Deus Rex Judaeorum by Emilia Lanier*. London: J. Cape, 1978. Pp. 144.
The introduction considers religious themes in her writings.

98   Travitsky, Betty. "'The Lady Doth Protest': Protest in the Popular Writings of Renaissance English Women," *ELR* 14 (1984): 255-84.
Studies six works by middle-class women against contemporary

attacks denigrating women and focuses on the differences in these writings from the male polemics.

99   Utley, Francis Lee. *The Crooked Rib*. Columbus: Ohio State, 1944. Pp. 368.
     Considers the genres of satire and defense of women in English and Scottish literature to 1568.

100 Jardine, Lisa. *Still Harping on Daughters: Women and Drama in the Age of Shakespeare*. 1983; New York: Columbia, 1989. Pp. 202.
     Chapter 2 looks at the alleged "liberating" possibilities for women of this period in Protestantism, humanist education, and marital partnership; each, instead, is found to represent a double bind for women.

101 Rose, Mary Beth. *The Expense of Spirit: Love and Sexuality in English Renaissance Drama*. Ithaca: Cornell, 1988. Pp. 240.
     Argues that "a study of moral, religious and dramatic writing in the English Renaissance reveals that the Protestant idealization of marriage gained a distinct ascendancy as the predominant, authoritative sexual discourse" (5).

102 De Bruyn, Lucy. *Woman and the Devil in Sixteenth Century Literature*. Tisbury: Compton, 1979. Pp. 180.
     On the struggle for the ideal woman through her interaction with the devil.

103 Jones, Ann Rosalind. "Counterattacks on 'the Bayter of Women': Three Pamphleteers of the Early Seventeenth Century," in *The Renaissance Englishwoman in Print*, ed. Anne M. Haselkorn and Betty S. Travitsky. Amherst: Massachusetts, 1990. Pp. 45-62.
     Responses by Rachel Speght, Ester Sowernam, and Constantia Munda (the last two being pseudonyms) to Joseph Swetnam's 1615 misogynist pamphlet; attention to the use of Scripture to attack the antiwomanist position.

Women and the English Reformation

104   Willen, Diane. "Women and Religion in Early Modern Eng-
        land," in *Women in Reformation and Counter-Reformation
        Europe: Public and Private Worlds*, ed. Sherrin Marshall.
        Bloomington: Indiana, 1989. Pp. 140-65.
        A broad foundational essay, exploring the religious experiences
        of women in all social classes.

105   Thompsett, Fredrica Harris. "Women Inclined to Holiness:
        Our Reformation Ancestry," *HMPEC* 51 (1982): 337-45.
        On the participation of women as martyrs, in circles of
        friends, and as religious educators.

106   Cross, Claire. "'Great Reasoners in Scripture': The Activities
        of Women Lollards, 1380-1530," in *Medieval Women*, ed.
        Derek Baker. Oxford: Blackwell, 1978. Pp. 359-80.
        Shows how the late medieval lay religious phenomenon contin-
        ued into the sixteenth century (women represented one-third of
        those examined in Coventry in 1511-12).

107   Fines, John. "Heresy Trials in the Diocese of Coventry and
        Lichfield, 1511-12," *JEH* 14 (1963): 160-74.
        Discusses how evidence from the trials suggests a heavy in-
        volvement of women.

108   Davis, John. "Joan of Kent, Lollardy, and the English Refor-
        mation," *JEH* 33 (1982): 225-33.
        On the career of Joan Bocher, eventually burned to death in
        1550 for expressing an Anabaptist view of the Incarnation.

109   Aston, Margaret. "Segregation in Church," in *Women in the
        Church* (SCH 27), ed. W. J. Sheils and Diana Wood. Oxford:
        Blackwell, 1990. Pp. 237-94.
        On seating arrangements from the early medieval through the
        Reformation period; contends that the gradual Reformation
        shift from sex segregation to familial seating (opposed by
        church leaders) did not represent any improvement in the
        status of women in the church.

110   Dowling, Maria. "The Gospel and the Court: Reformation under Henry VIII," in *Protestantism and the National Church in Sixteenth-century England*, ed. Peter Lake and Maria Dowling. London: Croom Helm, 1987. Pp. 36-77.
Contains an extended discussion of the roles of Anne Boleyn and Katherine Parr.

111   Barstow, Anne Llewellyn. "An Ambiguous Legacy: Anglican Clergy Wives after the Reformation," in *Women in New Worlds: Historical Perspectives on the Wesleyan Tradition*, vol. 2, ed. Rosemary Skinner Keller, et al. Nashville: Abingdon, 1982. Pp. 97-111, 370-73 [slightly altered version appears as "The First Generations of Anglican Clergy Wives: Heroines or Whores?" *HMPEC* 52 (1983): 3-16].
On the events and attitudes surrounding the legalization of clerical marriage.

112   Prior, Mary. "Reviled and Crucified Marriages: The Position of Tudor Bishops' Wives," in *Women in English Society, 1500-1800*, ed. Mary Prior. London: Methuen, 1985. Pp. 118-48.
Discusses their difficult situation, "socially and legally disadvantaged compared with other women, and rendered all but invisible in public life" (141).

113   Carlson, Eric J. "Clerical Marriage and the English Reformation," *JBS* 31 (1992): 1-31.
Shows that though clerical marriage was affirmed in the Articles of Religion, it received very limited support among early reformers or among bishops and clergy.

114   Bainton, Roland H. *Women of the Reformation in France and England*. Minneapolis: Augsburg, 1973. Pp. 287.
In Part II, a focus on the Tudor queens, plus articles on John Foxe and the women martyrs and on Catherine Willoughby, duchess of Suffolk.

115   Levin, Carole. "Advice on Women's Behavior in Three Tudor Homilies," *IJWS* 6 (1983): 176-85.

Shows the Elizabethan government's use of the churches as a means of social control.

116   Christian, Margaret. "Elizabeth's Preachers and the Government of Women: Defining and Correcting a Queen," *SCJ* 24 (1993): 561-76.
       Examines sermons to show how the clergy tried to convince the queen to defer to their religious authority.

117   Wabuda, Susan. "Shunamites and Nurses of the English Reformation: The Activities of Mary Glover, Niece of Hugh Latimer," in *Women in the Church*, pp. 335-44.
       On the networks of hospitality offered by women to the clergy.

118   Collinson, Patrick. "The Role of Women in the English Reformation Illustrated by the Life and Friendships of Anne Locke," in *SCH* 2, ed. G. J. Cuming. London: Nelson, 1965. Pp. 258-72 [also in Collinson, *Godly People*. London: Hambledon, 1983. Pp. 273-87].
       Takes up Locke's career as a case, including her relationship with John Knox and marriage to Edward Dering.

119   Beilin, Elaine V. "Anne Askew's Self-Portrait in the *Examinations*," in *Silent but for the Word*, pp. 77-91.
       Argues that Askew intentionally created a self-image of a preacher/teacher of the plain style in her record of her imprisonment and interrogation: "She thus joined the process of redefining women's role in the Church and in her society, a process which was to concern some sixteenth-century women and many of their heirs in succeeding centuries" (91).

120   Bainton, Roland H. "Feminine Piety in Tudor England," in *Christian Spirituality: Essays in Honour of Gordon Rupp*, ed. Peter Brooks. London: SCM, 1975. Pp. 183-201.
       On the Cooke sisters and their inclinations to Puritan piety.

121   Lamb, Mary Ellen. "The Cooke Sisters: Attitudes Toward Learned Women in the Renaissance," in *Silent but for the Word*, pp. 107-25.

Compares their public representation with the energetic voices
that are visible in their correspondence.

The Church of England and Women

122   Sykes, Stephen.   "Richard Hooker and the Ordination of
       Women to the Priesthood," in *After Eve: Women, Theology
       and the Christian Tradition*, ed. Janet Martin Soskice. Lon-
       don: Marshall Pickering, 1990. Pp. 119-37.
       Uses Hooker's views of polity and history to argue for support
       for the ordination of women over against an unhistorical inter-
       pretation of tradition.

123   Bailey, Derrick S.   *Sexual Relation in Christian Thought*.
       New York: Harper, 1959. Chap. V.
       Shows how Anglican theology and ethics in this period reflect
       both an androcentric bias and some reforming interests as seen
       in simplified laws of marriage and rejection of clerical celiba-
       cy.

John Knox and the Gynecocracy Controversy

124   For studies of Knox's views regarding women rulers, as well
       as his personal engagements with women, see:
       Greaves, Richard L. "John Knox and the Ladies, or The Con-
            troversy over Gynecocracy," *Red River Valley Historical
            Journal* 2:1 (1977): 6-16 [also in *Theology and Revolution
            in the Scottish Reformation: Studies in the Thought of John
            Knox*. Grand Rapids, MI: Christian, 1980. Pp. 157-68].
       Lee, Patricia-Ann. "A Bodye Politique to Governe: Aylmer,
            Knox and the Debate on Queenship," *Historian* 52 (1990):
            242-61.
       Shephard, Amanda. "Gender and Authority in Sixteenth-Cen-
            tury England: The Debate about John Knox's *First Blast of
            the Trumpet against the Monstrous Regiment of Women.*"
            Ph.D., Lancaster, 1990. Pp. 450.
       Frankforter, A. Daniel. "Elizabeth Bowes and John Knox: A
            Woman and Reformation Theology," *Church History* 56
            (1987): 333-47.

Newman, Christine M.   "The Reformation and Elizabeth Bowes: A Study of a Sixteenth-century Northern Gentlewoman," in *Women in the Church*, pp. 325-33.

John Foxe and Women in the *Actes and Monuments*

125   Foxe's account of the fifty-five female Marian martyrs is examined in:

Levin, Carole.   "Women in *The Book of Martyrs* as Models of Behavior in Tudor England," *LJWS* 4 (1981): 196-207.

Bainton, Roland H.   "John Foxe and the Ladies," in *The Social History of the Reformation*, ed. Lawrence P. Buck and John Zophy.   Columbus: Ohio State, 1972.   Pp. 208-22.

Macek, Ellen.   "The Emergence of a Feminine Spirituality in *The Book of Martyrs*," *SCJ* 19 (1988): 63-80.

Thompsett, Fredrica Harris.   "Protestant Women as Victims and Subjects: Reformation Legacies from John Foxe's *Book of Martyrs*," in *This Sacred History: Anglican Reflections for John Booty*, ed. Don Armentrout.   Cambridge, MA: Cowley, 1990.   Pp. 182-98.

126   Levin, Carole.   "John Foxe and the Responsibilities of Queenship," in *Women in the Middle Ages and the Renaissance: Literary and Historical Perspectives*, ed. Mary Beth Rose.   Syracuse: Syracuse, 1986.   Pp. 113-33.
Explores Foxe's ambivalence toward women's rule.

The Puritan Movement

127   Did Puritan understandings represent new possibilities for women, and how did women participate in this movement?   For positive views, see:

Willen, Diane.   "Godly Women in Early Modern England: Puritanism and Gender," *JEH* 43 (1992): 561-80.

Greaves, Richard L.   "The Role of Women in Early English Nonconformity," *Church History* 52 (1983): 299-311 [also in *Triumph over Silence: Women in Protestant History*, ed. Richard L. Greaves (Westport, CT: Greenwood, 1985), pp.

75-92].

128   For views that Puritan understandings continued marriage and
       family relationships articulated much earlier and thus did not
       represent a significantly new perspective, see:
       Davies, Kathleen M.   "The Sacred Condition of Equal-
            ity—How Original were Puritan Doctrines of Marriage?"
            Social History 5 (May 1977): 563-80 [a version with a dif-
            ferent title is in *Marriage and Society: Studies in the Social
            History of Marriage*, ed. R. B. Outhwaite (London: Euro-
            pa, 1981), pp. 58-80].
       Todd, Margo.   "Humanists, Puritans, and the Spiritualized
            Household," *Church History* 49 (1980): 18-34.

129   Baskerville, Stephen.   "The Family in Puritan Political Theol-
            ogy," *Journal of Family History* 18 (1993): 157-78.
       Shifts the question somewhat to ask why Puritans felt the need
       to express their views in such detail, and suggests that these
       reflected anxieties over profound social changes taking place.

130   Some older discussions of Puritan teachings on love include:
       Haller, William and Malleville.   "The Puritan Art of Love,"
            Huntington Library Quarterly 5 (1941-42): 235-72.
       Sensabaugh, G. F.   "Platonic Love and the Puritan Rebellion,"
            Studies in Philology 37 (1940): 457-81.
       Frye, Roland M.   "The Teaching of Classical Puritanism on
            Conjugal Love," *Studies in the Renaissance* 2 (1955): 148-
            59.

131   Studies of Puritan theological writings on marriage are found
       in:
       Johnson, James Turner.   *A Society Ordained by God: English
            Puritan Marriage Doctrine in the First Half of the Seven-
            teenth Century*. Nashville: Abingdon, 1970. Pp. 219.
            _____.   "English Puritan Thought on the Ends of Mar-
            riage," *Church History* 38 (1969): 429-36.
            _____.   "The Covenant Idea and the Puritan View of Mar-
            riage," *JHI* 32 (1971): 107-18.
       Leites, Edmund.   "The Duty to Desire: Love, Friendship, and

Sexuality in Some Puritan Theories of Marriage," *JSH* 15 (1982): 383-408.

132   For Puritan attitudes to family and sexuality, see:
Schücking, Levin L. *The Puritan Family*. Trans. Brian Battershaw. 1929; New York: Schocken, 1970. Pp. 196.

Lucas, R. Valerie. "Puritan Preaching and the Politics of the Family," in *The Renaissance Englishwoman in Print*, pp. 224-40.

Leites, Edmund. *The Puritan Conscience and Modern Sexuality*. New Haven: Yale, 1986. Pp. 196.

De Welles, Theodore. "Sex and Sexual Attitudes in Seventeenth-Century England: The Evidence from Puritan Diaries," *Renaissance and Reformation* n.s. 12 (1988): 45-64.

Schnucker, Robert V. "Elizabethan Birth Control and Puritan Attitudes," *Journal of Interdisciplinary History* 4 (1975): 655-67.

_____. "La position puritaine à l'égard de l'adultere," *Annales: Economies, Sociétés, Civilisations* 27 (1972): 1379-88.

_____. "The English Puritans and Pregnancy, Delivery, and Breast Feeding," *History of Childhood Quarterly* 1 (1974): 637-58.

Coster, William. "Purity, Profanity, and Puritanism: The Churching of Women, 1500-1700," in *Women in the Church*, pp. 377-87.

133   Spufford, Margaret. "Puritanism and Social Control?" in *Order and Disorder in Early Modern England*, eds. Anthony Fletcher and John Stevenson. Cambridge: Cambridge, 1985. Pp. 41-57.
Argues that Puritans did not attempt any more social control than other groups had done. Moral cases brought to court were greater in the thirteenth century than in the Puritan era; a key factor in both eras was the increase in population.

134   Williams, George H. "Called by Thy Name, Leave Us Not: The Case of Mrs. Joan Drake," *Harvard Library Bulletin* 16 (1968): 111-28, 278-300.

Suggests that the theologian Thomas Hooker came to stress the doctrine of preparation because of his encounter with and ministry to Joan Drake (1585-1625); thus, Drake was to Hooker what Anne Hutchinson was to John Cotton.

135   Lake, Peter.   "Feminine Piety and Personal Potency: The 'Emancipation' of Mrs. Jane Ratcliffe," *Seventeenth Century* 2 (1987): 143-65.
A glimpse into the ways that moderate Puritan women could use a godly life as a source of personal potency or charisma.

Older studies of early Nonconformity include:
136   Powicke, Fred J.   "Lists of the Early Separatists," *TCHS* 1 (1902): 141-58.
Uses lists from 1567-96, showing numbers of women as well as men brought on charges of participating in conventicles.

137   Crippen, T. G.   "A Forgotten Chapter of Early Nonconformist History," *TCHS* 1 (1902): 192-94.
Studies examples of women preachers, c. 1620-46.

138   _____.   "The Females Advocate," *TCHS* 8 (1921): 96-101.
An exposition of the contents of a pamphlet arguing for the rights of women in dissenting churches.

Roman Catholicism

139   Bossy, John.   *The English Catholic Community, 1570-1850.* New York: Oxford, 1976. Pp. 446.
A broad survey; chapters 6 and 7 consider some roles of women in the Church.

140   Rowlands, Marie B.   "Recusant Women 1560-1640," in *Women in English Society, 1500-1800*, pp. 149-80.
On various activities of Catholic women in the era of Anglican dominance.

141   Duffy, Eamon.   "Holy Maydens, Holy Wyfes: The Cult of Women Saints in Fifteenth- and Sixteenth-century England," in

Women in the Church, pp. 175-96.
Uses evidence from rood screens.

142   Harris, Barbara J. "A New Look at the Reformation: Aristo-
        cratic Women and Nunneries, 1450-1540," *JBS* 32 (1993): 89-
        113.
        Despite significant religious interests, elite women seldom
        became nuns and did not support convents in their religious
        benefactions.

143   Greatrex, Joan. "On Ministering to 'Certayne Devoute and
        Religiouse Women': Bishop Fox and the Benedictine Nuns of
        Winchester Diocese on the Eve of the Dissolution," in *Women
        in the Church*, pp. 223-35.
        On Fox's translation of the *Rule of St. Benedict* to improve the
        spiritual life of the nuns.

144   Cross, Claire. "The Religious Life of Women in Sixteenth-
        century Yorkshire," in *Women in the Church*, pp. 307-24.
        Studies what happened to women religious after the dissolution
        of monasteries and the emergence of a new form of Catholi-
        cism in the latter half of the century.

145   For studies of institutions, see:
        Hamilton, Dom Adam. *The Chronicle of the English Augus-
            tinian Canonesses Regular of the Lateran at St. Monica's in
            Louvain.* 2 vols., London: Sands, 1904-06. Pp. 277 and
            219.
        Hardman, Anne. *English Carmelites in Penal Times.* Lon-
            don: Burns, Oates & Washbourne, 1936. Pp. 216.
        Rhodes, J. T. "Syon Abbey and Its Religious Publications in
            the Sixteenth Century," *JEH* 44 (1993): 11-25.

146   Studies of several Catholic religious and lay women can be
        found in:
        Mary Philip, Mother. *Companions of Mary Ward.* London:
            Burns, Oates & Washbourne, 1939. Pp. 176.
        Neame, Alan. *The Holy Maid of Kent: The Life of Elizabeth
            Barton, 1506-34.* London: Hodder and Stoughton, 1971.

Pp. 390.

Derrick, Michael. "Blessed Margaret of Salisbury," *Month* 177 (1941): 270-75.

Butler, Audrey. "Anne Boroeghe of Clerkenwell and Dingley," *Northamptonshire Past and Present* 5 (1977): 407-11.

Williams, J. Anthony. "Katherine Gawen, Papist," *Month* n.s. 29 (1963): 169-75.

Fischer, Sandra K. "Elizabeth Cary and Tyranny, Domestic and Religious," in *Silent but for the Word*, pp. 225-37.

Hanlon, Sister Joseph Damien. "These Be But Women," in *From the Renaissance to the Counter-Reformation*, ed. Charles H. Carter. New York: Random House, 1965. Pp. 371-400.

Norman, Marion. "Dame Gertrude More and the English Mystical Tradition," *Recusant History* 13 (1976): 196-211.

Gender Roles, Family, and Sexuality

147   Stone, Lawrence. *The Family, Sex and Marriage in England, 1500-1800*. New York: Harper & Row, 1977. Pp. 800; abridged ed., pp. 447.

_____. "The Rise of the Nuclear Family in Early Modern England. The Patriarchal Stage," in *The Family in History*, ed. Charles E. Rosenberg. Philadelphia: Pennsylvania, 1975. Pp. 13-57.

Traces the change from distance, deference, and patriarchy to affective individualism over three centuries.

148   Schwoerer, Lois G. "Seventeenth-century English Women Engraved in Stone?" *Albion* 16 (1984): 389-403.

A sharp critique of Stone's book for not dealing with women as individuals and not using gender as a viewpoint for studying the history of the family.

149   Houlbrooke, Ralph A. *The English Family, 1450-1700*. London: Longman, 1984. Pp. 272.

Challenges Stone's perception of significant change in familial forms and functions; discusses the role of the church and religious teaching on several related topics.

150   Amussen, Susan Dwyer. *An Ordered Society: Gender and Class in Early Modern England.* New York: Blackwell, 1988. Pp. 203.

_____. "Gender, Family and the Social Order, 1560-1725," in *Order and Disorder in Early Modern England*, pp. 196-215.

Studies in "social relationships and social hierarchies" (ix), such as the implications of the analogy between the state and the family.

151   James, Mervyn. *Family, Lineage, and Civil Society: A Study of Society, Politics, and Mentality in the Durham Region, 1500-1640.* Oxford: Clarendon, 1974. Pp. 223.

Chapter 5 gives special attention to religious changes and their relevance for the topic.

152   Several works on the subject of marriage in this period include:

Outhwaite, R. B., ed. *Marriage and Society: Studies in the Social History of Marriage.* New York: St. Martin's, 1981. Pp. 284; six of eleven essays deal with women and marriage in England.

Gillis, John R. *For Better, For Worse: British Marriages, 1600 to the Present.* New York: Oxford, 1985. Pp. 417.

Ingram, Martin. *Church Courts, Sex, and Marriage in England, 1570-1640.* Cambridge: Cambridge, 1987. Pp. 412.

_____. "The Reform of Popular Culture: Sex and Marriage in Early Modern England," in *Popular Culture in Seventeenth-Century England*, ed. B. Reay. London: Croom Helm, 1985. Pp. 129-65.

Powell, C. L. *English Domestic Relations, 1487-1653.* New York: Columbia, 1917. Pp. 274.

153   Fitz, Linda T. "What Says the Married Woman? Marriage Theory and Feminism in the English Renaissance," *Mosaic* 13:2 (1980): 1-22.

Against the view that sees the beginnings of feminism in the Renaissance view of women, Fitz argues that the literature is much more ambivalent and examines features of this attitude

that paved the way for modern feminism and those that have
not.

154   Thomas, Keith. "The Double Standard," *JHI* 20 (1959): 195-
216.
On the history of the idea that unchastity is a mild and par-
donable offense, at best, for a man, but a serious issue for a
woman; two historical currents that have run counter to the
double standard are Christianity and middle-class respectability.

155   Todd, Barbara. "The Remarrying Widow: A Stereotype Reconsidered," in *Women in English Society, 1500-1800*, pp. 54-
92.
Widows who could control their lives and estates often played
an important role in the religious life of the later seventeenth
century.

156   Harding, Davis P. "Elizabethan Betrothals and 'Measure for
Measure'," *Journal of English and German Philology* 49
(1950): 139-58.
Shows how the play represents popular morality of the day,
seeing little difference between the contract of marriage (in-
volving consent) and the church's blessing.

157   For studies of the role of religion in family life, see:
Collinson, Patrick. *The Birthpangs of Protestant England:
Religious and Cultural Change in the Sixteenth and Seven-
teenth Centuries.* New York: St. Martin's, 1988.
Chapter 3 includes consideration of the Protestant family and
the role and status of women.

Chrisman, Miriam. "Family and Religion in Two Noble
Families: French Catholic and English Puritan," *Journal of
Family History* 8 (1983): 190-210.
Wall, Alison. "Elizabethan Precept and Feminine Practice:
The Thynne Family of Longleat," *History* 75 (1990): 23-38.
Eales, Jacqueline. *Puritans and Roundheads: The Harleys of
Brampton Bryan and the Outbreak of the English Civil War.*

Cambridge: Cambridge, 1990. Pp. 225.

Macfarlane, Alan. *The Family Life of Ralph Josselin, A Seventeenth-Century Clergyman*. Cambridge: Cambridge, 1970. Pp. 241.

158   Considerations of reproduction and childbirth are found in:

McLaren, Angus. *Reproductive Rituals: The Perception of Fertility in England from the Sixteenth to the Nineteenth Century*. London: Methuen, 1984. Pp. 206.

Forbes, Thomas R. "The Regulation of English Midwives in the Sixteenth and Seventeenth Centuries," *Medical History* 8 (1964): 235-44.

Guy, John R. "The Episcopal Licensing of Physicians, Surgeons and Midwives," *Bulletin of the History of Medicine* 56 (1982): 528-42.

Atkinson, Colin B. and Stoneman, William P. "'Their griping greefes and pinching pangs': Attitudes to Childbirth in Thomas Bentley's *The Monument of Matrones* (1582)," *Sixteenth Century Journal* 21 (1990): 193-203.

Crawford, Patricia. "The Construction and Experience of Maternity in Seventeenth-century England," in *Women as Mothers in Pre-Industrial England*, ed. Valerie Fildes. London: Routledge, 1990. Pp. 3-38.

Wilson, Adrian. "The Ceremony of Childbirth and Its Interpretation," in *Women as Mothers in Pre-Industrial England*, pp. 68-107.

Otten, Charlotte F. "Women's Prayers in Childbirth in Sixteenth-century England," *Women and Language* 16:1 (1993): 18-21.

Cressy, David. "Purification, Thanksgiving and the Churching of Women in Post-Reformation England," *Past & Present* 141 (1993): 106-46.

Rushton, Peter. "Purification or Social Control? Ideologies of Reproduction and the Churching of Women after Childbirth," in *The Public and the Private*, ed. Eva Garmarnikow, et al. London: Heinemann, 1983. Pp. 118-31.

Witchcraft

159   Some broader European studies that include English illustra-
      tions and suggest the complexity of the topic are:
      Levack, Brian. *The Witch-Hunt in Early Modern Europe.*
      London: Longman, 1987. Pp. 267.
      Klaits, Joseph. *The Servants of Satan: The Age of the Witch
      Hunts.* Bloomington: Indiana, 1985. Pp. 212.
      Quaife, G. R. *Godly Zeal and Furious Rage: The Witch in
      Early Modern Europe.* New York: St. Martin's, 1987. Pp.
      235.

160   Thomas, Keith. *Religion and the Decline of Magic: Studies in
      Popular Beliefs in Sixteenth- and Seventeenth-Century England.*
      1971; Harmondsworth: Penguin, 1973. Pp. 716.
      Covers a wide range of subjects and includes women in all of
      the categories.

161   Macfarlane, Alan. *Witchcraft in Tudor and Stuart England: A
      Regional and Comparative Study.* London: Routledge &
      Kegan Paul, 1970. Pp. 334.
      _____. "Witchcraft in Tudor and Stuart Essex," in *Crime
      in England, 1550-1800*, ed. J. S. Cockburn. London:
      Methuen, 1977. Pp. 72-89.
      The monograph offers a comprehensive analysis of witchcraft
      cases, considering popular culture as well as social, economic,
      and religious themes. The article takes up the legal side of the
      question and finds no marked correlation between religious
      attitudes and attitudes to witchcraft.

162   Hole, Christina. *Witchcraft in England.* London: Batsford,
      1945. Pp. 167.
      _____. *A Mirror of Witchcraft.* London: Chatto & Win-
      dus, 1957. Pp. 260.
      Complementary volumes; a description of beliefs and practic-
      es, followed by selections from contemporary writings and
      trial reports.

163   Hester, Marianne. *Lewd Women and Wicked Witches: A Study*

of the Dynamics of Male Domination. London: Routledge, 1992. Pp. 239.

_____. "The Dynamics of Male Domination using the Witch Craze in 16th- and 17th-century England as a Case Study," *WSIF* 13 (1990): 9-19.

Hester takes up the subject of witchcraft accusations as an example of violence against women.

164   Some older studies include:

Holmes, Ronald. *Witchcraft in British History.* London: Muller, 1974. Pp. 272.

Haining, Peter, ed. *The Witchcraft Papers.* Secaucus, NJ: University Books, 1974. Pp. 240.

Rosen, Barbara, ed. *Witchcraft.* London: Edward Arnold, 1969. Pp. 407.

Kittredge, George Lyman. *Witchcraft in Old and New England.* Cambridge: Harvard, 1929. Pp. 641.

_____. "English Witchcraft and James I," in *Studies in the History of Religions.* New York: Macmillan, 1912. Pp. 1-65.

Notestein, Wallace. *History of Witchcraft in England from 1558 to 1718.* 1911; New York: Crowell, 1968. Pp. 442.

165   On Scottish witchcraft, see:

Larner, Christina. *Enemies of God: The Witch-hunt in Scotland.* London: Chatto & Windus, 1981. Pp. 244.

_____. *Witchcraft and Religion: The Politics of Popular Belief,* ed. Alan Macfarlane. Oxford: Blackwell, 1984. Pp. 192.

_____, et al. *A Source Book of Scottish Witchcraft.* Glasgow: Glasgow, 1977. Pp. 172.

Intended to replace the next item.

Black, George F. *A Calendar of Cases of Witchcraft in Scotland, 1510-1727.* 1938; New York: Arno, 1971. Pp. 102.

McLachlan, Hugh V. and Swales, J. K. "Stereotypes and Scottish Witchcraft," *Contemporary Review* 234 (1979): 88-94.

Contends that common stereotypes concerning the women involved and the nature of the trials are not confirmed in a review of cases between 1560 and 1730.

166   Seymour, St. John. *Irish Witchcraft and Demonology*. Dub-
       lin: Figgis, 1913. Pp. 256.
       Covers witchcraft cases from 1324 to 1913.

167   Deacon, Richard. *Matthew Hopkins: Witch Finder General*.
       London: Muller, 1976. Pp. 223.
       Although from the standpoint of the witch hunter (d. c. 1647),
       this work contains extensive discussion of accused women and
       of Puritan attitudes toward witchcraft.

168   Ewen, C. L'Estrange, ed. *Witch Hunting and Witch Trials:
       Indictments for Witchcraft from the Records of 1,272 Assiz-
       es held for the Home Circuit, 1559-1736*. London: Kegan,
       Paul, Trench, Trubner, 1929. Pp. 345.
       _____. *Witchcraft and Demonianism*. London: Heath
       Cranton, 1933. Pp. 495.
       Focuses on superstition as an explanation and is interested in
       the practitioners.

169   Walker, D. P. *Unclean Spirits: Possession and Exorcism in
       France and England in the Late Sixteenth and Early Seven-
       teenth Centuries*. Philadelphia: Pennsylvania, 1981. Pp. 116.
       A comparative study of cases of spirit possession and the
       churches' efforts to exorcise them.

170   Ross, Christina. "Calvinism and the Witchcraft Persecution in
          England," *JPHS* 12:1 (1960): 22-28.
       Teall, John L. "Witchcraft and Calvinism in Elizabethan Eng-
          land: Divine Power and Human Agency," *JHI* 23 (1962):
          21-36.
       Two arguments to relieve the Calvinist tradition of particular
       responsibility for the persecutions.

171   For different angles into the witchcraft question, see:
       Thomas, Keith. "The Relevance of Social Anthropology to the
       Historical Study of English Witchcraft," in *Witchcraft Confes-
       sions and Accusations*, ed. Mary Douglas. London: Tavi-

stock, 1970. Pp. 47-81.

Using the theme of *maleficium* (the power to do supernatural harm to others), Thomas argues that there are interesting parallels between English and other cultures' witchcraft beliefs.

Anglo, Sydney, ed. *The Damned Art: Essays in the Literature of Witchcraft*. London: Routledge & Kegan Paul, 1977. Pp. 258.

Of ten essays on literary sources, the following relate to Britain: Sydney Anglo, "Reginald Scot's *Discoverie of Witchcraft*: Scepticism and Sadduceeism," pp. 106-39; Alan Macfarlane, "A Tudor Anthropologist: George Gifford's *Discourse* and *Dialogue*," pp. 140-55; Stuart Clark, "King James's *Daemonologie*: Witchcraft and Kingship," pp. 156-81; Christina Larner, "Two Late Scottish Witchcraft Tracts: *Witchcraft Proven* and *The Tryal of Witchcraft*," pp. 227-45.

Matalene, Carolyn. "Women as Witches," *IJWS* 1 (1978): 573-87.

Argues that accusations were products of specific social purposes rather than responses to actual magical practices.

172   Holmes, Clive. "Popular Culture? Witches, Magistrates, and Divines in Early Modern England," in *Understanding Popular Culture*, ed. Stephen Kaplan. New York: Mouton, 1984. Pp. 85-111.

_____. "Women: Witnesses and Witches," *Past & Present* 140 (1993): 45-78.

These essays explore different aspects of the interaction between popular and elite culture.

173   Anderson, Alan and Gordon, Raymond. "Witchcraft and the Status of Women: The Case of England," *British Journal of Sociology* 29 (1978): 171-84.

Swales, J. K. and McLachlan, Hugh U. "Witchcraft and the Status of Women: A Comment," *ibid.* 30 (1979): 349-58.

A debate over the question of the role of scapegoating in the prosecutions; the second article challenges the claims of the first.

174   For local studies, see:
       Tyler, Philip. "The Church Courts at York and Witchcraft
           Prosecutions 1567-1640," *Northern History* 4 (1969): 84-
           110.
       Pollock, Adrian. "Social and Economic Characteristics of
           Witchcraft: Accusations in Sixteenth- and Seventeenth-cen-
           tury Kent," *Archaeological Cantiana* 95 (1979): 37-48.
       Rushton, Peter. "Women, Witchcraft, and Slander in Early
           Modern England: Cases from the Church Courts of Dur-
           ham, 1560-1675," *Northern History* 18 (1982): 116-32.

175   Sawyer, Ronald C. "'Strangely Handled in All Her Lyms':
       Witchcraft and Healing in Jacobean England," *JSH* 22 (1989):
       461-85.
       Analyses the casebooks of Richard Napier, Anglican clergy-
       man and astrological physician who practiced medicine be-
       tween 1597 and 1634.

176   Young, Alan R. "Elizabeth Lowys: Witch and Social Victim,
       1564," *History Today* 22 (1972): 879-85.
       Interrelated local communal tensions are illustrated in the case
       of the first person prosecuted under the 1563 statute against
       witchcraft.

Individuals

177   *Lady Margaret Beaufort (1443-1509)*
       The mother of Henry VII and prominent religious and educa-
       tional benefactor is studied most thoroughly in Michael K.
       Jones and Malcolm G. Underwood, *The King's Mother: Lady
       Margaret Beaufort, Countess of Richmond and Derby* (Cam-
       bridge: Cambridge, 1992). Other works include Linda Simon,
       *Of Virtue Rare: Margaret Beaufort, Matriarch of the House of
       Tudor* (Boston: Houghton Mifflin, 1982); E. M. G. Routh,
       Lady Margaret (London: Oxford, 1924); Malcolm G. Under-
       wood, "Politics and Piety in the Household of Lady Margaret
       Beaufort," *JEH* 38 (1987): 39-54; and Retha M. Warnicke,

"The Lady Margaret, Countess of Richmond (d. 1509), as seen by Bishop Fisher and by Lord Morley," *Moreana* 19 (June 1982): 47-55.

178   *Catherine of Aragon (1485-1536)*
Daughter of Ferdinand and Isabella of Spain, aunt to Charles V, and the first wife of Henry VIII; for monographic studies, see John E. Paul, *Catherine of Aragon and Her Friends* (New York: Fordham, 1966) and Garrett Mattingly, *Catherine of Aragon* (Boston: Little, Brown, 1941). Maria Dowling's "Humanist Support for Katherine of Aragon," *BIHR* 57 (1984): 46-55, argues that the royal divorce was not a conflict between traditional religion and reform.

179   *Anne Boleyn (c. 1507-37)*
There has been a resurgence of interest in the second wife of Henry VIII and some debate about the reasons for her fall. Retha M. Warnicke's *The Rise and Fall of Anne Boleyn* (Cambridge: Cambridge, 1989) reassesses the sources for interpreting her role in the royal court. Other recent studies include E. W. Ives, *Anne Boleyn* (Oxford: Blackwell, 1986); Carolly Erickson, *Anne Boleyn* (London: Macmillan, 1984); Norah Lofts, *Anne Boleyn* (London: Orbis, 1979); Hester W. Chapman, *Anne Boleyn* (London: J. Cape, 1974); and Marie Louise Bruce, *Anne Boleyn* (London: Collins, 1972).

The debate over the nature of Anne Boleyn's religious views and the extent of her interest in religious reform has been pursued in the journals. G. W. Bernard, "Anne Boleyn's Religion," *Historical Journal* 36:1 (1993): 1-20, challenges the claim that she was an evangelical in religion and a patron of reformers. Maria Dowling, "Anne Boleyn and Reform," *JEH* 35 (1984): 30-46, argues for her active interest in religious reform. Retha M. Warnicke's several articles take up disputed aspects in her biography: "Anne Boleyn's Childhood and Adolescence," *Historical Journal* 28 (1985): 939-52; "Sexual Heresy at the Court of Henry VIII," *Historical Journal* 30 (1987): 247-68; and "The Fall of Anne Boleyn: A Reassessment," *History* 70 (1985): 1-15.

Does the evidence support the accusations brought against

her? G. W. Bernard, in "The Fall of Anne Boleyn," *EHR* 106 (1991): 584-610 and "The Fall of Anne Boleyn: A Rejoinder," *EHR* 107 (1992): 665-74, says yes; while E. W. Ives, "The Fall of Anne Boleyn Reconsidered," *EHR* 107 (1992): 651-64, argues for her innocence. Retha Warnicke's "The Fall of Anne Boleyn Revisited," *EHR* 108 (1993): 653-65, argues for a third view, that her miscarriage in 1536 triggered the events that led to her death.

180   *Catherine Parr (c. 1514-48)*
The religious interests and humanist patronage of this final wife of Henry VIII are explored in Anthony Martienssen, *Queen Katherine Parr* (London: Secker & Warburg, 1973); James Michael Glass, "Silent Reform in Henry's Court: Katherine Parr and Her Court and Their Contribution to the English Reformation" (Ph.D., Southwestern Baptist Theological Seminary, 1991); C. Fenno Hoffman, Jr., "Catherine Parr as a Woman of Letters," *Huntingdon Library Quarterly* 23 (1960): 349-67; James K. McConica, *English Humanists and Reformation Politics Under Henry VIII & Edward VI* (Oxford: Clarendon, 1965), Chap. 7; William P. Haugaard, "The Religious Convictions of a Renaissance Queene," *Renaissance Quarterly* 22 (1969): 346-59; Minna F. Weinstein, "Queen's Power: The Case of Katherine Parr," *History Today* 26 (1976): 788-95; and John N. King, "Patronage and Piety: The Influence of Catherine Parr," in *Silent but for the Word*, pp. 43-60.

181   *Lady Jane Grey (1537-54)*
Following the death of Edward VI, her father-in-law sought to have her proclaimed queen; after nine days, she was overthrown by the forces of Mary, and within a year was executed for high treason. Her associations with the Protestant cause are explored in Alison Plowden, *Lady Jane Grey and the House of Suffolk* (London: Sidgwick & Jackson, 1985); Hester W. Chapman, *Lady Jane Grey* (London: J. Cape, 1962); Richard Davey, *The Nine Days' Queen: Lady Jane Grey and Her Times* (London: Methuen, 1909); and Carole Levin, "Lady Jane Grey: Protestant Queen and Martyr," in *Silent but for the*

Word, pp. 92-106.

182   *Mary Tudor (1516-58)*
       The life of the Catholic queen has most recently been studied
       by David Loades; see *Mary Tudor: A Life* (Oxford: Blackwell,
       1989); *The Reign of Mary Tudor: Politics, Government, and
       Religion in England, 1553-1558* (New York: St. Martin's,
       1979); and "The Reign of Mary Tudor: Historiography and
       Research," *Albion* 21 (1989): 547-58. Other works include
       Robert Tittler, *The Reign of Mary I* (London: Longman,
       1983); Jasper Ridley, *The Life and Times of Mary Tudor* (Lon-
       don: Weidenfeld and Nicolson, 1973); H. F. M. Prescott,
       Mary Tudor (1940; London: Eyre & Spottiswoode, 1952); and
       Elizabeth Russell, "Mary Tudor and Mr. Jorkins," *Historical
       Research* 63 (1990): 263-76.

183   *Elizabeth I (1533-1603)*
       A number of different approaches as well as assessments char-
       acterize the recent work on Elizabeth. Anne Somerset, *Eliza-
       beth I* (London: Weidenfeld and Nicholson, 1991) tries to
       present a comprehensive portrait; Philippa Berry, *Of Chastity
       and Power: Elizabethan Literature and the Unmarried Queen*
       (London: Routledge, 1989) and Susan Bassnett, *Elizabeth I: A
       Feminist Perspective* (Oxford: Berg, 1988) offer feminist
       analyses; Christopher Haigh, *Elizabeth I* (New York: Long-
       man, 1988) examines her exercise of political power, including
       over the church; Jasper Ridley, *Elizabeth I* (London: Consta-
       ble, 1987) gives significant attention to religious issues; Alison
       Plowden, *Two Queens in One Isle: The Deadly Relationship of
       Elizabeth I & Mary, Queen of Scots* (Brighton: Harvester,
       1984) explores political and familial intrigues; Carolly Erick-
       son, *The First Elizabeth* (London: Macmillan, 1983), provides
       a very unflattering portrait, while Paul Johnson, *Elizabeth I: A
       Biography* (New York: Holt, Rinehart & Winston, 1974),
       offers a quite positive view. Two older views are those of
       Elkin C. Wilson, *England's Eliza* (Cambridge: Harvard, 1939)
       and John E. Neale, *Queen Elizabeth I* (London: Jonathan
       Cape, 1934). For studies of the specifically religious dimen-
       sions of her life and reign, see William P. Haugaard, *Elizabeth*

and the English Reformation (Cambridge: Cambridge, 1968) and Carl S. Meyer, *Elizabeth I and the Religious Settlement of 1559* (St. Louis: Concordia, 1960).

Some recent articles have focused on gender, image, and religion, including Peter McClure and Robin Headlam Wells, "Elizabeth I as a Second Virgin Mary," *Renaissance Studies* 4 (1990): 38-70; Carole Levin's "'Would I could give you help and succor': Elizabeth I and the Politics of Touch," *Albion* 21 (1989): 191-205, and "Power, Politics and Sexuality: Images of Elizabeth I," in *The Politics of Gender in Early Modern Europe*, ed. Jean R. Brink, et al. (Kirksville, MO: SCJ, 1989), pp. 95-110; and Mark Breitenberg, "'. . . the hole matter opened': Iconic Representation and Interpretation in 'The Quenes Majesties Passage'," *Criticism* 28 (1986): 1-25. Other articles related to the subject of religion include Susan Doran, "Religion and Politics at the Court of Elizabeth I: The Hapsburg Marriage Negotiations of 1559-1567," *EHR* 104 (1989): 908-26; Michael G. Brennan, "Two Private Prayers by Queen Elizabeth I," *Notes and Queries* 32 (1985): 26-28; Pamela Joseph Benson, "Rule, Virginia: Protestant Theories of Female Regiment in *The Fairy Queene*," *ELR* 15 (1985): 277-92; Anne Lake Prescott, "The Pearl of the Valois and Elizabeth I: Marguerite de Navarre's *Mirror* and Tudor England," in *Silent but for the Word*, pp. 61-76; Esther Clifford, "Marriage of True Minds," *SCJ* 15 (1984): 37-46; Norman L. Jones, "Elizabeth, Edification, and the Latin Prayer Book of 1560," *Church History* 53 (1984): 174-86; William P. Haugaard, "Elizabeth Tudor's *Book of Devotions*: A Neglected Clue to the Queen's Life and Character," *SCJ* 12 (1981): 79-106; and Frances A. Yates, "Queen Elizabeth as Astraea," *Journal of the Warburg and Courtauld Institutes* 10 (1947): 27-82.

184   *Mary, Queen of Scots (1542-87)*
Jenny Wormald's *Mary Queen of Scots: A Study in Failure* (London: George Philip, 1988) focuses on her brief rule as queen instead of on her person, and concludes that she was a failure as a ruler and a tragic figure because she was unable to cope with the responsibilities of power and showed complete indifference to the religion of her realm. The volume edited

by Michael Lynch, *Mary Stewart, Queen in Three Kingdoms* (Oxford: Blackwell, 1988), contains nine essays, including two on religious issues: Ian B. Cowan, "The Roman Connection: Prospects for Counter-Reformation during the Personal Reign of Mary, Queen of Scots," pp. 105-22; and Julian Goodare, "Queen Mary's Catholic Interlude," pp. 154-70. Other studies of varying quality include Jean Plaidy, *Mary Queen of Scots: The Fair Devil of Scotland* (London: Hale, 1975); Gordon Donaldson, *Mary Queen of Scots* (London: English Universities, 1974); Antonia Fraser, *Mary, Queen of Scots* (London: Methuen, 1969); and Andrew Dakers, *The Tragic Queen: A Study of Mary Queen of Scots* (London: Hutchinson, 1931).

185   *Lady Anne Clifford (1590-1676)*
There are few separate studies of this powerful individual and her interest in the church. The most suggestive is R. T. Spence, "Lady Anne Clifford, Countess of Dorset, Pembroke, and Montgomery (1590-1676): A Reappraisal," *Northern History* 15 (1979): 43-65; he writes that "Anne drew strength and conviction from adhering to and applying the assumptions of patriarchalism, not by rejecting them" (53). Other works include Martin Holmes, *Proud Northern Lady: Lady Anne Clifford, 1590-1676* (London: Phillimore, 1975); George C. Williamson, *Lady Anne Clifford* (Kendal: T. Wilson, 1922); and Wallace Notestein, *Four Worthies* (New Haven: Yale, 1957), pp. 123-68.

186   *Margaret Clitherow (c. 1553-86)*
One of the Elizabethan Catholic martyrs, her story is told and has been remembered in largely heroic dimensions. See Margaret T. Monro, *Blessed Margaret Clitherow* (London: Burns, Oates & Washbourne, 1946); Mary Claridge, *Margaret Clitherow, 1556?-1586* (New York: Fordham, 1966), and "Blessed Margaret Clitherow and the York Plays," *Month* n.s. 31 (1964): 347-54; Katherine M. Longley, "The 'Trial' of Margaret Clitherow," *Ampleforth Journal* (1970): 335-64; and Claire Cross, "An Elizabethan Martyrologist and his Martyr: John Mush and Margaret Clitherow," in *Martyrs and Martyrologies*, ed. Diana Wood (SCH 30; Oxford: Blackwell, 1993), pp. 271-

81.

187   *Mary Sidney, Countess of Pembroke (1561-1621)*
Patron of religion and literature, active supporter of the Protestant cause, she encouraged devotional writing and translated
the works of others. Several recent studies have featured or
included her, as Margaret P. Hannay's *Philip's Phoenix: Mary
Sidney, Countess of Pembroke* (New York: Oxford, 1990), and
earlier articles: "'Princes you as men must dy': Genevan Advice to Monarchs in the *Psalmes* of Mary Sidney," *ELR* 19
(1989): 22-41; and "'Doo What Men May Sing': Mary Sidney
and the Tradition of Admonitory Dedication," in *Silent but for
the Word*, pp. 149-65. Mary Ellen Lamb's *Gender and Authorship in the Sidney Circle* (Madison: Wisconsin, 1990),
considers women's writing in the context of a culture hostile to
women's speech; and her article "The Countess of Pembroke
and the Art of Dying," in *Women in the Middle Ages and the
Renaissance*, pp. 207-26, considers the way in which her
translations "embody a female literary strategy through which
women could be represented as heroic without challenging the
beliefs of the patriarchal culture of Elizabethan England"
(209). G. F. Waller's *Mary Sidney, Countess of Pembroke*
(Salzburg: Salzburg, 1979) was the first modern study of her;
his articles, "The text and Manuscript Variants of the Countess
of Pembroke's Psalms," *Review of English Studies* n.s. 26
(1975): 1-18, and "The Countess of Pembroke and Gendered
Reading," in *The Renaissance Englishwoman in Print*, pp.
327-45, take up textual and interpretive questions. Two articles by Beth Wynne Fisken, "'The Art of Sacred Parody' in
Mary Sidney's *Psalmes*," *TSWL* 8 (1989): 223-39, and "Mary
Sidney's *Psalmes*: Education and Wisdom," in *Silent but for
the Word*, pp. 166-83, explore aspects of her translations. A
bibliographical account and assessment is provided in Josephine A. Roberts, "Recent Studies in Women Writers of Tudor
England. Part II: Mary Sidney, Countess of Pembroke," *ELR*
14 (1984): 426-39. An older study is Frances Berkeley
Young, *Mary Sidney, Countess of Pembroke* (London: D.
Nutt, 1912).

188   *Mary Ward (1585-1645)*
Founder of a religious order for women on the Jesuit model
but greatly opposed by Rome and the English Catholic clergy,
Ward's reputation was not fully rehabilitated outside the order
until the twentieth century. Most studies have been hagiogra-
phic or have focused on her spirituality. The special issue of
The Way entitled *Mary Ward: Journey into Freedom* (Supplement 53, Summer 1985), celebrating the four hundredth anni-
versary of her birth, contains eleven essays on several dimensions of her legacy. M. Emmanuel Orchard, ed., *Till God
Will: Mary Ward Through her Writings* (London: Darton,
Longman and Todd, 1985), has an extended introduction to
her life and religious context. Antonia Fraser's "Mary Ward:
A 17th-Century Reformer," *History Today* 31 (May, 1981):
14-18, briefly traces her career, as does Mary Margaret Little-
hales in *Mary Ward (1585-1645): A Woman for All Seasons*
(London: Catholic Truth Soc., 1974). Popular biographies for
a church audience include M. M. O'Connor, *That Incompara-
ble Woman* (Montreal: Palm, 1962); Mary Oliver, *Mary Ward,
1585-1645* (New York: Sheed and Ward, 1959); M. Pauline
Parker, *The Spirit of Mary Ward* (1945; Bristol: Thomas
More, 1963); and Mother M., *Mary Ward: A Foundress of the
Seventeenth Century* (London: Burns & Oates, 1901). Substantial studies are provided by Josef Grisar: *Die Ersten Ankla-
gen in Rom Gegen das Institut Maria Wards (1622)* and *Mary
Wards Institut vor Römischen Kongregationen (1616-1630)*
(Rome: Pontificia Università Gregoriana, 1959 and 1966); and
"Die beiden ältesten Leben Maria Wards der Grunderin der
Englischen Fraulein," *Historisches Jahrbuch* 70 (1951): 154-
89. John P. Marmion studies the meaning of the fifty paintings of Ward commissioned by her followers in "Some Notes
on the 'Painted Life' of Mary Ward," *Recusant History* 18
(1987): 318-22. While rather old, the articles by Leo Hicks,
"Mary Ward's Great Enterprise," *Month* 151 (1928): 137-46,
317-26; 152 (1928): 40-52, 231-38; 153 (1929): 40-48, 223-
36, contain much useful detail.

Others

189   Read, Evelyn. *Catherine, Duchess of Suffolk.* London: J.
       Cape, 1962. Pp. 205.
       Goff, Cecilie. *A Woman of the Tudor Age.* London: J. Mur-
       ray, 1930. Pp. 326.
       Studies of Catherine Willoughby (1519-80), who was involved
       in the development of English Protestantism.

190   Warnicke, Retha M. "Lady Mildmay's Journal: A Study in
       Autobiography and Meditation in Reformation England,"
       SCJ 20 (1989): 55-68.
       Weigall, Rachel. "An Elizabethan Gentlewoman: The Journal
       of Lady Mildmay, circa 1570-1617, Unpublished,"
       Quarterly Review 215 (1911): 119-38.
       Grace Mildmay (1552-1620) married into a Puritan family; her
       journal is an important source for women's religious experi-
       ence in this period.

191   Notestein, Wallace. "Brilliana Lady Harley," in *English Folk:
       A Book of Characters.* New York: Harcourt, Brace, 1938.
       Pp. 227-63.
       In this volume of thirteen sketches, three are on women; Har-
       ley (1598-1643) was part of a Puritan family.

192   Meads, Dorothy M., ed. *Diary of Lady Margaret Hoby.*
       London: Routledge, 1930. Pp. 289.
       The introduction provides an extended biography (1571-1633).

CHAPTER 3

1640-1740:
CIVIL WAR AND RESTORATION;
WOMEN IN THE QUAKER MOVEMENT
AND THE LARGER CULTURE

Bibliographies, Guides, and Anthologies

193   Backscheider, Paula, et al., eds. *An Annotated Bibliography of Twentieth-Century Critical Studies of Women and Literature, 1660-1800.* New York: Garland, 1977. Pp. 287.
Includes books and articles published between 1900 and 1975.

194   Smith, Hilda L. and Cardinale, Susan, eds. *Women and the Literature of the Seventeenth Century: An Annotated Bibliography Based on Wing's Short-Title Catalogue.* New York: Greenwood, 1990. Pp. 332.
A list of 637 titles by women in the period 1641-1700, some 55% concerning religion and 27% by Quakers; and a second list of 973 titles for and about women. The annotations provide information about authors, as known.

195   Crawford, Patricia. "Women's Published Writings 1600-1700," in *Women in English Society, 1500-1800*, pp. 211-82.
A detailed analysis of the development of women's interest to write for publication, together with an extended bibliography of these published writings.

196   Todd, Janet, ed. *A Dictionary of British and American Women Writers, 1660-1800.* Totowa, NJ: Rowman & Allenheld,

1985. Pp. 344.
Biographical entries on more than 450 women, plus a substantial contextual introduction by the editor.

197   Greaves, Richard L. and Zaller, Robert, eds. *Biographical
      Dictionary of British Radicals in the Seventeenth Century.* 3
      vols., Brighton: Harvester, 1982-84.
      Includes entries for some 40 women, chiefly Quakers and
      other sectaries.

198   Goreau, Angeline, ed. *The Whole Duty of a Woman: Female
      Writers in Seventeenth-Century England.* Garden City, NY:
      Dial, 1985. Pp. 344.
      A wide-ranging selection of writings by and about women:
      ideals and prescriptions attending women's education, male
      critiques and women's responses, and some examples of wom-
      en's writings.

199   Graham, Elspeth, et al., eds. *Her Own Life: Autobiographical
      Writings by Seventeenth-century Englishwomen.* London:
      Routledge, 1989. Pp. 250.
      Twelve selections from 1616 to 1691, together with an ex-
      tended introduction; for the most part, these are spiritual auto-
      biographies reflecting several different religious and social
      contexts.

General Historical Studies

200   Clark, Alice. *Working Life of Women in the Seventeenth
      Century.* London, 1919. Pp. 328.
      This important early work argues that the split between the
      private and public spheres, enhanced by the Industrial Revo-
      lution, limited opportunities for women workers.

201   Reynolds, Myra. *The Learned Lady in England, 1650-1760.*
      Boston: Houghton Mifflin, 1920. Pp. 489.
      Explores the general state of education of women, attitudes
      toward women scholars, and the contributions of individual
      women.

202   Hole, Christina. *The English Housewife in the Seventeenth Century.* London: Chatto & Windus, 1953. Pp. 248.
The domestic round, from marriage to death; the importance of religion in seventeenth-century family life is considered.

203   Knox, Ronald A. *Enthusiasm: A Chapter in the History of Religion with Special Reference to the XVII and XVIII Centuries.* Oxford: Clarendon, 1950. Pp. 622.
A sweeping and occasionally jaunty history, from the New Testament to nineteenth-century revivals; the special focus is on Jansenism and Quietism, but also includes Quakers, Methodists, Shakers, and nineteenth-century holiness women. For Knox, "enthusiasm is not a wrong tendency but a false emphasis" (590).

204   Rowbotham, Sheila. *Women, Resistance and Revolution: A History of Women and Revolution in the Modern World.* London: Allen Lane The Penguin Press, 1972; rept, 1974. Pp. 288.
From its beginnings in the Puritan experience to recent revolutions in Cuba, Algeria, etc. Chapter 1 focuses on women, religion, and revolution in England from the sixteenth to the eighteenth centuries and discusses the secularization of ideas.

205   _____. *Hidden from History.* London: Pluto, 1973. Pp. 182.
A breezy, sweeping history of the oppression of women and responses to it, from the seventeenth to the early twentieth century, with a focus on economic issues and the more radical responses.

206   Thompson, Roger. *Women in Stuart England and America: A Comparative Study.* London: Routledge & Kegan Paul, 1974. Pp. 276.
The comparison is pursued across a number of topics, including economic opportunities, religion, courtship and marriage, family, and education; the general conclusion is that American women had a more attractive position in society, regardless of class.

207   Eisenstein, Zillah. *The Radical Future of Liberal Feminism*.
        New York: Longman, 1981. Pp. 260.
        Takes up the theoretical debate over the shape of liberalism,
        including the contributions of Mary Wollstonecraft and J. S.
        Mill toward a justification of women's civil and legal equality.

208   Smith, Hilda L. *Reason's Disciples: Seventeenth-Century
        English Feminists*. Urbana: Illinois, 1982. Pp. 237.
        Identifies a dozen female intellectuals in the second half of the
        century who shifted the notion of the educated woman by their
        writings about women as a group, their defense of women's
        rational abilities, and their insight into the social definition of
        sex roles. Most of this group were Anglican in religion and
        Tories politically.

209   _____. "Intellectual Bases for Feminist Analysis: The
        Seventeenth and Eighteenth Centuries," in *Women and Reason*,
        ed. Elizabeth D. Harvey and Kathleen Okruhlik. Ann Arbor:
        Michigan, 1992. Pp. 19-38.
        This article continues the themes of the previous volume.

210   Mendelson, Sara Heller. *The Mental World of Stuart Women:
        Three Studies*. Amherst: Massachusetts, 1987. Pp. 235.
        Through biographies of Margaret Cavendish, Duchess of
        Newcastle; Mary Rich, Countess of Warwick; and Aphra
        Behn, playwright and author, a view of women's mental world
        emerges by focusing on "female life stages, patriarchalism in
        theory and practice, the control of female sexuality, the limita-
        tions inherent in women's conventional role and the reactions
        provoked by those who sought to challenge them" (11). The
        chapter on Rich includes extended discussion of women's
        devotional life.

211   George, Margaret. *Women in the First Capitalist Society:
        Experiences in Seventeenth-Century England*.   Urbana:
        Illinois, 1988. Pp. 260.
        _____. "From Goodwife to Mistress: The Transformation
        of the Female in Bourgeois Culture," *Science and Society*
        37 (1973): 152-77.

Explorations into the development of the bourgeois women's world, including the influential rationale provided by Protestant preachers of the spiritualized family with the woman in charge.

212   Gallagher, Catherine. "Embracing the Absolute: The Politics of the Female Subject in Seventeenth-Century England," *Genders* 1 (1988): 24-39.
On the convergence of Toryism and feminism in Margaret Cavendish and Mary Astell, which eventually gave birth to the idea of "emancipated" female subjectivity.

213   Ruether, Rosemary Radford. "Prophets and Humanists: Types of Religious Feminism in Stuart England," *Journal of Religion* 70 (1990): 1-18.
Considers three types of responses challenging women's subordination in religion in this period: 1) a continuation of the *querelle des femmes* tradition representing the end of a Renaissance genre; 2) mid-century millenarian and apocalyptic female prophets and Quaker women; and 3) late seventeenth-century emphases on reason and women's rights to education.

214   Norman, Marion. "Eve's Daughters at School," *Atlantis* 3 (Spring 1978): 66-81.
Studies some of the forerunners to the educational developments for women that took place in the eighteenth and nineteenth centuries; examples from Anglican, Nonconformist, and Catholic contexts.

215   Hill, Bridget. "A Refuge from Men: The Idea of a Protestant Nunnery," *Past & Present* 117 (November 1987): 107-30.
Explores the recurrence of the idea of a "Protestant nunnery" from the sixteenth to the nineteenth century, with special attention to the religious dimension of these interests; from these foundations, Hill notes, emerged separate women's colleges in the late nineteenth century.

216   Schnorrenberg, Barbara B. "A Paradise Like Eve's: Three Eighteenth-century English Female Utopias," *Women's Studies* 9 (1982): 263-73.

Considers proposals for reform through the creation of communities of women that came from Mary Astell, Sarah Scott, and Clara Reeve; each was centered on an Anglican understanding of religious training.

Literary Studies

217   Hobby, Elaine. *Virtue of Necessity: English Women's Writing 1649-1688*. London: Virago, 1988. Pp. 269.
Uses the writings of some two hundred women to discern how they responded to the limits they encountered within the family, education, and religion, and contributed to the re-shaping of their own identities.

218   Todd, Janet. *The Sign of Angellica: Women, Writing and Fiction, 1660-1800*. New York: Columbia, 1989. Pp. 328.
On the entrance of women into literature as a profession, with attention to the moral and didactic elements in much of this literature and to those writers nurtured in Dissenting circles. "If the natural world and its control in technology were not their concern, then manners and morals surely were" (25).

219   Nussbaum, Felicity. *The Autobiographical Subject: Gender and Ideology in Eighteenth-Century England*. Baltimore: Johns Hopkins, 1990. Pp. 264.
A study of the ideologies of self-biography from John Bunyan to Hester Thrale; an important dimension in this developing genre is the spiritual autobiography, and an important aspect of the emergence of gendered subjectivity is the production of women's spiritual autobiographies.

220   Thickstun, Margaret Olofson. *Fictions of the Feminine: Puritan Doctrine and the Representation of Women*. Ithaca: Cornell, 1988. Pp. 176.
Explores the influence of Puritan theology and domestic theory on the representation of women in Spenser, Milton, and Bunyan, and later in the novels of Richardson and Hawthorne.

221   Adburgham, Alison. *Women in Print: Writing, Women and*

Women's Magazines from the Restoration to the Accession of Victoria. London: Allen & Unwin, 1972. Pp. 302.
Includes discussion of Mary Astell's ambitious proposals for the education of women and the moral uplift literature by Sarah Trimmer and Hannah More a century later.

222   Wallas, Ada. *Before the Bluestockings.* London: Allen & Unwin, 1929. Pp. 223.
Six essays that explore the position of educated Englishwomen between 1660 and 1730, including one on Mary Astell.

223   Phillips, Margaret and Tomkinson, W. S. *English Women in Life and Letters.* Oxford: Oxford, 1926. Pp. 408.
The focus here is on 1650-1800, with only occasional references to religion.

224   Pomerleau, Cynthia S. "The Emergence of Women's Autobiography in England," in *Women's Autobiography: Essays in Criticism*, ed. Estelle C. Jelinek. Bloomington: Indiana, 1980. Pp. 21-38.
Although secular examples receive greater attention, these are juxtaposed with observations on the number and influence of religious autobiographies.

225   Rose, Mary Beth. "Gender, Genre, and History: Seventeenth-Century English Women and the Art of Autobiography," in *Women in the Middle Ages and the Renaissance: Literary and Historical Perspectives*, pp. 245-78.
Considers the contributions of four aristocratic Anglican women to the development of secular autobiography; though all are pious, they write of their activities in a social world.

226   Hobby, Elaine. "'Discourse so unsavoury': Women's Published Writings of the 1650s," in *Women, Writing, History: 1640-1740*, ed. Isobel Grundy and Susan Wiseman. Athens: Georgia, 1992. Pp. 16-32.
An overview of the decade which saw the first significant appearance of women's published writings in English; Hobby points to the complexity of the relationships between femininity

and religious belief in this decade.

227   Parish, Debra L. "The Power of Female Pietism: Women as
       Spiritual Authorities and Religious Role Models in Seven-
       teenth-century England," *JRH* 17 (1992): 33-46.
       Through funeral sermons and ministerial devotional writings,
       Parish examines "the nature and extent of the religious power
       and influence which these ministers gave to their female sub-
       jects" (36).

228   Lilley, Kate. "Blazing Worlds: Seventeenth-century Women's
       Utopian Writing," in *Women, Texts, and Histories, 1575-1760*,
       pp. 102-33.
       Discusses works by five authors, including Mary Cary (1651)
       and Mary Astell (1694) who represent the radical sectarian and
       conservative poles of the religious discourse on the subject.

229   Mendelson, Sara Heller. "Stuart Women's Diaries and Occa-
       sional Memoirs," in *Women in English Society, 1500-1800*,
       pp. 181-210.
       A study of twenty-three women who left such writings, some
       three-fourths of which contain considerable devotional content.

230   Bishop, Barbara Jean. "'Tis Good to Cry Out When We Are
       Assaulted': The Christian Heroine from *The Pilgrim's Prog-
       ress* to *Little Dorrit*." Ph.D., UCLA, 1992. Pp. 305.
       Analyses the effects of gendered religious ideology on Chris-
       tian heroines and the literary texts that contain them.

231   Maurer, Shawn Lisa. "Reforming Men: Gender, Sexuality,
       and Class in the Early English Periodical." Ph.D., Michigan,
       1991. Pp. 232.
       Argues that an understanding of the development of gender
       roles must include an analysis of men's place in the discourse
       of domesticity.

232   Marshall, Madeleine Forell. *The Poetry of Elizabeth Singer
       Rowe (1674-1737)*. Lewiston, NY: Edwin Mellen, 1987.
       Pp. 369.

Stecher, Henry F. *Elizabeth Singer Rowe, the Poetess of Frome: A Study in Eighteenth-Century English Pietism*. Frankfort: Peter Lang, 1973. Pp. 265.

Two studies of her life and poetical writings, within the context of eighteenth-century literary, religious, and moral ideas; Stecher's is flawed by a rather loose understanding of Pietism.

233   Green, Mary Elizabeth. "Elizabeth Elstob: 'The Saxon Nymph' (1683-1756)," in *Female Scholars: A Tradition of Learned Women Before 1800*, ed. J. R. Brink. Montreal: Eden, 1980. Pp. 137-60.

Elstob was a remarkable linguist and scholar of Anglo-Saxon, who published a translation of a homily of Aelfric, tenth-century archbishop of Canterbury, in 1709.

234   Graham, Elspeth. "Authority, Resistance, and Loss: Gendered Difference in the Writings of John Bunyan and Hannah Allen," in *John Bunyan and His England, 1628-88*, ed. Anne Laurence, et al. London: Hambledon, 1990. Pp. 115-30.

A comparison of their spiritual autobiographies.

235   Blanchard, Rae. "Richard Steele and the Status of Women," *Studies in Philology* 26 (1929): 325-55.

Considers three groups of writers, 1650-1725, interested in the subject of women: conservatives, wits, and reformers; Blanchard suggests that while Steele does not fit neatly with any of these, he has some affinities with each.

John Milton and Women

236   Since the beginnings of a debate in the 1970s, the question of Milton's attitude toward women has become one of the most vigorous in Milton scholarship; its relevance here stems from its association with a religious grounding and its representation (or not) of the age in which he lived. Milton scholarship is, of course, massive and has its own reference literature; what is included here is a sample of the discussion of this issue. Two useful bibliographies are:

Patrides, C. A., ed. *An Annotated Critical Bibliography of*

John Milton. Brighton: Harvester, 1987. Pp. 200.

Huckaby, Calvin, ed. *John Milton: An Annotated Bibliography, 1929-1968.* Rev. ed., Pittsburgh: Duquesne, 1969. Pp. 392.

237   McColley, Diane Kelsey. *Milton's Eve.* Urbana: Illinois, 1983. Pp. 232.
Aims "to extricate Eve from a reductive critical tradition . . . and to establish a regenerative reading of her role" (4), thus making a case for Milton's being in advance of the thinking of his age.

238   Turner, James G. *One Flesh: Paradisal Marriage and Sexual Relations in the Age of Milton.* Oxford: Clarendon, 1987. Pp. 320.
A study of interpretations of the first chapters of Genesis, considering understandings of sexuality, views of womanhood and the nature of marriage, and the conflicts involved in living in a fallen world.

239   Wittreich, Joseph. *Feminist Milton.* Ithaca: Cornell, 1987. Pp. 173.
Argues that "Milton was not just an ally of feminists but their early sponsor" (ix).

240   Walker, Julia M., ed. *Milton and the Idea of Woman.* Urbana: Illinois, 1988. Pp. 262.
Twelve essays explore different aspects of the topic, most with reference to a particular text; as an example, see Dayton Haskins, "Milton's Portrait of Mary as a Bearer of the Word," pp. 169-84.

241   Gallagher, Philip J. *Milton, the Bible, and Misogyny.* Columbia: Missouri, 1990. Pp. 185.
Focusing on the doctrines of creation, fall, and redemption, Gallagher proposes that Milton "set about to rehabilitate Scripture by repudiating its misogynistic spirit even as he preserved its very letter" (174).

242   Landy, Marcia. "Kinship and the Role of Women in *Paradise
       Lost*," *Milton Studies* 4 (1972): 3-18.
       Lewalski, Barbara K. "Milton on Women—Yet Once More,"
       Milton Studies 6 (1974): 3-20.
       _____. "Milton on Women—Yet Again," in *Problems for
       Feminist Criticism*, ed. Sally Minogue. London: Routledge,
       1990. Pp. 46-69.
       An example of the debate over Milton. Landy holds that while
       not a misogynist, Milton was a representative of Protestant
       patriarchy; Lewalski urges attention to what is universal in
       Milton's concerns, rather than what is historically conditioned.

243   Bowers, Mary Beacom. "Milton's Conception of Woman,"
       Ohio Journal of Religious Studies 4:1 (1976): 19-33.
       Contends that while Milton gave great importance to woman's
       role, he set this firmly within a hierarchical order subordinate
       to man.

244   One position in this discussion acknowledges Milton's belief in
       universal hierarchy and the subordination of woman to man,
       but notes ways in which Milton transcended his age; some of
       this is seen in the following articles:
       Isaak, Jo-Anne. "The Education of Eve: Milton," *Atlantis* 2
       (Spring 1977): 114-22.
       Webber, Joan Malory. "The Politics of Poetry: Feminism and
       Paradise Lost," *Milton Studies* 14 (1980): 3-24.
       Farwell, Marilyn R. "Eve, the Separation Scene, and the
       Renaissance Idea of Androgyny," *Milton Studies* 16 (1982):
       3-20.
       McChrystal, Dierdre Keenan. "Redeeming Eve," *ELR* 23
       (1993): 490-508.
       Siegel, Paul N. "Milton and the Humanist Attitude Toward
       Women," *JHI* 11 (1950): 42-53.
       Radzinowicz, Mary Ann Nevins. "Eve and Dalila: Renovation
       and the Hardening of the Heart," in *Reason and the Imagi-
       nation: Studies in the History of Ideas, 1600-1800*, ed. J.
       A. Mazzeo. New York: Columbia, 1962. Pp. 155-82.
       Mollenkott, Virginia R. "Milton and Women's Liberation: A
       Note on Teaching Method," *Milton Quarterly* 7 (1973): 99-

103.
Halpern, Richard. "Puritanism and Maenadism in *A Mask*," in
*Rewriting the Renaissance: The Discourses of Sexual Differ-
ence in Early Modern Europe*, eds. Margaret W. Ferguson,
et al. Chicago: Chicago, 1986. Pp. 88-105.

Religion, Prophecy, and Radical Activity

245   Hill, Christopher. *The World Turned Upside Down: Radical
        Ideas during the English Revolution.* New York: Viking,
        1972. Pp. 351.
        An exploration of the "revolt within the Revolution" (13), as
        represented by such groups as Levellers, Diggers, Ranters,
        and the various sects. Chapter 15 discusses Puritan and radi-
        cal understandings of the role of women as well as their atti-
        tudes to sexuality.

246   McArthur, Ellen A. "Women Petitioners and the Long Par-
        liament," *EHR* 24 (1909): 698-709.
        This early article focuses on the activity of claiming an equal
        interest with men in matters of national importance, but does
        not take up the connection to religious roots for the claim.

247   Higgins, Patricia. "The Reactions of Women, with Special
        Reference to Women Petitioners," in *Politics, Religion, and
        the English Civil War*, ed. Brian Manning. London: E. Ar-
        nold, 1973. Pp. 179-222.
        Higgins both expands and corrects McArthur's investigations,
        exploring both activities and arguments; regarding the claim
        for equality, she declares that "puritan insistence on individual
        salvation and on the equality of man and woman in Christ . . .
        had given it a new vigour and freshness" (215).

248   _____. "Women in the English Civil War." M. A., Man-
        chester, 1965. Pp. 297.
        Studies different roles undertaken by women between 1640-49,
        showing how the decade was important in enlarging the status
        of women; religious interests and activities are given promi-
        nence, especially the roles of preachers, prophets, and writers,

as well as the influence of sectarian teaching and practice concerning the place of women in society.

249   McEntee, Ann Marie. "'The [Un]Civill-Sisterhood of Oranges and Lemons': Female Petitioners and Demonstrators, 1642-53," *Prose Studies* 14:3 (1991): 92-111.
On the increasingly bold demand for political rights, including the use of biblical imagery to assert these claims.

250   Smith, Nigel. *Perfection Proclaimed: Language and Literature in English Radical Religion 1640-1660*. Oxford: Clarendon, 1989. Pp. 396.
Within this broader topic, Smith notes the centrality of recounting religious experiences, dreams and visions, especially in the writings of women prophets such as Sarah Wight and Anna Trapnel.

251   Gentles, Ian. "London Levellers in the English Revolution: The Chidleys and Their Circle," *JEH* 29 (1978): 281-309.
Katherine and Samuel Chidley (mother and son) were religious pamphleteers and evangelists and defenders of separatism and religious toleration; Katherine led the women's protest against the imprisonment of the Leveller leader, John Lilburne.

252   Berg, Christine and Berry, Philippa. "'Spiritual Whoredom': An Essay on Female Prophets in the Seventeenth Century," in *1642: Literature and Power in the Seventeenth Century*, ed. Frances Barker, et al. Essex: Essex, 1981. Pp. 37-54.
Argues that the threat of prophetic speech lay particularly in its feminine character, challenging conventional modes of expression and control with seventeenth-century patriarchal society; the threat lay in the possibility that a woman could possess and transmit the word of God.

253   Lennon, Thomas M. "Lady Oracle: Changing Conceptions of Authority and Reason in Seventeenth-Century Philosophy," in *Women and Reason*, ed. Elizabeth D. Harvey and Kathleen Obruhlik. Ann Arbor: Michigan, 1992. Pp. 39-61.
Contends that objections to prophetic discourse occurred be-

cause it ran counter to the new understanding of reason as universal and self-evident, not because it was perceived as feminine.

254   Mack, Phyllis. "Women as Prophets during the English Civil War," *Feminist Studies* 8 (1982): 19-45 [also in *The Origins of Anglo-American Radicalism*, ed. M. Jacob and J. Jacob (London: Allen & Unwin, 1984), pp. 214-30].

_____. "The Prophet and Her Audience: Gender and Knowledge in the World Turned Upside Down," in *Reviving the English Revolution: Reflections and Elaborations on the Work of Christopher Hill*, ed. Geoff Eley and William Hunt. London: Verso, 1988. Pp. 139-52.

Two articles on the use of feminine religious symbols and imagery. The second probes the question of why the most radical of the sectarian groups, the Diggers, had programs which preserved a patriarchal order, while those groups with the least political programs and the most mystical theology (especially the Quakers) integrated women into their activities.

255   Dailey, Barbara Ritter. "The Visitation of Sarah Wight: Holy Carnival and the Revolution of the Saints in Civil War London," *Church History* 55 (1986): 438-55.

A tale of the public role of piety, told by Henry Jessey, of the illness and threat of impending death of Sarah Wight in 1647, which, in the carnival dramas of role reversal, became the occasion of her public teaching in a time of national crisis.

256   Trubowitz, Rachel. "Female Authority and Male Wives: Gender and Authority in Civil War England," *Prose Studies* 14:3 (1991): 112-33.

Considers some paradoxes in gender relations in the 1640s, where "irrational and ecstatic modes of female inspiration are sanctioned alongside rationalist and new scientific efforts to control and domesticate 'female' nature" (128).

257   Wiseman, Sue. "Unsilent Instruments and the Devil's Cushions: Authority in Seventeenth-Century Women's Prophetic Discourse," in *New Feminist Discourses*, ed. Isobel Arm-

strong. London: Routledge, 1992. Pp. 176-96.
On how women prophets used codes of prophecy and biblical
exegesis to support their status as prophets and to open up
potentially anti-patriarchal conceptualizations of political and
religious authority.

258   Purkiss, Diane. "Producing the Voice, Consuming the Body:
       Women Prophets of the Seventeenth Century," in *Women,
       Writing, History: 1640-1740*, pp. 139-58.
       Argues "that the visibility of the woman prophet's body was a
       means by which she negotiated a space to speak within the
       constraints of seventeenth-century religious discourse, and
       hence a way for her to threaten established orders and hier-
       archies" (141).

259   Burrage, Champlin. "Anna Trapnel's Prophecies," *EHR* 26
       (1911): 526-35.
       Burrage identified the author of a recently purchased folio
       volume of 1659, containing prophecies in poem form, as
       Trapnel.

260   Rogers, Philip G. *The Fifth Monarchy Men*. London: Ox-
              ford, 1966. Pp. 168.
       Capp, B. S. *Fifth Monarchy Men: A Study in Seventeenth-
              century English Millenarianism*. London: Faber & Faber,
              1972. Pp. 315.
       These are general studies, with very limited attention to the
       role of women participants such as Mary Cary and Anna
       Trapnel.

261   Cohen, Alfred. "The Fifth Monarchy Mind: Mary Cary and
              the Origins of Totalitarianism," *Social Research* 31 (1964):
              195-213.
                     . "Prophecy and Madness: Women Visionaries
              During the Puritan Revolution," *Journal of Psychohistory*
              11 (1983-84): 411-30.
       Two rather critical essays; the first probes the ideological
       affinity between revolutionary chiliasm and modern authori-
       tarianism in Cary's writings, while the second suggests that

many women prophets were, in fact, if perhaps temporarily, mad.

Puritans, Sectarians, and Nonconformists

262   Williams, Ethyn Morgan. "Women Preachers in the Civil War," *Journal of Modern History* 1 (1929): 561-69.
       Traces the appearance of women pamphleteers and preachers among Independents from 1641-46, especially Katherine Chidley and Elizabeth Warren.

263   Thomas, Keith. "Women and the Civil War Sects," *Past & Present* 13 (1958): 42-62 [also in *Crisis in Europe 1560-1660*, ed. T. H. Aston (New York: Basic Books, 1965), pp. 317-40].
       A widely-cited article on the impact of the separatist religious groups on the patriarchal view of family in general and on women in particular. Much of the religious expression in this period encouraged self-expression for women, wider spheres of influence, and an asceticism which could emancipate from ties of family life; all this posed a major threat to the established order, but was only one of the challenges to the patriarchal family.

264   Cross, Claire. "He-Goats Before the Flocks: A Note on the Part Played by Women in the Founding of Some Civil War Churches," in *Popular Belief and Practice* (SCH 8), ed. G. J. Cuming and Derek Baker. Cambridge: Cambridge, 1972. Pp. 195-202.
       On the tradition of independent action by laywomen coming to fruition in the Civil War but having roots back to the Henrician Reformation; Cross uses the examples of Dorothy Hazzard, Katherine Chidley, and the company of godly women who formed the Bedford church in 1650.

265   Ludlow, Dorothy. "'Arise and Be Doing': English 'Preaching' Women, 1640-1660." Ph.D., Indiana, 1978. Pp. 404.
       _____. "Shaking Patriarchy's Foundations: Sectarian Women in England, 1641-1700," in *Triumph Over Silence: Women in Protestant History*, pp. 93-123.

The dissertation deals with the writings and activities of eight preaching women as products of their society who had a distinctive sense of Christian calling. Ludlow's article offers a comparison between the revolutionary and Restoration eras regarding the situation for women, showing both changes and continuities.

266   Field, Clive D. "Adam and Eve: Gender in the English Free Church Constituency," *JEH* 44 (1993): 63-79.
This is the first article covering the extent of female activity in Nonconformity from 1650 to the present, using categories of membership, attendance, and profession; over six hundred Baptist and Congregational church membership lists provide the basic source material. One tentative judgment: "the less that is required by way of active involvement or personal sacrifice, the greater the number of men" (78).

267   Greaves, Richard L. "The Ordination Controversy and the Spirit of Reform in Puritan England," *JEH* 21 (1970): 225-41.
Discusses the issue of the right to preach without ordination between 1644-55; in addition to differences over freedom and order, the issue divided along class lines.

268   Briggs, John. "She-preachers, Widows and Other Women: The Feminine Dimension in Baptist Life Since 1600," *Baptist Quarterly* 31 (1986): 337-52.
This survey covering nearly four hundred years is necessarily sketchy, but a good starting point for studying the contributions of Baptist women; besides noting numerous individuals and their work, Briggs probes the continuing resistance to full equality for women in this century.

269   McBeth, Leon. *Women in Baptist Life.* Nashville: Broadman, 1979. Pp. 27-37.
This short section looks at the contributions of women in the establishment of Baptist congregations after 1640.

270   Caffyn, John. *Sussex Believers: Baptist Marriage in the 17th and 18th Centuries.* Worthing: Churchman, 1988. Pp. 319.

In exploring Baptist attitudes and practices, Caffyn discovers that all but a small minority married within their communion; and since women outnumbered men significantly in the congregations, many would have remained spinsters.

271 Wadsworth, Kenneth W. "A Tercentenary—Elizabeth Gaunt," *JURCHS* 3 (1986): 316-20.
On the last female burned to death at Tyburn for her Anabaptist religious beliefs, in 1685.

272 More, Ellen S. "Congregationalism and the Social Order: John Goodwin's Gathered Church, 1640-60," *JEH* 38 (1987): 210-35.
A microscopic look at one congregation to see if contemporary fears that congregationalism would prove subversive to the stability of family, parish, and kingdom were justified; individual women could become members, but they did not hold office or engage in any public role.

273 Laurence, Anne. "A Priesthood of She-believers: Women and Congregations in Mid-seventeenth-century England," in *Women in the Church*, pp. 345-63.
Argues that despite the prominence of women in the radical sects, their position with respect to church organization and authority was no different from that of women in the Anglican or Roman Catholic churches.

274 Yoshioka, Barbara G. S. "Imaginal Worlds: Women as Witch and Preacher in Seventeenth-Century England," Ph.D., Syracuse, 1977. Pp. 656.
Contends that women as preachers and witches shared a common theme of the body being connected with the spirit.

275 Braund, Elizabeth. "Mrs. Hutchinson and Her Teaching," *Evangelical Quarterly* 31 (1959): 72-81.
Hutchinson's two works, published some 150 years after they were written, are considered as examples of Puritan theology.

276 Smith, Charlotte Fell. *Mary Rich, Countess of Warwick*

(1625-1678): Her Family and Friends. London: Longmans, Green, 1901. Pp. 377.

Fraser, Antonia. "Mary Rich, Countess of Warwick: A Good Woman and a Great Lady," *History Today* 31 (June 1981): 48-51.

Studies of Rich (1625-78) as an example of Puritan womanhood.

277   Jenkins, Philip. "Mary Wharton and the Rise of the 'New Woman'," *National Library of Wales Journal* 22 (1981): 170-86.

From an aristocratic, puritan background, Wharton (1649-99) had advanced views on marriage, family, and children.

278   Bell, Maureen. "Hannah Allen and the Development of a Puritan Publishing Business, 1646-51," *Publishing History* 26 (1989): 5-66.

In the period between the death of her husband and her remarriage, Allen published official fast and thanksgiving sermons as well as other political/religious pamphlets.

279   Keeble, N. H. "'Here is her Glory, even to be under Him': The Feminine in the Thought and Work of John Bunyan," *Baptist Quarterly* 32 (1988): 380-92.

On the role assigned to women in Bunyan's writing; "his imaginative sympathy for women is never so intense as to jeopardise patriarchy" (390).

280   Eales, Jacqueline. "Samuel Clarke and the 'Lives' of Godly Women in Seventeenth-century England," in *Women in the Church*, pp. 365-76.

Shows how the spiritual biographies, often from funeral sermons, included in Clarke's *Lives* (1683) help one to appreciate the role of women in the Puritan tradition.

281   Crawford, Patricia. "Katherine and Philip Henry and Their Children: A Case Study in Family Ideology," *Transactions of the Historic Society of Lancashire and Cheshire* 134 (1984): 39-73.

On the importance of family life in a late seventeenth-century Nonconformist minister's household; in such a family, Crawford suggests, "religion increased the distance between the prestige of the men's and women's domains" (57).

282   Bell, Patricia L.   "Agnes Beaumont of Edworth," *Baptist Quarterly* 35 (1993): 3-17.
A narrative of her life (1652-1728), including her association with the Bunyan meeting in Bedford.

283   Hamblin, F. J.   "A Minister's Wife of the Eighteenth Century," *TUHS* 10 (1954): 185-92.
A glimpse of religious life from the vantage point of Elizabeth Lawrence Lloyd Bury (1644-1720).

Quakers

284   Although the literature on the role of women in the Society of Friends is extensive, there is a marked difference between the material produced from within the movement and that emerging since the 1970s from scholars interested in gender issues, questions of authority and power, and other related topics. Relevant early studies include:
Braithwaite, William C. *The Beginnings of Quakerism.* 1912; Cambridge: Cambridge, 1970. Pp. 607.
_____. *The Second Period of Quakerism.* 1919; Cambridge: Cambridge, 1961. Pp. 735.
Jorns, Auguste. *The Quakers as Pioneers in Social Work.* Trans. Thomas K. Brown. 1912; New York: Macmillan, 1931. Pp. 269.
Brailsford, Mabel R. *Quaker Women, 1650-1690.* London: Duckworth, 1915. Pp. 340.
Wright, Luella M. *The Literary Life of the Early Friends, 1650-1725.* New York: Columbia, 1932. Pp. 309.
Lloyd, Arnold. *Quaker Social History, 1669-1738.* London: Longmans, Green, 1950. Pp. 207.
Vann, Richard T. *The Social Development of English Quakerism, 1655-1755.* Cambridge: Harvard, 1969. Pp. 259.
Vipont, Elfrida. *The Story of Quakerism Through Three Cen-

turies. London: Bannisdale, 1954. Pp. 310.

_____. *George Fox and the Valiant Sixty*. London: H. Hamilton, 1975. Pp. 141.

285   Gadt, Jeannette Carter. "Women and Protestant Culture: The Quaker Dissent from Puritanism." Ph.D., UCLA, 1974. Pp. 347.
Argues that there was a necessary and compelling connection between the Quaker doctrine of the indwelling spirit and the large participation of women in the movement.

286   Luder, Hope Elizabeth. *Women and Quakerism*. Wallingford, PA: Pendle Hill, 1974. Pp. 36.
Leach, Robert J. *Women Ministers: A Quaker Contribution*. Wallingford, PA: Pendle Hill, 1979. Pp. 29.
Two pamphlets on women's involvement from the beginnings of the movement.

287   Speizman, Milton D. and Kronick, Jane C. "A Seventeenth-Century Quaker Women's Declaration," *Signs* 1 (1975): 231-45.
An introduction to a previously unpublished extended letter that represents "a codification of the thought and experience of women's meetings" (234).

288   Mullett, Michael, ed. *Early Lancaster Friends*. Occasional Paper, No. 5; Centre for North-West Regional Studies, Univ. of Lancaster, 1978. Pp. 56.
Of the four essays, two deal with women's activities: Michael Mullett, "The Social Organization of Lancashire Friends," pp. 12-21; and Beatrice Carré, "Early Quaker Women in Lancaster and Lancashire," pp. 43-53.

289   Huber, Elaine C. "'A Woman Must Not Speak': Quaker Women in the English Left Wing," in *Women of Spirit: Female Leadership in the Jewish and Christian Traditions*, ed. Rosemary Ruether and Eleanor McLaughlin. New York: Simon and Schuster, 1979. Pp. 153-81.
Considers the role of women in the context of the movement's

early characteristics: simplicity, empowerment in the present moment, a sense of adventure, and opportunity for full participation.

290   Scott, Janet. "Women in the Society of Friends," in *A Quaker Miscellany for Edward H. Milligan*, ed. David Blamires, et al. Manchester: Headley, 1985. Pp. 125-31.
A brief and broad overview across three centuries.

291   Barbour, Hugh. "Quaker Prophetesses and Mothers in Israel," in *Seeking the Light: Essays in Quaker History in Honor of Edwin B. Bronner*. ed. J. Wm. Frost and John M. Moore. Wallingford, PA: Pendle Hill, 1986. Pp. 41-60.
On these two special roles for women in the movement.

292   Dunn, Richard S. and Mary Maples, eds. *The World of William Penn*. Philadelphia: Pennsylvania, 1986.
Of twenty essays, two are of special interest here: Carole Shammas, "The World Women Knew: Women Workers in the North of England During the Late Seventeenth Century," pp. 99-115; and Michael J. Galgano, "Out of the Mainstream: Catholic and Quaker Women in the Restoration Northwest," pp. 117-37.

293   Brown, Elisabeth Potts and Stuard, Susan Mosher, eds. *Witnesses for Change: Quaker Women over Three Centuries*. New Brunswick: Rutgers, 1989. Pp. 190.
Of five essays covering England and America, Susan Mosher Stuard's "Women's Witnessing: A New Departure," pp. 3-25, sets the early Quakers in the context of the prevailing gender ideology and discusses the contributions of Quaker women in challenging it; Phyllis Mack's "Gender and Spirituality in Early English Quakerism, 1650-1665," pp. 31-68, opposes several lines of traditional scholarship by emphasizing Quaker freedom from selfhood, noting several important differences between northern and southern women, and distinguishing Quaker preaching from that of other contemporary visionaries.

294   Trevett, Christine. *Women and Quakerism in the 17th Centu-*

ry. York: Sessions, 1991. Pp. 171.
Surprisingly, the first book on the subject since Mabel Brailsford's (1915); three chapters address the role of women in the
early years, their work as ministers and their activities in the
home, and the establishment of structures of separate meetings
and patterns of life concerning marriage, children, and education. Very suggestive for further work.

295   _____. "The Women around James Naylor, Quaker: A
Matter of Emphasis," *Religion* 20 (1990): 249-73.
Trevett gives a fresh look at the history and historiography of
Naylor's 1656 journey into Bristol, with an eye to Quaker
women's experience; she argues that by emphasizing the role
of women in this event (unfairly, relative to the role of men),
presentations of it have reinforced the restrictions on women's
ministry instituted soon after.

296   Mack, Phyllis. *Visionary Women: Ecstatic Prophecy in Seventeenth-Century England.* Berkeley: California, 1992. Pp.
465.
Part One, "Feminine Symbolism and Female Prophecy," provides a foundation for a detailed gender analysis of the early
Quaker movement in Parts Two and Three, which take up
issues of gender and women's activity during the sharply
different periods of its beginnings and institutionalization. In
the first period the writings and activities of women prophets
transcend gender, dissolve individual personality, and conflate
masculine and feminine symbols; in the second, gender is
recognized, women's meetings are organized, and women's
activities are both more clearly defined and controlled.

297   Schofield, Mary Anne. "'Womens Speaking Justified': The
Feminine Quaker Voice, 1662-1797," *TSWL* 6 (1987): 61-77.
On the development of the female voice in Quakerism and the
differences in eighteenth-century writings from earlier works.

298   Dailey, Barbara Ritter. "The Husbands of Margaret Fell: An
Essay on Religious Metaphor and Social Change," *Seventeenth
Century* 2 (1987): 55-71.

Considers gender distinctions and language as means both of social change and continuity.

299   Mason, Gillian. "Quaker Women and Education, 1642-1840." M.A., Lancaster, 1987. Pp. 102.
       Argues that despite the foundation of religious equality, Quakers soon lost this radical perspective and dealt with education of girls in a manner similar to the larger society.

300   Bacon, Margaret Hope. "Quaker Women in Overseas Ministry," *Quaker History* 77 (Fall 1988): 93-109.
       Follows the work of some 47 American women (one-third of the total) who travelled to Britain between 1685-1835 to pursue ministerial activities among their fellow Quakers.

301   Kunze, Bonnelyn Young. "Religious Authority and Social Status in Seventeenth-Century England: The Friendship of Margaret Fell, George Fox, and William Penn," *Church History* 57 (1988): 170-86.
       Investigates the role of class and gender in this three-way relationship.

302   _____. "'Poore and in Necessity': Margaret Fell and Quaker Female Philanthropy in Northwest England in the Late Seventeenth Century," *Albion* 21 (1990): 559-80.
       Shows the workings of an organized pattern of poor relief for members and neighbors that functioned outside of the state system and was based on the religious principle of gender equality.

303   _____. "'vesells fitt for the masters us[e]': A Transatlantic Community of Religious Women, The Quakers 1675-1753," in *Court, Country, and Culture: Essays on Early Modern British History*, ed. Bonnelyn Young Kunze and Dwight D. Brautigam. Rochester, NY: Rochester, 1992. Pp. 177-97.
       A study of female religious culture as it is seen in their correspondence.

304   Mack, Phyllis. "Feminine Behavior and Radical Religious

Movements: Franciscans, Quakers, and the Followers of Gandhi," *Signs* 11:3 (1986): 457-77 [a briefer version with an altered title is in *Disciplines of Faith: Studies in Religion, Politics, and Patriarchy*, ed. Jim Obelkevich, et al. (London: Routledge & Kegan Paul, 1987), pp. 115-30].

Explores the feminine images and symbolism employed by Francis, George Fox, and Gandhi in their various cultural critiques and expressions of social and intellectual nullity, and suggests that their attitudes toward actual women were ambivalent.

305   Scheffler, Judith. "Prison Writings of Early Quaker Women: 'We Were Stronger Afterward than Before,'" *Quaker History* 73 (Fall 1984): 25-37.

From the works of six traveling ministers, Scheffler contends that they are a form of a "literature of sufferings," in which the writers go beyond self-centered themes to concern for the welfare of fellow inmates and the world outside.

306   Hodgkin, L. V. *Gulielma: Wife of William Penn*. London: Longmans, Green, 1947. Pp. 227.

A perspective on her life (1644-94), largely from the journals of those closest to her.

307   Manners, Emily. *Elizabeth Hooton: First Quaker Woman Preacher, (1600-1672)*. London: Headley Brothers, 1914. Pp. 95.

A study of her life as a Quaker, drawn primarily from her letters and journals.

308   Bell, Maureen. "Mary Westwood, Quaker Publisher," *Publishing History* 23 (1988): 5-66.

Westwood published works by twenty-seven different Quaker authors between 1658 and 1662.

309   Kohler, Charles. *A Quartet of Quakers: Isaac and Mary Penington, John Bellers, John Woolman*. London: Friends Home Service Community, 1978. Pp. 60.

Blecki, Catherine LaCourreye. "Alice Hayes and Mary Pen-

ington: Personal Identity within the Tradition of Quaker
Spiritual Autobiography," *Quaker History* 65 (1976): 19-31.

Ingle, H. Larry. "A Quaker Woman on Women's Roles:
Mary Penington to Friends, 1678," *Signs* 16 (1991): 587-
96.

Some studies of Mary Penington (c. 1624-82), author of a
spiritual autobiography and defender of particular work for
women within the Society of Friends.

310   The *Journal of the Friends Historical Society* has published a
number of articles on the work of women in the movement;
see

Manners, Emily. "Notes Relating to Elizabeth Heath, of
Mansfield, Foundress of Heath's Charity," 10 (1913): 61-
64.

Fox, R. Hingston. "Women's Meetings in Cornwall in the
Early Days of the Society," 11 (1914): 32-34.

Smith, Charlotte Fell. "Isabel Yeamans," 12 (1915): 53-58.

Edwards, Irene L. "The Women Friends of London," 47
(1955): 3-21.

Rickman, Lydia L. "Esther Biddle and Her Mission to Louis
XIV," 47 (1955): 38-45.

Mortimer, R. S. "Marriage Discipline in Early Friends," 48
(1957): 175-95.

Carroll, Kenneth L. "Martha Simmonds, A Quaker Enigma,"
53 (1972): 31-52.

Mortimer, Jean E. "An Early Quaker Poet: Mary (South-
worth) Mollineux, d. 1696," 53 (1973): 125-47.

Tual, Jacques. "Sexual Equality and Conjugal Harmony: The
Way to Celestial Bliss. A View of Early Quaker Matrimo-
ny," 55 (1988): 161-74.

311   Cadbury, Henry J. "George Fox and Women's Liberation,"
Friends' Quarterly 18 (1974): 370-76.
Considers Fox as sympathetic and responsive to women's
interests in participating in the new movement, more than an
innovator in these matters.

312   Ford, Linda. "William Penn's Views on Women: Subjects of

Friendship," *Quaker History* 72 (1983): 75-102.
Argues that despite holding many traditional views of a proper
woman's role in family and society, Penn's belief in women's
spiritual equality meant that he encouraged their active participation in religious life and supported the establishment of
women's meetings.

Roman Catholicism

313   Grundy, Isobel.   "Women's History: Writings by English
       Nuns," in *Women, Writing, History: 1640-1740*, pp. 126-38.
       Reflections on the life stories of individual nuns or of whole
       communities, which focus more on personal and family details
       than on abstractions of piety.

314   Roberts, Alasdair F. B.   "The Role of Women in Scottish
       Catholic Survival," *Scottish Historical Review* 70 (1991): 129-
       50.
       On their importance during this period, a time of general
       religious suppression; aristocratic women were key figures,
       Roberts notes, but were later replaced by women from lower
       social ranks as the Catholic community itself became impov-
       erished.

315   Forster, Ann M. C.   "The Chronicles of the English Poor
       Clares of Rouen," *Recusant History* 18 (1986): 59-102, 149-
       91.
       A narrative of the English convent established in 1644, down
       to the move to its present location at Darlington in 1857; the
       convent first moved to England in 1795, as a result of events
       of the French Revolution.

316   Hardman, Anne.   *Mother Margaret Mostyn, Discalced Car-
       melite, 1625-79*. London: Burns, Oates & Washbourne, 1937.
       Pp. 149.
       A Welsh Catholic who entered the English convent at Antwerp
       in 1644, Mother Margaret was prioress for twenty-five years.

317   _____. *Two English Carmelites*. London: Burns, Oates &

Washbourne, 1939. Pp. 176.
Lives of women in the same convent: Catherine Burton (1668-1714), Mother Mary Xaveria; and Margaret Wake (1617-78), Mother Mary Margaret.

Women and Religion in Ireland

318   MacCurtain, Margaret and O'Dowd, Mary, eds. *Women in Early Modern Ireland, 1500-1800.* Edinburgh: Edinburgh, 1991.
        Of twenty-one essays, two deal with religion in this period: Paul Kilroy's "Women and the Reformation in Seventeenth-Century Ireland," pp. 179-96, studies the contrasting experiences of Quaker and Catholic religious women; Patrick J. Cornish's "Women and Religious Practice," pp. 212-20, discusses the importance of the Irish mother as the Catholic Counter-Reformation developed in modern Ireland, especially as religious practice was centered in the home.

319   Concannon, Helena. *The Poor Clares in Ireland (A.D. 1629-1929).* Dublin: Gill and Son, 1929. Pp. 181.
        Arriving in Dublin in 1629, the Poor Clares suffered religious persecution and secession over the years that followed, but eventually established additional houses of the community.

Gender Roles, Marriage, and Family

320   Michel, Robert H. "English Attitudes Towards Women, 1640-1700," *Canadian Journal of History* 13 (1978): 35-60.
        On the limits placed on women by law, scripture, and theories of their physical and mental characteristics, as seen in the writings of clergy, lawyers, wits, and other authors. With the household rather than the individual the fundamental unit of society, the law defined the proprietary and civil incapacity of woman, seen as under the control first of her father and then of her husband.

321   Nadelhaft, Jerome. "The Englishwoman's Sexual Civil War: Feminist Attitudes Toward Men, Women, and Marriage, 1650-

1740," *JHI* 43 (1982): 555-79.
Considers the large body of literature in this period that attacks men's attitudes toward and treatment of women; lacking a practical alternative, these writers focused on the need for education, self-identity, and the development of networks of support.

322   Brown, Irene Q. "Domesticity, Feminism, and Friendship: Female Aristocratic Culture and Marriage in England, 1660-1760," *Journal of Family History* 7 (1982): 406-24.
Argues that the development of a rational or Enlightenment domesticity among the upper classes created a distinctive culture; it encouraged an equality among heterosocial relationships, promoted the value of friendship, was influenced by the form of Christian humanism found in latitudinarian Anglicanism, and enabled public as well as private roles for women.

323   Shanley, Mary Lyndon. "Marriage Contract and Social Contract in Seventeenth-Century English Political Thought," in *The Family in Political Thought*, ed. Jean Bethke Elshtain. Amherst: Massachusetts, 1984. Pp. 80-95.
On the shift from a hierarchical to a social contract view of political authority and its implications for familial authority, as natural law arguments replace scriptural ones; this promoted an egalitarian understanding of marriage and the possibility of divorce.

324   Osmond, Rosalie E. "Body, Soul, and the Marriage Relationship: The History of an Analogy," *JHI* 34 (1973): 283-90.
How the use of an image supports subordination; here Osmond is interested in the English understanding that the soul is masculine and the body feminine, combined with the interpretation of Genesis that the body first tempted the soul.

325   Beougher, Tim. "The Puritan View of Marriage: The Nature of the Husband/Wife Relationship in Puritan England as Taught and Experienced by a Representative Puritan Pastor, Richard Baxter," *Trinity Journal* 10 (1989): 131-60.
Explores the theme of authority and responsibility in the con-

text of a hierarchy of function that is understood to be established by God.

326   Thomas, John A. "A Moral Voice for the Restoration Lady: A Comparative View of Allestree and Vives," *Journal of the Rocky Mountain Medieval and Renaissance Association* 7 (1986): 123-42.
Argues that the similarity in views between the writings of Allestree (1673) and Vives (1523) illustrate a continuing conservative, religiously-centered, set of convictions only slightly altered for the Restoration.

327   Marshall, Rosalind K. *The Days of Duchess Anne: Life in the Household of the Duchess of Hamilton, 1656-1716.* New York: St. Martin's, 1974. Pp. 256.
Studies the life of an aristocratic Scottish woman, a leading supporter of Presbyterianism.

Medical and Physiological Aspects

328   Crawford, Patricia. "Attitudes to Pregnancy from a Woman's Spiritual Diary, 1687-8," *Local Population Studies* 21 (Autumn 1978): 43-45.
Shows how the diary of Sarah Savage reveals deep longing for a child and fear of barrenness when she did not conceive soon after her marriage; after initial disappointments, she eventually had nine children.

329   _____. "Attitudes to Menstruation in Seventeenth-Century England," *Past & Present* 91 (May 1981): 47-73.
Covers scientific and religious understandings, as well as women's ideas on the subject; "while men saw in menstruation evidence of women's ambiguous position—a position of both weakness and power—women saw menstruation as a normal part of their lives" (71-72).

330   Smith, Ginnie. "Thomas Tryon's Regimen for Women: Sectarian Health in the Seventeenth Century," in *The Sexual Dynamics of History*, ed. The London Feminist History Group.

London: Pluto, 1983. Pp. 47-65.

A radical Dissenter and author of popular medical advice books, Tryon (1634-1703) advocated ascetic and temperate measures to recover the moral and medical constitution of pure natural womanhood; his view "was a powerful individual contribution to a mythology and ethic of female domesticity" (65).

Witchcraft and Madness

331   Neale, Chris. *The Seventeenth-Century Witch Craze in West Fife: A Guide to the Printed Sources*. Dunfermline: District Libraries, 1980. Pp. 30.
       Narratives on the phenomenon in six parishes.

332   Adam, Isabel. *Witch Hunt: The Great Scottish Witchcraft Trials of 1697*. London: Macmillan, 1978. Pp. 256.
       Accusations of a young girl, Christian Shaw, and the investigations of court and presbytery.

333   Rushton, Peter. "Crazes and Quarrels: The Character of Witchcraft in the North-East of England, 1649-80," *Bulletin of the Durham County Local History Society* 31 (December 1983): 2-40.
       Analyses over one hundred cases, showing the complexity of the issue and the difficulty of single explanations for a cause.

334   Geis, G. "Lord Hale, Witches, and Rape," *British Journal of Law and Society* 5 (1978): 26-44.
       McLachlan, Hugh V. and Swales, J. K. "Lord Hales, Witches, and Rape," *Ibid.*: 251-61.
       A debate over the appropriate conclusions to draw from Hale's activity as judge at a trial of two women in 1662, especially over whether women were treated more harshly than men.

335   Guskin, Phyllis J. "The Context of Witchcraft: The Case of Jane Wenham (1712)," *Eighteenth-Century Studies* 15 (1981): 48-71.
       Kingsbury, J. B. "The Last Witch of England," *Folk-lore* 61

(September 1950): 134-45.

Gerish, W. B. *A Hertfordshire Witch; or, The Story of Jane Wenham, The "Wise Woman" of Walkern.* Hertfordshire Folk-Lore, 4. Bishop's Stortford, 1906. Pp. 13.

Three studies of the same case include consideration of religious belief and the role of Anglican clergy in such events.

336   MacDonald, Michael. "Women and Madness in Tudor and Stuart England," *Social Research* 53 (1986): 261-81.

Pursues the question of why madness was not regarded as a female malady in this period as it was later, and suggests that a feminization of madness emerged from "a shift in the locus of patriarchal authority away from communal institutions sanctioned by religious beliefs and toward professional institutions sanctioned by secular beliefs" (281).

Liberalism and the Early English Enlightenment

337   Perry, Ruth. "Radical Doubt and the Liberation of Women," *Eighteenth-Century Studies* 18 (1985): 472-93.

On the intellectual liberation of women in the late seventeenth century through their association with early Enlightenment and platonist philosophers whose ideas on rationality and whose personal support encouraged them.

338   Schwoerer, Lois G. "Women and the Glorious Revolution," *Albion* 18 (1986): 195-218.

Focuses on three writers, each of whom was deeply religious, to illustrate the participation of women in the issues and events of the Revolution: Anne Docwra, a Quaker; Elinor James, an Anglican; and Joan Whitrowe, an independent prophet.

339   Clark, Lorenne. "Women and Locke: Who Owns the Apples in the Garden of Eden?" *Canadian Journal of Philosophy* 7 (1977): 699-724 [also in *The Sexism of Social and Political Theory: Women and Reproduction from Plato to Nietzsche*, ed. Lorenne Clark and Lynda Lange (Toronto: Toronto, 1979), pp. 16-40].

Butler, Melissa A. "Early Liberal Roots of Feminism: John

Locke and the Attack on Patriarchy," *American Political Science Review* 72 (1978): 135-50.

O'Donnell, Sheryl R. "Mr. Locke and the Ladies: The Indelible Words on the *Tabula Rasa*," *Studies in Eighteenth-Century Culture* 8 (1979): 151-64.

Did Locke's philosophical and theological works support or undermine a patriarchal understanding? Clark contends that his use of Genesis built a natural disadvantage into a rigid understanding of women's subordination. Butler argues that he departed from traditional views in favor of an individualistic approach, supporting education for women and female preaching. O'Donnell believes that while Locke encouraged women's education, many of the women who used Locke to advance their aspirations "could not afford to examine their own dependence upon the definition of woman by the Christian patriarchy" (161).

Individuals

340 *Mary Astell (1666-1731)*

Rediscovered in the late 1970s after long neglect, Astell has become a favorite of those looking for feminist antecedents to the modern women's movement; but despite being an advocate for women's education and for a certain independence from men, she was conservative socially, politically, and religiously. Bridget Hill's *The First English Feminist: Reflections on Marriage and Other Writings by Mary Astell* (New York: St. Martin's, 1986), contains a substantial introduction to a selection of her writings that discusses her thought on a number of subjects. The most complete biography is Ruth Perry, *The Celebrated Mary Astell: An Early English Feminist* (Chicago: Chicago, 1986); she has also discussed Astell's resistance to sexuality, her platonist philosophy, and her critique of liberal political theory: see "The Veil of Chastity: Mary Astell's Feminism," *Studies in Eighteenth-Century Culture* 9 (1979): 25-43; "Mary Astell's Response to the Enlightenment," in *Women and the Enlightenment*, ed. Margaret Hunt, et al. (New York: Haworth, 1984), pp. 13-40; and "Mary Astell and the Feminist Critique of Possessive Individualism," *Eighteenth-*

Century Studies 23 (1990): 444-57. The first extended study was Florence M. Smith's *Mary Astell* (New York: Columbia, 1916). Other dimensions of her thought are considered in Joan K. Kinnaird, "Mary Astell and the Conservative Contribution to Feminism," *JBS* 19:1 (1979): 53-75; Hilda L. Smith, "'All Men and Both Sexes': Concepts of Men's Development, Women's Education, and Feminism in the Seventeenth Century," in *Man, God, and Nature in the Enlightenment*, ed. Donald C. Mell, Jr., et al. (East Lansing, MI: Colleagues, 1988), pp. 75-84; Catherine Shamrock, "De-ciphering Women and De-scribing Authority: The Writings of Mary Astell," in *Women, Writing, History: 1640-1740*, pp. 109-24; and D. N. Deluna, "Mary Astell: England's First Feminist Literary Critic," *Women's Studies* 22 (1992-93): 231-42. Shamrock argues that Astell's critique of patriarchy is both limited and flawed.

341 *Lady Eleanor Davies (c. 1590-1652)*
Prophet of the apocalypse and author of over sixty tracts between 1625 and 1652, Davies was regarded by many contemporaries as mad; hence the contemporary anagram of her name in the titles of Esther S. Cope's works: *Handmaid of the Holy Spirit. Dame Eleanor Davies: Never Soe Mad a Ladie* (Ann Arbor: Michigan, 1992), and "'Dame Eleanor Davies Never Soe Mad a Ladie?'" *Huntington Library Quarterly* 50 (Spring 1987): 133-44. Other studies include Beth Nelson, "Lady Elinor Davies: The Prophet as Publisher," *WSIF* 8 (1985): 403-409; Theodore Spencer, "The History of an Unfortunate Lady," *Harvard Studies and Notes in Philology* 20 (1938): 43-59; and C. J. Hindle, "A Bibliography of the Printed Pamphlets and Broadsides of Lady Eleanor Douglas, the 17th Century Prophetess," *Papers of the Edinburgh Bibliographical Society* 15 (1930-35): 35-54.

342 *Margaret Fell (1614-1702)*
Much material on this important early leader of the Quaker movement and wife of George Fox can be found in the works included under the movement itself; still, it is surprising how few separate studies of her life and work have appeared. Bonnelyn Young Kunze's *Margaret Fell and the Rise of Quak-*

erism (Stanford: Stanford, 1994) investigates the social, political, economic, and religious aspects of her life in order to
produce a reassessment of her person and role in the movement. Previously, the standard biography was Isabel Ross,
Margaret Fell, Mother of Quakerism (London: Longmans,
Green, 1949); a much earlier study is Helen G. Crosfield,
Margaret Fox of Swarthmoor Hall (London: Headley Brothers,
1913). Judith Kegan Gardiner's "Re-Gendering Individualism:
Margaret Fell Fox and Quaker Rhetoric," in *Privileging Gender in Early Modern England*, pp. 205-24, explores Fell's role
in the development of an ungendered yet authoritative language
that overcame the distinction between individual and community. Margaret Olofson Thickstun's "'This Was a Woman that
Taught': Feminist Scriptural Exegesis in the Seventeenth Century," *Studies in Eighteenth-Century Culture* 21 (1991): 149-
58, compares the work of Fell and Astell and argues the contemporary feminist scholars give greater place to Astell because they privilege the voice of reason over revelation and
underestimate the power of religious authority in the seventeenth century and today; but Astell does not challenge male
interpretations of Scripture, while Fell, in her confrontation of
these views, begins "to wrest the interpretation of Scripture,
and therefore of women, from patriarchal control" (157).

343   *Anne Finch, Lady Conway (1631-79)*
       Author of *The Principles of the Most Ancient and Modern
       Philosophy* and an acquaintance of many seventeenth-century
       philosophers, Conway has received only limited study, most
       notably in a collection of papers in the *Guilford Review* 23
       (Spring 1986), including Carolyn Merchant, "Anne Conway:
       Quaker and Philosopher," pp. 2-13; John Stoneburner, "Henry
       More and Anne Conway," pp. 24-35; and Carol Stoneburner,
       "A Comparison of Margaret Fell Fox and Anne Conway," pp.
       64-70. Allison Coudert's "A Cambridge Platonist's Kabbalist
       Nightmare," *JHI* 36 (1975): 633-52, considers F. M. van
       Helmont's friendship with and influence on her.

344   *Margaret Godolphin (1652-78)*
       An example of seventeenth-century Anglican piety, Godolphin

is studied in W. G. Hiscock, *John Evelyn and Mrs. Godolphin* (London: Macmillan, 1951) and Margaret Cropper, *Flame Touches Flame* (London: Longmans, Green, 1949), pp. 155-81.

345   *Jane Lead (1624-1704)*
Prophet, mystic, and a founder of the Philadelphian Society in the 1690s, Lead explored the possibilities of feminine imagery of the divine and the unity of God and the human soul. Three articles by Catherine F. Smith pursue aspects of her thought: "Jane Lead: The Feminist Mind and Art of a Seventeenth-Century Protestant Mystic," in *Women of Spirit*, pp. 183-203; "Jane Lead: Mysticism and the Woman Cloathed with the Sun," in *Shakespeare's Sisters: Feminist Essays on Women Poets*, ed. Sandra Gilbert and Susan Gubar (Bloomington: Indiana, 1981), pp. 3-18, 316-18; and "Jane Lead's Wisdom: Women and Prophecy in Seventeenth-Century England," in *Poetic Prophecy in Western Literature*, ed. Jan Wojcik and Raymond-Jean Frontain (Cranbury, NJ: Associated University Presses, 1984), pp. 55-63. See also Elizabeth Keiser, "Jane Lead and the Philadelphian Society: Connections with Anne Conway and Quakers," *Guilford Review* 23 (Spring 1986): 72-89; Joanne M. Sperle, "God's Healing Angel: A Biography of Jane Ward Lead" (Ph.D., Kent State, 1985); and Nils Thune, *The Behmenists and the Philadelphians: A Contribution to the Study of English Mysticism in the 17th and 18th Centuries* (Uppsala: Almqvist and Wiksells, 1948).

346   *Bathsua Makin (1608?-75?)*
A strong advocate of the education of women, including in matters of religion, Makin is studied in Mitzi Myers, "Domesticating Minerva: Bathsua Makin's 'Curious' Argument for Women's Education," *Studies in Eighteenth-Century Culture* 14 (1985): 173-92; and in two articles by J. R. Brink: "Bathsua Makin: Scholar and Educator of the Seventeenth Century," *IJWS* 1 (1978): 417-26; and "Bathsua Makin: Educator and Linguist (1608?-1675?)," in *Female Scholars: A Tradition of Learned Women Before 1800*, pp. 86-100.

347   *Susanna Wesley (1669-1742)*
       Most often presented as the mother of John and Charles, Su-
       sanna Wesley has received only limited study on her own.
       Some bibliographical assistance is offered to that end in John
       A. Newton, "Susanna Wesley (1669-1742): A Bibliographical
       Survey," *PWHS* 37:2 (1969): 37-40; his monograph, *Susanna
       Wesley and the Puritan Tradition in Methodism* (London:
       Epworth, 1968), provides considerable insight into her piety
       and theology.   Maldwyn Edwards offers a family portrait in
       *Family Circle: A Study of the Epworth Household in Relation
       to John and Charles Wesley* (London: Epworth, 1949). Two
       articles by Charles Wallace, Jr., "Susanna Wesley's Spirituali-
       ty: The Freedom of a Christian Woman," *Methodist History* 22
       (1983-84): 158-73, and "'Some Stated Employment of Your
       Mind': Reading, Writing, and Religion in the Life of Susanna
       Wesley," *Church History* 58 (1989): 354-66, present her as an
       important transitional figure in the history of women and
       western religion and consider the resources of her intellectual
       life.   Some popular biographies are Mabel R. Brailsford,
       Susanna Wesley: The Mother of Methodism (London: Charles
       H. Kelly, 1910; rept, 1938); Rebecca L. Harmon, *Susanna,
       Mother of the Wesleys* (Nashville: Abingdon, 1968); and Rita
       F. Snowden, *Such a Woman: The Story of Susanna Wesley*
       (Nashville: Upper Room, 1962).   Frank Baker explores her
       several religious roles in "Salute to Susanna," *Methodist Histo-
       ry* 7:3 (1969): 3-12; "Susanna Wesley, Apologist for Method-
       ism," *PWHS* 35 (1965-66): 68-71; and "Susanna Wesley:
       Puritan, Parent, Pastor, Protagonist, Pattern," in *Women in
       New Worlds* 2: 112-31, 373-77.   Other studies include Eliza-
       beth Hart, "Susanna Wesley and Her Editors," *PWHS* 48
       (1992): 202-209; 49 (1993): 1-10; Samuel J. Rogal, "The
       Epworth Women: Susanna Wesley and Her Daughters," *Wes-
       leyan Theological Journal* 18:2 (1983): 80-89; Robert Walms-
       ley, "John Wesley's Parents: Quarrel and Reconciliation,"
       PWHS 29 (1953-54): 50-57.

Others

348   Kirchberger, C.   "Elizabeth Burnet, 1661-1709," *Church*

Quarterly Review 148 (1949): 17-51.
Burnet was one of the last of the seventeenth century's "devout ladies," faithful members of the Church of England.

349   Smith, Julia J. "Susanna Hopton: A Biographical Account," *Notes and Queries* 236 (1991): 165-72.
A brief study of an Anglican devotional writer (1627-1709).

350   Schwoerer, Lois G. *Lady Rachel Russell: "One of the Best of Women."* Baltimore: Johns Hopkins, 1988. Pp. 321.
Shows how Russell (1637-1723) used her influence on the patronage networks of both Church and state, but was also sympathetic to Dissent.

CHAPTER 4

1740-1850:
THE EVANGELICAL REVIVAL
AND THE IDEAL OF WOMANHOOD

Bibliographies, Guides, and Anthologies

351   Schnorrenberg, Barbara Brandon. "Toward a Bibliography of
        Eighteenth-Century Englishwomen," *Eighteenth-Century Life* 1
        (1975): 50-52.
        A brief survey of books on the subject.

352   Kanner, Barbara, ed. *Women in English Social History, 1800-
        1914: A Guide to Research.* 3 vols., New York: Garland,
        1987-90.
        A large, annotated bibliography, organized within subject areas
        chronologically, with a combination of primary and secondary
        sources. Volumes I and II contain twelve chapters, including
        Religion and Spiritualism (Chap. V) and Philanthropy, Social
        Service, and Social Reform (Chap. VIII); volume III deals
        with autobiographical writings.

353   Palmegiano, E. M. "Women and British Periodicals, 1832-
        1867: A Bibliography," *Victorian Periodicals Newsletter* 9
        (March 1976): 3-36.
        Within this larger subject, many religious publications are
        listed.

354   Banks, Olive. *The Biographical Dictionary of British Femi-
        nists.* New York: New York, 1985. Vol. 1: 1800-1930. Pp.
        239.

Provides sketches of 126 individuals.

355   Spender, Dale, ed. *Feminist Theorists: Three Centuries of Key Women Thinkers*. New York: Pantheon, 1983. Pp. 402.
Essays on twenty-one individuals, including eight British women: Aphra Behn, Mary Astell, Mary Wollstonecraft, Harriet Martineau, Barbara Bodichon, Millicent Garrett Fawcett, Christabel Pankhurst, and Vera Brittain.

356   _____. *Women of Ideas and What Men Have Done to Them. From Aphra Behn to Adrienne Rich*. London: Ark, 1982. Pp. 800.
Short essays on individual women.

357   Malmgreen, Gail, ed. *Religion in the Lives of English Women*, 1760-1930. Bloomington: Indiana, 1986. Pp. 295.
Ten essays on a wide range of topics, listed separately in this bibliography because of their importance to the subject.

358   Helsinger, Elizabeth K., et al., eds. *The Woman Question: Society and Literature in Britain and America, 1837-1883*. 3 vols., Chicago: Chicago, 1983. Pp. 146, 260, and 237.
Essays on dimensions of the Anglo-American debate in the middle class over woman's nature and place: volume I contains six essays on representative figures and texts that illuminate the debate; the second traces the development of the issue in law, science, work, and religion; and the third follows literary debates to illustrate cultural assumptions, the constraints of the separate sphere ideology, and the functions of literary heroines.

359   Johnson, Dale A., ed. *Women in English Religion, 1700-1925*. New York: Edwin Mellen, 1983. Pp. 353.
Some sixty selections in six chapters, with contextual introductions.

360   Bell, Susan Groag and Offen, Karen M., eds. *Woman, the Family, and Freedom: The Debate in Documents*. 2 vols., Stanford: Stanford, 1983. Pp. 561 and 474.

Broad coverage of viewpoints in Europe and America through this collection, setting prevailing views against challenges to those views; the volumes treat the years 1750-1880 and 1880-1950, respectively.

361   Hill, Bridget, ed. *Eighteenth-Century Women: An Anthology.* London: Allen and Unwin, 1984. Pp. 280.
Beginning with images of womanhood, where the only selections having to do with religion are included, this collection focuses on social and economic topics.

362   Jones, Vivien, ed. *Women in the Eighteenth Century: Constructions of Femininity.* London: Routledge, 1990. Pp. 257.
Contains fifty-one selections under the topics of conduct, sexuality, education, writing, and feminisms.

363   Hellerstein, Erna Olafson, et al., eds. *Victorian Women: A Documentary Account of Women's Lives in Nineteenth-Century England, France, and the United States.* Stanford: Stanford, 1981. Pp. 534.
From c. 1830-1880; over one hundred documents, several showing the influence of religion in the lives of many nineteenth-century women, and organized by stages of life.

General Historical Studies
A. Eighteenth Century

364   Barker-Benfield, G. J. *The Culture of Sensibility: Sex and Society in Eighteenth-Century Britain.* Chicago: Chicago, 1992. Pp. 520.
A cultural history that puts gender at the center of pre-industrial Britain, showing the high price paid for the identification of sensibility with women: "If sensibility was a form of religion, the evidence suggests that it was overwhelmingly a religion of women" (262).

365   Rogers, Katharine M. *Feminism in Eighteenth-Century England.* Urbana: Illinois, 1982. Pp. 291.
On the different forms of feminism that emerged in this peri-

od, including rationalist and romantic, and provided the foundation for later systematic feminist thought and awareness; Rogers concludes that the emphasis on female chastity was the limiting factor in eighteenth-century feminism.

366   Browne, Alice. *The Eighteenth-Century Feminist Mind.* Brighton: Harvester, 1987. Pp. 237.
Sets feminist responses against eighteenth-century notions of woman; a range of didactic, devotional, and religious autobiographical literature is considered in the process. By the end of the century feminist writing had shifted religious arguments into a secular context, Browne contends.

367   Taylor, Gordon Rattray. *The Angel-Makers: A Study in Psychological Origins of Social Change, 1750-1850.* London: Heinemann, 1958. Pp. 388.
Asks how the England known for immorality in the eighteenth century became known for morality in the nineteenth, and concludes that a primary factor is that the former period was predominantly matrist while the latter was patrist (that is, reflecting the psychological influence of a mother- or father-figure).

368   Okin, Susan Moller. "Patriarchy and Married Women's Property in England: Questions about Some Current Views," *Eighteenth-Century Studies* 17 (1983-84): 121-38.
Argues against some current contentions that the patriarchal powers of husbands had weakened significantly in the upper classes by the end of the century and that there was a growing egalitarianism in marriages.

369   Soulbury, Viscount. "Women of Influence, 1750-1800," *Quarterly Review* 297 (1959): 400-407.
A survey of some prominent women in these years, including some persons in the area of religion.

370   Carmichael, Kay. "Protestantism and Gender," in *Sermons and Battle Hymns: Protestant Popular Culture in Modern Scotland,* ed. Graham Walker and Tom Gallagher. Edinburgh:

Edinburgh, 1990. Pp. 213-30.
A sweeping history, full of sharp polarities, focusing on the
cultural burdens placed upon women by Protestantism since the
Reformation.

B. Early Nineteenth Century

371   O'Malley, Ida B. *Women in Subjection: A Study of the Lives
       of English Women Before 1832.* London: Duckworth, 1933.
       Pp. 365.
       A pioneering study that includes women's responses to sub-
       jection, as in their important contributions to the eighteenth-
       century evangelical movement; O'Malley sees Hannah More
       and Mary Wollstonecraft as "fellow-workers in the vindication
       of women" (150), even though More disapproved of Woll-
       stonecraft's work.

372   Dunbar, Janet. *The Early Victorian Woman: Some Aspects of
       Her Life, 1837-1857.* London: Harrap, 1953. Pp. 192.
       Attempts to counter stereotypes of the middle-class woman.
       But Dunbar is too preoccupied with servants, shops, food,
       fashion, etc., to give full dimension to that; and while ac-
       knowledging that this was a serious religious age, she does not
       explore any such association with women.

373   Houghton, Walter E. *The Victorian Frame of Mind, 1830-
       1870.* New Haven: Yale, 1957. Pp. 467.
       Analyses the character of the age; chap. 13, "Love," treats the
       importance of the home and perceptions of womanhood and
       sexuality, as well as understandings of love.

374   Delamont, Sara and Duffin, Lorna, eds. *The Nineteenth-Cen-
       tury Woman: Her Cultural and Physical World.* London:
       Croom Helm, 1978. Pp. 213.
       Six essays explore conflicts between the culture and developing
       feminist consciousness, chiefly in science and education.

375   Bolt, Christine. *The Women's Movement in the United States
       and Britain from the 1790s to the 1920s.* Amherst: Massachu-

setts, 1993. Pp. 390.
A broad, comparative study.

376   Banks, Olive. *Faces of Feminism: A Study of Feminism as a
      Social Movement.* New York: St. Martin's, 1981. Pp. 285.
      Discusses three intellectual traditions with origins in the eigh-
      teenth century that contributed to the development of and
      tensions within the feminist movement in England and Ameri-
      ca: evangelical Christianity, Enlightenment philosophy, and
      communitarian socialism.   The main thrust of evangelical
      feminism, Banks declares, was philanthropic, and it empha-
      sized a traditional view of marriage and the family.

377   Weeks, Jeffrey. *Sex, Politics and Society: The Regulation of
      Sexuality Since 1800.* London: Longman, 1981. Pp. 306.
      On the historical construction of sexuality and developments
      that include the Victorian family, regulation movements, birth
      control, the construction of homosexuality, and the impact of
      feminism and socialism on understandings of sexuality.   Al-
      though not interested in religious dimensions of the subject,
      Weeks provides a comprehensive background to several related
      topics.

378   Thomis, Malcolm I. and Grimmett, Jennifer. *Women in Pro-
      test 1800-1850.* London: Croom Helm, 1982. Pp. 166.
      In their various protests, working-class women "found a moral
      defence of their political behavior, which became a series of
      'hallowed endeavors' and 'sacred duties,' justified by the
      Biblical texts which came easily to their tongues and their
      pens" (115); thus, the authors conclude that a chapel back-
      ground helped to develop leadership abilities in those women
      who participated in social and industrial protests.

379   Robertson, Priscilla. *An Experience of Women: Pattern and
      Change in Nineteenth-Century Europe.* Philadelphia: Temple,
      1982. Pp. 673.
      A comparative study of four countries: England, France,
      Germany, and Italy, with a description of expected patterns
      and discussion of individuals who rebelled against or broke them.

380   Taylor, Barbara. *Eve and the New Jerusalem: Socialism and Feminism in the Nineteenth Century.* New York: Pantheon, 1983. Pp. 394.

_____. "The Woman-Power: Religious Heresy and Feminism in Early English Socialism," in *Tearing the Veil: Essays on Femininity,* ed. Susan Lipshitz. London: Routledge & Kegan Paul, 1978. Pp. 119-44.

Considers the role of women and the development of feminism within Owenite socialism, together with the conflict between evangelical Christianity and "rational religion" over their respective religious images and understandings. The article discusses the influence of Joanna Southcott's protest against masculine power on the development of a radical feminist vision of social change.

381   Rendall, Jane. *The Origins of Modern Feminism: Women in Britain, France and the United States, 1780-1860.* New York: Schocken, 1984. Pp. 382.

A comparative and synthetic study, which notes the difference between French and Anglo-American developments. Chapter 3 considers the role of evangelicalism, and chapter 7 deals with the connection between religion, moral reform, and philanthropy.

382   Kestner, Joseph. *Protest and Reform: The British Social Narrative by Women, 1827-1867.* London: Methuen, 1985. Pp. 242.

Discusses the nature of British social protest fiction, including the place of religion in some of these writings.

383   Davidoff, Leonore and Hall, Catherine. *Family Fortunes: Men and Women of the English Middle Class, 1780-1850.* Chicago: Chicago, 1987. Pp. 576.

A study of ideologies, institutions, and practices, with a focus on the place of the family and delineations of gender difference in a time of rapid social change. Contributing to the religious foundation of this system was a dual link, between religion and commerce and between religion, godliness, and the family, the authors contend.

384   Hall, Catherine.   "Gender Divisions and Class Formation in
       the Birmingham Middle Class, 1780-1850," in *People's Histo-
       ry and Socialist Theory*, ed. Raphael Samuel.   London: Rout-
       ledge & Kegan Paul, 1981. Pp. 164-75.
       Shows how the separation of spheres was a fundamental orga-
       nizing characteristic of the middle-class society and how it was
       supported in Nonconformist and Evangelical Anglican church-
       es.

385   Davidoff, Leonore.   "'Life is Duty, Praise and Prayer': Some
       Contributions of the New Women's History." Fawcett Library
       Papers No. 4; London: LLRS Publications, 1981. Pp. 22.
       Considers the writings of Ann and Jane Taylor, who came
       from a devout Nonconformist family in the early nineteenth
       century and helped through their widely popular poems and
       stories for children to create the idea of home as a separate
       woman's domain.

386   Smith, Ruth L. and Valenze, Deborah M.   "Mutuality and
       Marginality: Liberal Moral Theory and Working-Class Women
       in Nineteenth-Century England," *Signs* 13 (1988): 277-98.
       Considers the conflict between the individualistic dimensions of
       liberal moral theory and themes of mutuality as understood by
       working-class women; Owenite socialism and popular evangel-
       icalism in the form of "cottage religion" were early nineteenth-
       century continuations of this theme.

387   Liddington, Jill. *The Road to Greenham Common: Feminism
       and Anti-Militarism in Britain Since 1820*.   Syracuse: Syra-
       cuse, 1991. Pp. 349. (Published in Britain under the title,
       The Long Road to Greenham. London: Virago, 1989.)
       The history of women's peace campaigns from the largely
       Quaker beginnings in the early nineteenth century to the 1980s
       demonstrations at Greenham Common.

Literary Studies
A. Eighteenth Century

388   Todd, Janet. *Sensibility: An Introduction*. London: Methuen,
        1986. Pp. 169.
        On the cultivation of the faculty of feeling in the mid-eigh-
        teenth century; Todd shows how changes in the understanding
        of class, family, and the position of women contributed to its
        emergence and how the language of evangelicalism supported
        and encouraged it in religion.

389   Lonsdale, Roger, ed. *Eighteenth-Century Women Poets: An
        Oxford Anthology*. Oxford: Oxford, 1989. Pp. xlvii + 555.
        The extended introduction explains the development in the
        literary status of women, and is followed by selections from
        more than one hundred authors.

390   Brophy, Elizabeth Bergen. *Women's Lives and the 18th-Cen-
        tury English Novel*. Tampa: South Florida, 1991. Pp. 291.
        Were novels realistic in their portrayals of women, and what
        influence did they have on their women readers?   Brophy
        basically says yes to the first question, exploring conduct
        books and writings of women before comparing them with the
        portrayals of women in the works of seven novelists.

391   Göller, Karl Heinz. "The Emancipation of Women in Eigh-
        teenth-Century English Literature," *Anglia* 101 (1983): 78-98.
        Contends that feminist pamphlets of the late seventeenth and
        early eighteenth centuries helped to steer women writers to-
        ward the field of creative literature; often their attacks were
        directed at representatives of the church.

392   Samuel Richardson's novels *Clarissa* and *Pamela* are important
        documents in the discussion of women's lives in the literature
        of the period; for guides to works on Richardson, see:
        Smith, Sarah W. R. *Samuel Richardson: A Reference Guide*.
            Boston: G. K. Hall, 1984. Pp. 425.
        Hannaford, Richard Gordon. *Samuel Richardson: An Anno-
            tated Bibliography of Critical Studies*. New York: Garland,

1980. Pp. 292.

393   Yoder, R. Paul. "Clarissa Regained: Richardson's Redemp-
       tion of Eve," *Eighteenth Century Life* 13:2 (1989): 87-99.
       An example of analysis of one of Richardson's novels; Yoder
       suggests that he uses Milton's *Paradise Regained* to create a
       story in which Clarissa plays the role of Christ.

394   Rogers, Katharine. "The Feminism of Daniel Defoe," in
       Woman in the 18th Century, and Other Essays, ed. Paul Fritz
       and Richard Morton. Toronto: S. Stevens, 1976. Pp. 3-24.
       Argues that Defoe stands out among the male writers of his
       century for his advanced views of women, such as advocating
       mutuality in marriage and a single moral standard for men and
       women.

395   Ehrenpreis, Irvin and Halsband, Robert. *The Lady of Letters
       in the Eighteenth Century*. Los Angeles: Clark Library, 1969.
       Two essays here; Ehrenpreis's "Letters of Advice to Young
       Spinsters," pp. 3-27, discusses Swift's views of women as
       advanced for their time; and Halsband's "Ladies of Letters in
       the Eighteenth Century," pp. 31-51, considers the writings of
       Lady Mary Wortley Montagu, a bridge figure to later profes-
       sional women writers at the end of the century.

396   The lives and writings of a group of learned and fashionable
       women who attempted to combine their learning with virtue
       are explored in the following works:
       Myers, Sylvia Harcstark. *The Bluestocking Circle: Women,
       Friendship, and the Life of the Mind in Eighteenth-Century
       England*. Oxford: Clarendon, 1990. Pp. 342.
       _____. "Learning, Virtue, and the Term 'Bluestocking',"
       Studies in Eighteenth-Century Culture 15 (1986): 279-88.
       Schnorrenberg, Barbara Brandon. "The Blue Stocking As-
       sembly: A Comment on Women's Lives in Eighteenth-
       Century England," in *Views of Women's Lives in Western
       Tradition*, ed. Frances Richardson Keller. Lewiston, NY:
       Edwin Mellen, 1990. Pp. 360-91.
       Scott, Walter S. *The Bluestocking Ladies*. London: J. Green,

1947. Pp. 212.

Wheeler, Ethel R. *Famous Blue-stockings*. London: Methuen, 1910. Pp. 352.

Williamson, Marilyn L. "Who's Afraid of Mrs. Barbauld? The Blue Stockings and Feminism," *IJWS* 3 (1980): 89-102.

397   Williams, Carolyn D. "Fielding and Half-Learned Ladies," *Essays in Criticism* 38 (1988): 22-34.
Argues that Fielding's satire was aimed at women who only pretended at learning, not at those who took education seriously.

398   McIlquham, Harriett. "Some Further Eighteenth-Century Advocates of Justice for Women," *Westminster Review* 159 (1903): 167-79.
A review of the position of the women's rights question to the time of Mary Wollstonecraft, especially as seen in minor women writers.

B. Early Nineteenth Century

399   Jay, Elisabeth. *The Religion of the Heart: Anglican Evangelicalism and the Nineteenth Century Novel*. Oxford: Clarendon, 1979. Pp. 297.
A study of the contribution of Evangelical ideas and practices to the development and direction of the English novel; while not directly on the subject of women, Jay considers the works of a number of Evangelical women writers from Hannah More to Hesba Stretton, with separate chapters on George Eliot and Mrs. Worboise.

400   Krueger, Christine L. *The Reader's Repentance: Women Preachers, Women Writers, and Nineteenth-Century Social Discourse*. Chicago: Chicago, 1992. Pp. 350.
Explores the impact of Methodist women's preaching on four writers (More, Tonna, Gaskell, and Eliot), showing how evangelical language provided a double-voiced discourse which could both disguise its subversive power and enable women's literary empowerment; thus, it is both women and patriarchy

who are called to repentance in these writings.

401   Agress, Lynne. *The Feminine Irony: Women on Women in Early Nineteenth-Century English Literature*. Rutherford, NJ: Fairleigh Dickinson, 1978. Pp. 190.
Asks how women writers and intellectuals fostered and perpetuated society's stereotypes of and biases against women; Hannah More and other evangelical writers are featured prominently.

402   Cunningham, Valentine. *Everywhere Spoken Against: Dissent in the Victorian Novel*. Oxford: Clarendon, 1975. Pp. 311.
On the various literary perceptions of Nonconformity, with substantial attention to the works of the Brontës, Gaskell, Eliot, and Mrs. Oliphant.

403   Basch, Françoise. *Relative Creatures: Victorian Women in Society and the Novel*. New York: Schocken, 1974. Pp. 360.
A consideration of Victorian women in fiction between the years 1837 and 1867, in a comparison of the sanctified image of wife and mother with the negative images of the single woman and the impure woman.

404   Colby, Vineta. *Yesterday's Woman: Domestic Realism in the English Novel*. Princeton: Princeton, 1974. Pp. 269.
Chapter 4 discusses the evangelical novel, including works by Hannah More, Mrs. Sherwood, and others.

405   Bald, Marjory Amelia. *Women-Writers of the Nineteenth Century*. Cambridge: Cambridge, 1923. Pp. 288.
Essays on Jane Austen, the Brontës, Gaskell, Eliot, Mrs. Browning, and Christina Rossetti, with some discussion of their religious perspectives, especially in Eliot and Rossetti.

406   Nathan, Rhoda B., ed. *Nineteenth-Century Women Writers of the English-Speaking World*. New York: Greenwood, 1986.
Twenty-three essays on British and American authors; see especially Robert N. Keane, "Christina Rossetti: A Reconsideration," pp. 99-106; Coral Lansbury, "The Price of Love:

Gaskell versus Eliot," pp. 107-13; and Alison G. Sulloway, "Jane Austen's Meditative Voice," pp. 193-99.

407   Newton, Judith Lowder. *Women, Power, and Subversion: Social Strategies in British Fiction, 1778-1860.* Athens: Georgia, 1981. Pp. 202.
Representations of women's activity and competence in the context of the emergence of an ideology of woman's sphere.

408   Gilbert, Sandra. "Patriarchal Poetry and Women Readers: Reflections on Milton's Bogey," *PMLA* 93 (1978): 368-82; response by Philip J. Gallagher and reply by Gilbert in *PMLA* 94 (1979): 319-22.
From an expression by Virginia Woolf and a characterization of Milton as "the first of the masculinists" (especially in *Paradise Lost*), Gilbert explores "the implications of Milton's ideas for women" (381, n. 8), most particularly the shadow of misogyny cast over later readers. The response and reply focus on charges and counter-charges of misreading texts.

409   Gilbert, Sandra and Gubar, Susan. *The Madwoman in the Attic: The Woman Writer and the Nineteenth-Century Literary Imagination.* New Haven: Yale, 1979. Pp. 719.
In a large study of women writers that focuses on the theme of confinement, Part III: "How Are We Fal'n?: Milton's Daughters," takes up the subject of religious imagery, including the "Milton's Bogey" essay as well as "Mary Shelley's Monstrous Eve" and "Emily Brontë's Bible of Hell."

410   Kowaleski-Wallace, Beth. "Milton's Daughters: The Education of Eighteenth-Century Women Writers," *Feminist Studies* 12 (1986): 275-93.
Discusses the prominence of the "benevolent patriarch" in the educating father; Hannah More's situation as a self-styled "daughter of Eve" is considered at length.

411   McDermid, Jane. "Conservative Feminism and Female Education in the Eighteenth Century," *History of Education* 18 (1989): 309-22.

Argues that although their legacy is ambiguous, the conservative advocates for the education of women at the end of the
century provided a more positive evaluation of women's domestic and religious role and sought to develop the reasoning
powers of women, to the end of greater social and moral
cohesion in society.

412   Corbett, Mary Jean.   "Feminine Authorship and Spiritual
       Authority in Victorian Women Writers' Autobiographies,"
       Women's Studies 18 (1990): 13-29.
       How three evangelical autobiographers (Mary Martha Stewart,
       Charlotte Tonna, and Mary Anne Schimmelpenninck) used the
       language of piety to give them authority to deal with the com-
       peting tensions between public and private worlds.

413   A number of works have explored the religious themes in the
       novels of Jane Austen; for bibliographical resources, see:
       Roth, Barry and Weinsheimer, Joel, eds. *An Annotated Bibli-
            ography of Jane Austen Studies, 1952-1972.*   Char-
            lottesville: Virginia, 1973. Pp. 272.
            _____, ed.   *An Annotated Bibliography of Jane Austen
            Studies, 1973-83.*   Charlottesville: Virginia, 1985.   Pp.
            359.

414   Examples of specific works on Austen include:
       Koppel, Gene. *The Religious Dimension of Jane Austen's
            Novels.* Ann Arbor: UMI Research, 1988. Pp. 141.
       MacDonagh, Oliver. *Jane Austen: Real and Imagined Worlds.*
            New Haven: Yale, 1991.   Chap. 1, "Religion: *Mansfield
            Park.*"
       Bush, Douglas. *Jane Austen.* New York: Collier, 1975. Pp.
            205.
       Kantrov, Ilene M.   "'A Deep and Enlightened Piety': The
            Religious Background of Jane Austen's Fiction."   Ph.D.,
            Tufts, 1980. Pp. 293.
       Willis, Lesley. "Religion in Jane Austen's *Mansfield Park*,"
            English Studies in Canada 13 (1987): 65-78.
       Monaghan, David. "*Mansfield Park* and Evangelicalism: A
            Reassessment," *Nineteenth-Century Fiction* 33 (1978-79):

215-30.

Jackson, Michael. "Jane Austen's View of the Clergy," *Theology* 78 (1975): 531-38.

415   For work on the Brontë sisters, see:

Barclay, Janet M., ed. *Emily Brontë Criticism, 1900-1982: An Annotated Check List*. Westport, CT: Meckler, 1984. Pp. 162.

Passel, Anne, ed. *Charlotte and Emily Brontë: An Annotated Bibliography*. New York: Garland, 1979. Pp. 359.

DuVal, Katherine Niell. "The Quiet Heretics: Religion and the Craft of the Brontë Sisters." Ph.D., Arkansas, 1991. Pp. 329.

Miller, J. Hillis. *The Disappearance of God: Five Nineteenth-Century Writers*. Cambridge: Harvard, 1963. Pp. 157-211.

Lawson, Kate. "The Dissenting Voice: *Shirley's* Vision of Women and Christianity," *Studies in English Literature, 1500-1900* 29 (1989): 729-43.

Phillips, Marion J. "Charlotte Brontë's Favourite Preacher: Frederick Denison John Maurice (1805-1872)," *Brontë Society Transactions* 20 (1990): 77-88.

Larson, Janet L. "'Who is Speaking?' Charlotte Brontë's Voices of Prophecy," in *Victorian Sages and Cultural Discourse: Renegotiating Gender and Power*, ed. Thäis E. Morgan. New Brunswick: Rutgers, 1990. Pp. 66-86.

Ohmann, Carol. "Historical Reality and 'Divine Appointment' in Charlotte Brontë's Fiction," *Signs* 2 (1977): 757-78.

Gilbert, Sandra M. "Plain Jane's Progress," *Signs* 2 (1977): 779-804.

416   Kowaleski-Wallace, Elizabeth. *Their Fathers' Daughters: Hannah More, Maria Edgeworth, and Patriarchal Complicity*. New York: Oxford, 1991. Pp. 235.

Contrary to some estimates of these writers as moderate feminists, Kowaleski-Wallace sees them as women who have been empowered from within patriarchal discourse, making their contributions limited and their strategies inadequate.

417   Atkinson, Colin B. and Jo. "Sydney Owenson, Lady Morgan: Irish Patriot and First Professional Woman Writer," *Erie-Ireland* 15:2 (1980): 60-90.
An Anglican in Ireland, Morgan (1776-1859) portrayed Catholics in a favorable light in her many writings and criticized the tithe as "the greatest of all Irish grievances."

Ideals and Images

418   Branca, Patricia. *Silent Sisterhood: Middle-Class Women in the Victorian Home.* London: Croom Helm, 1975. Pp. 170.
Focuses on the period 1830-80 and discusses such topics as homemaking, health, motherhood, child care, and birth control by applying the category of the process of modernization; concludes that "religion lost some of its meaning for middle-class women" (147), despite the persistence of this group's image as extremely pious and religious.

419   Gorham, Deborah. *The Victorian Girl and the Feminine Ideal.* London: Croom Helm, 1982. Pp. 223.
Uses the concepts of separate spheres and the cult of domesticity to explore the construction of gender roles in a middle-class context; Gorham argues that religion became a foundation for the appeals to feminine virtues of self-abnegation and self-sacrifice as well as self-control and respectability.

420   LeGates, Marlene. "The Cult of Womanhood in Eighteenth-Century Thought," *Eighteenth-Century Studies* 10 (1976): 21-39.
On the transition from misogyny to a "cult of true womanhood," with the image of the disorderly woman replaced by that of the chaste maiden and obedient wife.

421   Chambers-Schiller, Lee. "The Single Woman Reformer: Conflicts Between Family and Vocation, 1830-1860," *Frontiers* 3 (Fall 1978): 41-48.
How single women shared many of the ideological and familial encumbrances of their married sisters, and thus were not substantially more free to commit themselves to service to others;

such ambivalence often generated stress and illness.

422   Hall, Catherine. "The Early Formation of Victorian Domestic
       Ideology," in *Fit Work for Women*, ed. Sandra Burman. New
       York: St. Martin's, 1979. Pp. 15-32.
       Between 1780 and 1830, a new bourgeoisie recodified ideas
       about womanhood; Hall shows how evangelicalism played a
       crucial role with its themes of new seriousness and respect-
       ability in life, together with a stress on a religion of the hous-
       ehold.

423   Tyrrell, Alexander. "'Woman's Mission' and Pressure Group
       Politics in Britain (1825-60)," *BJRL* 63 (1980): 194-230.
       Argues that while cultural values inhibited a public role for
       women, they still "nourished the belief that in a special way
       women were qualified to invoke a version of this 'moral lan-
       guage' of reform, and that as a consequence they too could
       step onto the national scene as an acknowledged source of
       public opinion" (204); the result was a feminization of the
       religious and philanthropic world.

424   Kelly, J. C. "The Creation of 'Moral Woman': A Sociologi-
       cal History, with reference to Britain in the Nineteenth and
       Twentieth Centuries." Ph.D., London School of Economics,
       1986.

425   Williams, J. T. "Bearers of Moral and Spiritual Values: The
       Social Roles of Clergymen and Women in British Society, c.
       1790 - c. 1880, as Mirrored in Attitudes to Them as Foxhunt-
       ers." D.Phil., Oxford, 1988. Pp. 390.
       On the changing attitudes to clergy and women, as new models
       for each assigned greater responsibility for maintaining moral
       and spiritual values in the society.

426   Gelling, A. "Middle-Class Women and the Ideology of Do-
       mestic Femininity circa 1820-1860." M. Litt., Oxford, 1989.
       Traces the development of a new ideology based on evangeli-
       cal Christianity.

Alfred Lord Tennyson and Women

427 Tennyson's relevance to the subject of this bibliography
     emerges in the debate over whether his works (especially *The
     Princess*) support or undercut the emerging ideology for wom-
     en; see the following reference works and an example of the
     debate:
     Shaw, Marion. *An Annotated Critical Bibliography of Alfred,
        Lord Tennyson*. New York: St. Martin's, 1989. Pp. 134.
     Beetz, Kirk H. *Tennyson: A Bibliography, 1827-1982*. Me-
        tuchen, NJ: Scarecrow, 1984. Pp. 528.
     Hall, Donald E. "The Anti-Feminist Ideology of Tennyson's
        The Princess," *Modern Language Studies* 21:4 (1991): 49-
        62.

Sexuality and Attitudes toward Women

428 Bristow, Edward J. *Vice and Vigilance: Purity Movements in
     Britain Since 1700*. London: Gill and Macmillan, 1978. Pp.
     274.
     A broad study, from societies for the reformation of manners
     to the campaigns for social purity led by Mary Whitehouse in
     the 1960s and 1970s; the Christian support for "social purity"
     in the nineteenth century is central to the story.

429 Trudgill, Eric. *Madonnas and Magdalens: The Origins and
     Development of Victorian Sexual Attitudes*. London: Heine-
     mann, 1976. Pp. 336.
     A history of change and conflict over understandings of
     womanhood, the significance of the home, and fear of sex.
     Evangelical moralists from the 1790s affect the evolution of
     more stringent moral codes by the 1830s, but a reaction
     against these from the 1850s results in the diminution of moral
     restraints by the end of the century.

430 Nevill, M. "Women and Marriage Breakdown in England,
     1832-1857." Ph.D., Essex, 1989.
     A consideration of legal options available to women who
     wished to separate from their husbands in the years before

civil divorce became legal; includes discussion of the work of ecclesiastical courts.

431   Anderson, Nancy F. "The 'Marriage with a Deceased Wife's Sister Bill' Controversy: Incest Anxiety and the Defense of Family Purity in Victorian England," *JBS* 21:2 (1982): 67-86.

Gullette, Margaret M. "The Puzzling Case of the Deceased Wife's Sister: Nineteenth-Century England deals with a Second-Chance Plot," *Representations* 31 (1990): 142-66.

Two articles on a long parliamentary debate, with insights into views of marriage and family, the nature of sexuality, and the stake of the Church of England in upholding perceived moral norms.

Industrial Revolution, Economics, and Employment for Women

432   Pinchbeck, Ivy. *Women Workers in the Industrial Revolution, 1750-1850.* London: Routledge, 1930. Pp. 342.

Covers the dramatic changes in women's employment, as epitomized in the shift of work from home to factory, and concludes that "the Industrial Revolution has on the whole proved beneficial to women" (4) in creating greater leisure and reducing drudgery and monotony.

433   Neff, Wanda F. *Victorian Working Women: An Historical and Literary Study of Women in British Industries and Professions,* 1832-1850. London: Allen & Unwin, 1929. Pp. 288.

Considers textile and other factory workers, the dressmaker, governess, and idle woman, with occasional discussion of the role of religion in their lives.

434   Malmgreen, Gail. *Neither Bread nor Roses: Utopian Feminists and the English Working Class, 1800-1850.* Brighton: Noyce, 1978. Pp. 41.

On the interaction of utopian socialists, working-class reformers, trade unionists, and Chartists on issues relating to the emancipation of women; Malmgreen's narrative helps to account for the apolitical quietism of working-class women.

435   Peterson, M. Jeanne. *Family, Love, and Work in the Lives of Victorian Gentlewomen*. Bloomington: Indiana, 1989. Pp. 241.

_____. "No Angels in the House: The Victorian Myth and the Paget Women," *AHR* 89 (1984): 677-709.

A study of three generations of the Paget family (1799-1914) in order to counter what Peterson sees as a distorted picture of Victorian gentlewomen, where rank mattered more than gender; the family's extensive ties to the ecclesiastical world are a major part of the story. The article contends that the continuing stereotypes surrounding this class of women did not much exist in reality.

436   Saville, John. "Robert Owen on the Family and the Marriage System of the Old Immoral World," in *Rebels and Their Causes*, ed. Maurice Cornforth. Atlantic Highlands, NJ: Humanities, 1979. Pp. 107-21.

How Owen's critique of the marriage system involved a critique of organized religion and aroused intense hostile reaction.

The Spirit of Reform

437   Harrison, Brian. "A Genealogy of Reform in Modern England," in *Anti-Slavery, Religion and Reform*, ed. Christine Bolt and Seymour Drescher. Folkstone: Dawson, 1980. Pp. 119-48.

Covers the nineteenth-century reforming tradition and its advocacy of progress and liberty; its associations with the middle class, with Nonconformist churches and liberal and evangelical Anglicans, and family connections; significant attention is given to women's participation in the reforming causes.

438   Myers, Mitzi. "Reform or Ruin: A Revolution in Female Manners," *Studies in Eighteenth-Century Culture* 11 (1982): 199-216.

In a comparison of Mary Wollstonecraft and Hannah More, Myers suggests that the radical and Evangelical models of moral reform are more parallel than contrasting female responses to political upheaval.

439   Halbersleben, Karen I. *Women's Participation in the British Antislavery Movement*, 1824-1865. Lewiston, NY: Edwin Mellen, 1993. Pp. 246.
Focuses on some forty auxiliaries formed by middle-class women; most were conservative and chiefly Anglican, while a few were radical and Nonconformist (chiefly Quaker and Unitarian). These organizations became a bridge into later activity on behalf of women's rights.

440   Ferguson, Moira. "British Women Writers and an Emerging Abolitionist Discourse," *Eighteenth Century* 33 (1992): 3-23.
On the creation of a new genre of abolitionist writing in Hannah More's "Slavery, A Poem" (1788); it signalled the beginning of active engagement by evangelical women in the abolitionist cause.

441   Midgley, Clare. *Women Against Slavery: The British Campaigns, 1780-1870*. New York: Routledge, 1992. Pp. 281.
Argues that women played a significant part in the anti-slavery movement on both local and national levels, with much of the impulse for this coming from religious identifications; within this foundation, however, a hierarchical model of society supported by evangelicals was increasingly challenged by an egalitarian vision articulated by radicals.

442   _____. "Anti-Slavery and Feminism in Nineteenth-Century Britain," *Gender & History* 5 (1993): 343-62.
Explores the boundaries of gender and race that were challenged by women's involvement in anti-slavery campaigns, as well as the tensions between "maternal activists" and "egalitarian feminists."

443   Billington, Louis and Rosamund. "'A Burning Zeal for Righteousness': Women in the British Anti-Slavery Movement, 1820-1860," in *Equal or Different: Women's Politics, 1800-1914*, ed. Jane Rendall. Oxford: Blackwell, 1987. Pp. 82-111, 248-60.
How women became leading participants in the cause, with Unitarians and Quakers especially prominent.

444   Hurwitz, Edith F. *Politics and the Public Conscience: Slave Emancipation and the Abolitionist Movement in Britain.* London: Allen & Unwin, 1973. Pp. 179.
       Chapter 4 discusses the role of religion, especially Dissent, in the movement, as well as the role of religiously-motivated women who founded a number of associations to further the cause.

445   Ware, Vron. *Beyond the Pale: White Women, Racism, and History.* London: Verso, 1992. Pp. 263.
       From a contemporary interest in the relationship between racism and the feminist movement, Ware explores the involvement of Anglo-American white women in three historical movements: anti-slavery campaigns, imperialism, and the anti-lynching campaign.

446   Klingberg, Frank J. "Harriet Beecher Stowe and Social Reform in England," *AHR* 43 (1937-38): 542-52.
       How Stowe's writings and trips to England encouraged identification with reform causes; one response, the "Stafford House Address," objected to slavery on moral and religious grounds and was signed by more than half a million British women.

447   For discussions of women's involvement in the issue of prison reform, see:
       Cooper, Robert A. "The English Quakers and Prison Reform, 1809-1823," *Quaker History* 68 (1979): 3-19.
       Dobash, Russell P., et al. *The Imprisonment of Women.* Oxford: Blackwell, 1986. Pp. 255.
       Hinde, R. S. E. *The British Penal System, 1773-1950.* London: Duckworth, 1951. Pp. 255.

Women and Philanthropy

448   Rodgers, Betsy. *Cloak of Charity: Studies in Eighteenth-Century Philanthropy.* London: Methuen, 1949. Pp. 185.
       A consideration of various motives for charitable activity for the relief of poverty, such as religious, social, and political

ones, followed by discussion of the work of several individuals
and their causes—including chapters on the schools established
by Sarah Trimmer and Hannah More.

449   Owen, David E. *English Philanthropy, 1660-1960*. Cam-
       bridge: Harvard, 1964. Pp. 610.
       From benevolence to the welfare state; in a larger framework
       of organizations and benefactions, Owen gives some attention
       to the work and roles of women such as Octavia Hill and
       Angela Burdett-Coutts.

450   Dunlop, A. Ian. "Provision for Ministers' Widows in Scot-
       land—Eighteenth Century," *RSCHS* 17 (1971): 233-48.
       On the development of the Scottish Ministers' Widows' Fund
       from 1744, which provided annuities chiefly from income
       produced from annual rates paid by ministers.

451   Prochaska, F. K. *Women and Philanthropy in Nineteenth-
       Century England*. Oxford: Clarendon, 1980. Pp. 301.
       A major study, in two parts: The Power of the Purse and The
       Power of the Cross; in the latter, topics include home visiting,
       the development of work in public and charitable institutions
       (prisons, orphanages, asylums, and the like), and activities
       toward the reclamation of prostitutes.

452   _____. *The Voluntary Impulse: Philanthropy in Modern
       Britain*. London: Faber and Faber, 1988. Pp. 106.
       Not as detailed as the earlier volume; here the aim is to put
       contemporary philanthropic interests in historical perspective,
       and the coverage is from the mix of evangelicalism and liber-
       alism in the early nineteenth century to the dominance of state
       welfare after the Second World War. Contributions of women
       to this work are featured prominently.

453   _____. "Women in English Philanthropy, 1790-1830,"
       IRSH 19 (1974): 426-45.
       An early exploration into the role of charitable women by
       studying subscription lists, contributions, and kinds of work
       undertaken; Prochaska notes that "as a religion of action,

philanthropy slowly challenged the complaisancy of women, gave them practical experience and responsibility, and perhaps most importantly, it heightened their self-confidence and self-respect" (441).

454 _____. "Charity Bazaars in Nineteenth-Century England," *JBS* 16 (Spring 1977): 62-84.
Bazaars became popular in the early part of the century, largely supported by articles made by women and events organized by female philanthropic societies; some churchpersons worried about the frivolity of the activity, and others feared "that the Church was in danger of being 'womanized'" (82).

455 Summers, Anne. "A Home from Home—Women's Philanthropic Work in the Nineteenth Century," in *Fit Work for Women*, pp. 33-63.
On the voluntary visiting of the poor by leisured women for philanthropic activity and spiritual missions; Summers suggests that these initiatives were both reactionary (stemming from very conservative political views) and progressive (in raising questions for the participants).

Education and the Sunday School Movement

456 Turner, Barry. *Equality for Some: The Story of Girls' Education.* London: Ward Lock Educational, 1974. Pp. 233.
A broad history, focusing on the eighteenth century to the present. Discusses the role of the church in early education for girls, especially in promoting a Christian ideal of womanhood; despite attempts to challenge this, it was an important dimension of education, including at the collegiate level, until the early twentieth century.

457 Kasbekar, Veena P. "Power over Themselves: The Controversy about Female Education in England, 1660-1820." Ph.D., Cincinnati, 1980. Pp. 389.
An analysis of the literary debate that eventually produced two opposing views on the subject, the progressive and the conservative.

458   Laqueur, Thomas W. *Religion and Respectability: Sunday
        Schools and Working Class Culture, 1780-1850.* New Haven:
        Yale, 1976. Pp. 293.
        Argues that "the Sunday school was largely the creation of the
        working-class community" (24); while not specifically con-
        cerned with the role of women in this activity, Laqueur gives
        many examples of their participation and their contributions.

459   Sangster, Paul. *Pity My Simplicity: The Evangelical Revival
        and the Religious Education of Children, 1738-1800.* London:
        Epworth, 1963. Pp. 200.
        Includes some discussion of the contributions of individual
        women as writers and teachers.

460   Cutt, M. Nancy. *Mrs. Sherwood and Her Books for Children.*
        London: Oxford, 1974. Pp. 157.
        Author of over four hundred titles, Sherwood (1775-1851) in
        her Evangelical period, c. 1810-26, wrote about the impor-
        tance of family and religious duty, the need for missions,
        Sunday schools, and the evils of slavery.

461   Wolter, Helen. "Give the Children Something Good to Read,"
        Christianity Today 24 (Sept. 5, 1980): 956-58.
        Considers the work of three authors who produced religious
        books for children for the new market for evangelical reading
        material: Sarah Trimmer (1741-1810), Hannah More (1745-
        1833), and Mary Sherwood.

Evangelical Religion

462   Rupp, Gordon. *Religion in England, 1688-1791.* Oxford:
        Clarendon, 1986. Pp. 584.
        In a broad survey, Rupp has sections on women in the evan-
        gelical movement: early Methodism, the Countess of Hunt-
        ingdon, and the ministries of Sarah Trimmer and Hannah
        More.

463   Brown, Ford K. *Fathers of the Victorians.* Cambridge: Cam-
        bridge, 1961. Pp. 569.

A strong critique of the Evangelical program of moral reform, with major attention to the work of Hannah More, whom Brown calls its "greatest publicist" (11).

464   Bradley, Ian. *The Call to Seriousness: The Evangelical Impact on the Victorians*. London: Cape, 1976. Pp. 224.
Studies Anglican Evangelicalism in the first half of the nineteenth century, with attention to the role of women in its activities on behalf of "vital religion."

465   Heasman, Kathleen. *Evangelicals in Action: An Appraisal of Their Social Work in the Victorian Era*. London: G. Bles, 1962. Pp. 310.
A study of the voluntary organizations that represented Evangelical activity on a number of social issues.

466   Carwardine, Richard. *Transatlantic Revivalism: Popular Evangelicalism in Britain and America, 1790-1865*. Westport, CT: Greenwood, 1978. Pp. 249.
In this exploration of American influence on British evangelical life, Carwardine considers the work of Phoebe Palmer as a traveling evangelist.

467   Kent, John. *Holding the Fort: Studies in Victorian Revivalism*. London: Epworth, 1978. Pp. 381.
Studies the British experience of revivalism across the nineteenth century; the work of Phoebe Palmer is featured prominently, and the activities of other women, such as Catherine Booth and Hannah Smith, are noted.

468   Lewis, Donald M. "'Lights in Dark Places': Women Evangelists in Early Victorian Britain, 1838-1857," in *Women in the Church*, pp. 415-27.
On the employment of women as full-time evangelists by interdenominational agencies; they were visitors and readers and offered practical assistance to persons in need, and by the 1850s they worked with men as well as women.

469   Field-Bibb, Jacqueline. "The Worst of Heresies," *MC* 33:4

(1992): 13-22.

An exploration of the ministries of women between 1790 and 1830, as exhibited in Zechariah Taft's *Biographical Sketches of the Lives and Public Ministry of Various Holy Women* (2 vols., 1825 and 1828).

470   Valenze, Deborah.   "Cottage Religion and the Politics of Survival," in *Equal or Different: Women's Politics, 1800-1914*, pp. 31-56, 243-46.
       On the world of laboring women who became preachers in the years 1790-1860 and active agents in the struggle to maintain and uphold community and family, with special attention to the Primitive Methodist preacher, Mary Porteous (1783-1861); this activity represented a challenge to liberal individualism and to the middle-class notion of separate spheres.

471   Penny, N. B.   "English Church Monuments to Women Who Died in Childbed between 1780-1835," *Journal of the Warburg and Courtauld Institutes* 38 (1975): 314-32.
       Two conventions are traced here: portrayals of the woman as she dies, with varying degrees of idealization, and the ascension into heaven of the dead mother and child.

472   Landsman, Ned.   "Evangelists and Their Hearers: Popular Interpretations of Revivalist Preaching in Eighteenth-Century Scotland," *JBS* 28:2 (1989): 120-49.
       Includes discussion of the responses of many women.

473   Smout, T. C.   "Born Again at Cambuslang: New Evidence on Popular Religion and Literacy in Eighteenth-Century Scotland," *Past & Present* 97 (1982): 114-27.
       Reflections on the local minister's interviews of 110 participants in the 1742 religious revival, two-thirds of whom were women.

Millenarian Religion

474   Schwartz, Hillel. *The French Prophets: The History of a Millenarian Group in Eighteenth-Century England*. Berkeley:

California, 1980. Pp. 382.
Schwartz provides extensive discussion of the role of women prophets and followers in this early eighteenth-century movement; although excluded from power in its beginnings, women represented more than half of the prophets, nearly half of the followers, and most of the excluded "false prophets." In the second generation revival after 1730, women such as Hannah Wharton provided both leadership and a source for the later millenarian thought of Ann Lee.

475   "Friends and the French Prophets," *JFHS* 22 (1925): 1-9.
Random information concerning Quaker women and men who either left the movement for the Prophets or who had connections with them.

476   Garrett, Clarke. *Spirit Possession and Popular Religion: From the Camisards to the Shakers.* Baltimore: Johns Hopkins, 1987. Pp. 294.
On the origins of the Shakers in the radical religious experience of possession and prophecy in Europe and America, including the emergence of Ann Lee in Manchester and the establishment of Shakerism in America.

477   _____. *Respectable Folly: Millenarians and the French Revolution in France and England.* Baltimore: Johns Hopkins, 1975. Pp. 237.
A study of the impact of the French Revolution on the development of millenarian ideas in France and England, including the association of Richard Brothers and Joanna Southcott.

478   Andrews, Edward Deming and Faith. *The People Called Shakers.* New York: Oxford, 1953; 2nd ed., 1963. Pp. 309.
Chapter 1 deals with the English roots of Ann Lee in Manchester, with her connections to Quakers and the possibilities of influence from the Camisards, or French Prophets.

479   MacDiarmid, Hugh. *Scottish Eccentrics.* London: Routledge, 1936.
Includes a study of the messianic leader Elspeth Buchan (1738-

91), pp. 160-93, a forerunner of Joanna Southcott in claiming
to be a fulfiller of biblical prophecy.

The Methodist Movement
A. Bibliographies and Guides

480   For bibliographies of Methodist history (the general works
      include much material on American topics), see:
      Eltscher, Susan M., ed. *Women in the Wesleyan and United
          Methodist Traditions: A Bibliography*. Madison, NJ: Gen-
          eral Commission on Archives and History, 1992. Pp. 158.
      Jarboe, Betty M., ed. *John and Charles Wesley: A Bibliogra-
          phy*. Metuchen, NJ: Scarecrow, 1987. Pp. 404.
      Rowe, Kenneth E. *Methodist Women: A Guide to the Litera-
          ture*. Lake Junaluska, NC: General Commission on Ar-
          chives and History, 1980. Pp. 50.

481   Davies, Rupert, et al., eds. *A History of the Methodist Church
      in Great Britain* 4 vols., London: Epworth, 1965-88.
      Volume 4 (1988) contains illustrative documents (with four
      units on women) and a substantial bibliography that includes
      three small sections on women in this tradition.

B. General Studies

482   For general studies of Methodist beginnings that give some
      attention to the role and participation of women in the
      movement, see:
      Church, Leslie F. *The Early Methodist People*.   London:
          Epworth, 1948. Pp. 286.
      _____. *More About the Early Methodist People*. London:
          Epworth, 1949. Pp. 324.
      Wearmouth, Robert F. *Methodism and the Common People of
          the Eighteenth Century*. London: Epworth, 1945. Pp. 276.
      Whitely, J. H. *Wesley's England: A Survey of XVIIIth Centu-
          ry Social and Cultural Conditions*.   London: Epworth,
          1938. Pp. 380.

C. John Wesley and Women

483   The founder of Methodism had difficult personal relationships
       with women, yet gave many of his female followers opportuni-
       ties for leadership and public visibility in the movement that
       were well in advance of his age. Of the large number of
       Wesley biographies, some of the better and more recent that
       attend to such matters are:
       Rack, Henry D. *Reasonable Enthusiast: John Wesley and the
           Rise of Methodism*. London: Epworth, 1989. Pp. 656.
       Ayling, Stanley. *John Wesley*. London: Collins, 1979. Pp.
           350.
       Green, V. H. H. *John Wesley*. London: Nelson, 1964. Pp.
           168.

484   Abelove, Henry. *The Evangelist of Desire: John Wesley and
           the Methodists*. Stanford: Stanford, 1990. Pp. 136.
       _____. "The Sexual Politics of Early Wesleyan Method-
           ism," in *Disciplines of Faith*, pp. 86-99.
       In part of this study of Wesley's influence on his followers,
       Abelove addresses issues of sexuality, e.g., his preference for
       the single state over marriage and his organization of meetings
       into single-sex groups; "women continued to find scope in
       Methodism for devaluing and breaking the ties they disliked"
       (65).

485   Edwards, Maldwyn. *My Dear Sister: The Story of John Wes-
           ley and the Women in his Life*. Manchester: Penwork, 1980.
           Pp. 124.
       From his mother to some of his most committed followers,
       with a focus on individuals rather than their activity in the
       movement.

486   Harrison, G. Elsie. *Son to Susanna: The Private Life of John
           Wesley*. London: Nicholson and Watson, 1937. Pp. 353.
       Bowen, Marjorie. *Wrestling Jacob: A Study of the Life of
           John Wesley and Some Members of the Family*. London:
           Watts, 1937. Pp. 261.
       Two older studies on the influence of women in his life.

487   Ethridge, Willie Snow. *Strange Fires: The True Story of John Wesley's Love Affair in Georgia*. New York: Vanguard, 1971. Pp. 254.

A novelistic recounting of his relationship with Sophey Hopkey.

488   Hayes, Alan L. "John Wesley and Sophey Hopkey: A Case Study in Wesley's Attitude toward Women," in *Women in New Worlds* 2: 29-44, 359-61.

Explores this relationship during Wesley's ministry in Georgia (1736-37) in terms of his understanding of the role of women in the church and his tendency to distance himself emotionally from others.

489   Lawson, Albert B. *John Wesley and the Christian Ministry*. London: SPCK, 1963.

Contains a brief but helpful Appendix, "Wesley and the Ministry of Women," pp. 176-81.

490   Chilcote, Paul W. *John Wesley and the Women Preachers of Early Methodism*. Metuchen, NJ: Scarecrow, 1991. Pp. 375 [a briefer version is entitled *She Offered Them Christ: The Legacy of Women Preachers in Early Methodism* (Nashville: Abingdon, 1993)].

From the important role of women in the movement to the suppression of these activities by the early nineteenth century; appendices give biographical outlines of forty-two women preachers, sermon registers, and other relevant documents.

491   _____. "John Wesley as Revealed by the Journal of Hester Ann Rogers, July 1775-October 1784," *Methodist History* 20:3 (1982): 111-23.

Rogers (1756-94) first met Wesley when he visited Macclesfield in 1776; Chilcote uses her three-volume journal to see her view of Wesley as leader of the societies, pastor, and preacher.

492   Edwards, Maldwyn L. "Women in John Wesley's Life," *Methodist Magazine* (April 1967): 38-40.

This brief but substantial discussion of the complexity of Wesley's relationship with women suggests that he embraced, without consciously realizing it, the three-fold vows of poverty, chastity, and obedience; thus, he was a reluctant lover but a warm friend to many women.

493   Rogal, Samuel J. "John Wesley's Women," *Eighteenth Century Life* 1 (1974): 7-10.
Contends that Wesley's relations with women can be explained in relation to his central commitment to his cause; thus, those who shared this commitment received his encouragement.

494   Newton, John Anthony. "Wesley and Women," in *John Wesley: Contemporary Perspectives*, ed. John Stacey. London: Epworth, 1988. Pp. 129-37.
Focuses on his debt to his mother and gives a sample of his extended correspondence with women.

495   Lee, Umphrey. "John Wesley's Love Affairs," *Methodist Quarterly Review* 74 (1925): 476-93.
Reflections on why these experiences were such failures; Lee suggests that Wesley had a deep romantic tendency, was very ignorant "of the feminine mind," and had only one fundamental passion—religion.

496   Edwards, Maldwyn. "The Reluctant Lover: John Wesley as Suitor," *Methodist History* 12 (1974): 46-62.
Pursues the question of whether his relation to his mother affected his romantic relationships.

497   Baker, Frank. "John Wesley's First Marriage," *Duke Divinity School Review* 31 (1966): 175-88 and *London Quarterly and Holborn Review* 192 (1967): 305-15.
Maser, Frederick E. "John Wesley's Only Marriage," *Methodist History* 16 (1977-78): 33-41.
Baker, Frank. "Some Observations on John Wesley's Relationship with Grace Murray," *Ibid.*: 42-45.
A debate over the relationship of Wesley and Grace Murray which hinges on an understanding of marriage law at the time

and the character of the "contract" between them in 1749. Baker argues that the "marriage" was a legal contract rather than a personal relationship, in that there was no church cere- mony and no consummation, while Maser contends that the contract was destroyed because it contained conditional clauses that were never fulfilled.

498   Harrison, G. Elsie.   "Grace Murray," in *Methodist Good Companions*. London: Epworth, 1935. Pp. 13-32.
Considers Wesley from Murray's perspective.

499   Leger, Augustin. *Wesley's Last Love*. London: Dent, 1910. Pp. 300.
Although discussing Wesley and Grace Murray, Leger also considers Wesley's failed marriage to Molly Vazeille; an early effort at psychological explanation.

500   Rogal, Samuel J.   "John Wesley Takes a Wife," *Methodist History* 27 (1988-89): 48-55.
A brief narrative on the run-up to the marriage to Molly Va- zeille in 1751 and the strife that followed, especially after 1758.

501   Collins, Kenneth J.   "John Wesley's Relationship with his Wife as Revealed in his Correspondence," *Methodist History* 32:1 (1993): 4-18.
Considers Wesley's part in the failure of his marriage.

502   Rogal, Samuel J.   "John Wesley and Mary Queen of Scots: A Love Affair with History," *Methodist History* 24 (1980): 216- 26.
Contends that Wesley developed an infatuation from 1761 when he visited Holyrood House in Edinburgh.

503   Hull, James E.   "The Controversy Between John Wesley and the Countess of Huntingdon: Its Origin, Development and Consequences," Ph.D., Edinburgh, 1959. Pp. 353.
Traces the conflict from its beginnings in the 1740s to their deaths in the same year, 1791, and assesses the consequences

of it; personality clashes and disagreement over the doctrine of perfection divided them, despite common interests in the Evangelical Revival.

D. Women in Eighteenth-Century Methodism

504   Brown, Earl Kent. *Women of Mr. Wesley's Methodism*. New York: Edwin Mellen, 1983. Pp. 261.

        _____. "Standing in the Shadow: Women in Early Methodism," *Nexus* 17:2 (1974): 22-31.

        _____. "Women of the Word: Selected Leadership Roles of Women in Mr. Wesley's Methodism," in *Women in New Worlds: Historical Perspectives on the Wesleyan Tradition*, ed. Hilah F. Thomas and Rosemary Skinner Keller. Vol. 1; Nashville: Abingdon, 1981. Pp. 69-87, 384-86.

Brown's main study is organized around leadership roles of women: speakers, advisors and counselors, group leaders, school leaders, visitors, ministers' wives, itinerants, patrons, and models of the Christian life. This is followed by biographical studies of six prominent women and by a group portrait of the 110 women who are the subjects of this research.

505   _____. "Feminist Theology and the Women of Mr. Wesley's Methodism," in *Wesleyan Theology Today*, ed. Theodore Runyon. Nashville: Kingswood, 1985. Pp. 143-50.

Explores two topics in which eighteenth-century examples can provide resources for contemporary feminist theology: the use of experience as a source for theology and the occasions for sustenance and confirmation through worship, mutual ministry, reliance on God's "ownership" of their work, and the like.

506   Chilcote, Paul W. "The Women Pioneers of Early Methodism," in *Wesleyan Theology Today*, pp. 180-84.

In numbers (typically a 2:1 ratio to men in the individual communities) and influence, women were conspicuous as pioneers and sustainers, which gave them a working equality with Methodist males.

507   Keller, Rosemary S. "Women and the Nature of Ministry in
        the United Methodist Tradition," *Methodist History* 22:2
        (1984): 99-114.
        A rapid overview of three historic periods: 1) Methodist begin-
        nings, 2) the American revolutionary period, and 3) the found-
        ing of four major women's movements in the late nineteenth
        century.

508   Morrow, Thomas M. *Early Methodist Women.* London:
        Epworth, 1967. Pp. 119.
        Short biographical studies of five individuals: Sarah Crosby,
        Hannah Ball, Frances Pawson, Mary Fletcher, and Sarah
        Bentley.

509   Harrison, A. W. "An Early Woman Preacher—Sarah Cros-
            by," *PWHS* 14 (1923-24): 104-109.
        Baker, Frank. "John Wesley and Sarah Crosby," *PWHS* 27:4
            (1949): 76-82.
        Two articles on the first authorized woman preacher (1729-
        1804) of Methodism, whose preaching began in 1761.

510   Beresford, John B. "Wesley and Judith Beresford, 1734-
            1756," *London Quarterly Review* 147 (1927): 35-50.
        Bates, E. Ralph. "Sarah Ryan and Kingswood School,"
            PWHS 38 (1971-72): 110-14.
        Brooke, Susan C. "The Journal of Isabella Mackiver," *PWHS*
            28 (1951-52): 159-63.
        Nattrass, J. Conder. "Some Notes from the Oldest Register of
            the Great Yarmouth Circuit," *PWHS* 3 (1901-02): 73-77.
        Glimpses of generally unknown women in the movement; the
        last article includes information on the listing of female
        preachers in circuit rosters of early Methodism in 1785 and
        1787.

511   Banks, John. *"Nancy, Nancy": The Life Story of Ann Bolton
        Who Was the Friend, and Confidante, of John Wesley, Based
        on her Unpublished Journal and on Letters.* Wilmslow: Pen-
        work, 1984. Pp. 151.
        On their extensive correspondence and the view into their lives

that this provides.

512   Boulton, David J. "Women and Early Methodism," *PWHS* 43
       (1981): 13-17.
       Focuses on some of the work of those who were not preach-
       ers, but visited, began Sunday schools, supported itinerant
       preachers, and the like.

513   Gillespie, Joanna Bowen.   "Gasping for Larger Measures:
       Joanna Turner, Eighteenth-Century Activist," *Journal of Fem-
       inist Studies in Religion* 3:2 (1987): 31-55.
       From the memoirs of this evangelical activist (1732-84), an
       emphasis on the themes of self-development and independent
       ministry.

514   Collins, Vicki Tolar. "Perfecting a Woman's Life: Methodist
       Rhetoric and Politics in *The Account of Hester Ann Rogers*."
       Ph.D., Auburn, 1993. Pp. 292.
       An account of the publishing history of this work (containing a
       spiritual autobiography, a sermon preached at her funeral, and
       an essay by her husband), showing that the latter documents
       reshaped her memory in terms of her domestic virtues, includ-
       ing that she did not preach.

E. Local and Regional Methodist Activity

515   Malmgreen Gail. "Domestic Discords: Women and the Fam-
       ily in East Cheshire Methodism, 1750-1830," in *Disciplines of
       Faith*, pp. 55-70.
       Investigates the religious lives of ordinary Methodist women;
       they were more likely to be unmarried than male members,
       often traveled widely, and frequently joined societies in defi-
       ance of their parents' wishes. After being pushed from the
       center of Methodist life in the early nineteenth century, they
       turned to philanthropy and missions activity.

516   Harrison, A. W. "New Light on Methodism in the Isle of
       Man," *PWHS* 19:8 (1934): 195-202.
       Draws chiefly from the journal accounts of Mary Holder (d.

1836), who traveled with her preacher husband from their marriage in 1782.

517   Richardson, W. F. *Preston Methodism's 200 Fascinating Years, 1776-1976*. Preston, 1975. Pp. 219.
       Includes a brief account of Martha Thompson, the first person in Preston to become a Methodist (pp. 9-13).

518   Shaw, Thomas. *A History of Cornish Methodism*. Truro: Bradford, Barton, 1967. Pp. 145.
       As the Bible Christian Methodists began in Cornwall and had a prominent place for women in their early years, this regional study provides some illustrations of roles of women and the use of women preachers.

F. Nineteenth-Century Methodism

519   Swift, Wesley F. "The Women Itinerant Preachers of Early Methodism," *PWHS* 28 (1951-52): 89-94; 29 (1953-54): 76-83.
       Begins with women preachers in Wesleyan Methodism, but focuses on the Primitive Methodists and Bible Christians, who employed women as itinerants from their early nineteenth-century origins. Some seventy-one women served in the Bible Christian itinerancy between 1819 and 1861; Primitive Methodist itinerant women are more difficult to locate, but Swift discovered over forty.

520   Beckerlegge, Oliver A. "Women Itinerant Preachers," *PWHS* 30 (1955-56): 182-84.
       An extension of the previous article, showing additional itinerant women serving in Bible Christian stations in the 1890s and as ministers in the China mission from 1894 to 1907.

521   Jones, Margaret P. "Whose Characterisation? Which Perfection? Women's History and Christian Reflection," *Epworth Review* 20:2 (1993): 96-103.
       Looks at twenty biographies in the *Arminian/Methodist Magazine*, 1798-1821, to demonstrate how the public characteriza-

tion of women was under male control.

522   Werner, Julia Stewart. *The Primitive Methodist Connexion: Its Background and Early History.* Madison: Wisconsin, 1984. Pp. 251.
This denominational study focuses on the first generation of activity and gives some attention to the role of women as evangelists and preachers.

523   Graham, E. Dorothy. "Called by God: The Female Itinerants of Early Primitive Methodism." Ph.D., Birmingham, 1987. Pp. 376.
_____. *Chosen by God: A List of the Female Travelling Preachers of Early Primitive Methodism.* Bunbury, Cheshire: Wesley Hist. Soc., 1989. Pp. 31.
_____. "Chosen by God: The Female Travelling Preachers of Early Primitive Methodism," *PWHS* 49 (1993): 77-95.
_____. "Women Itinerants of Early Primitive Methodism," *Cirplan* 8 (1983-87): 106-15.
_____. "Mary Porteous, 1783-1861: Primitive Methodist Travelling Preacher," *Bulletin of the Wesley Historical Society, North-East Branch* 51 (February 1989): 5-21.
The dissertation traces ninety such women, but significant biographical data were found for only twenty (all born before 1816); the peak year was 1834 with twenty-six itinerant women, and the final retirement took place in 1862. Women preachers were used in evangelism and missions, but denied a voice in church courts and not given equal status with men in positions of power. The shorter pieces draw on material from the dissertation.

524   For studies of Primitive Methodists that give some attention to the contributions of women, see:
Wilkinson, John T. *Hugh Bourne, 1772-1852.* London: Epworth, 1952. Pp. 203.
Ritson, Joseph. *The Romance of Primitive Methodism.* London: Dalton, 1909. Pp. 312.
Kendall, H. B. *The Origin and History of the Primitive Methodist Church.* 2 vols., London, [1906]. Pp. 559 and 552.

525   For similar studies of Bible Christian Methodists, see:
       Pyke, Richard. *The Early Bible Christians*. London: Ep-
       worth, 1941. Pp. 46.
       _____. *The Golden Chain: The Story of the Bible Chris-
       tian Methodists, 1815-1907*. London: H. Hooks, 1915.
       Pp. 216.
       Shaw, Thomas. *The Bible Christians, 1815-1907*. London:
       Epworth, 1965. Pp. 120.
       Bourne, F. W. *The Bible Christians: Their Origin and Histo-
       ry*. London: Bible Christian Book Room, 1903. Pp. 567.
       Beckerlegge, Oliver A., comp. *United Methodist Ministers
       and Their Circuits*. London: Epworth, 1968. Pp. 268.

526   Valenze, Deborah M. *Prophetic Sons and Daughters: Female
       Preaching and Popular Religion in Industrial England*.
       Princeton: Princeton, 1985. Pp. 308.
       _____. "Pilgrims and Progress in Nineteenth-century
       England," in *Culture, Ideology and Politics: Essays for Eric
       Hobsbawm*, ed. R. Samuel and G. Stedman Jones. Lon-
       don: Routledge, 1982. Pp. 113-26.
       Probing studies of cottage religion (specifically, sectarian
       Methodism) in the first half of the nineteenth century and the
       special roles of women preachers who provided links between
       home and religion in a time of change for laboring people. As
       cottage religion declined after 1850, so also did the number
       and work of its women preachers.

527   Dews, D. Colin. "Ann Carr and the Female Revivalists of
       Leeds," in *Religion in the Lives*, pp. 68-87.
       Carr (1783-1841) was the leader of a secession from Primitive
       Methodism which had a worship atmosphere akin to later
       Pentecostalism; it did not continue long after her death.

528   Albin, Thomas R. *Full Salvation: The Spirituality of Anne
       Reynalds of Truro, 1775-1840*. Cornish Methodist Historical
       Association, 1981. Pp. 28.
       An account from her spiritual diary, written from 1799 to
       1838.

529   Waller, Dr. and Telford, John. "A Famous Lady Preacher,"
       Wesleyan Methodist Magazine 130 (1907): 538-44.
       On Mary Barritt Taft (1772-1851), the best known female
       evangelist of her day.

530   Parlby, William. "Diana Thomas, of Kington, Lay Preacher
       in the Hereford Circuit, 1759-1821," *PWHS* 14 (1923-24):
       110-11.
       Thomas joined the Methodists around 1800 and served as an
       evangelist with the support of the local superintendent, at least
       from 1809 to her death.

Quakers

531   Morton, Vanessa. "Quaker Politics and Industrial Change, c.
       1800-1850." Ph.D., Open University, 1988. Pp. 324.
       Chapters 3 and 4 analyze the role of women in Quaker poli-
       tics.

532   Wright, Sheila. "Quakerism and Its Implications for Quaker
       Women: The Women Itinerant Ministers of York Meeting,
       1780-1840," in *Women in the Church*, pp. 403-14.
       In contrast with an earlier eighteenth-century pattern, Quaker
       women ministers outnumbered men in the period from 1775 to
       1860. Wright compares these women with their Methodist
       counterparts to determine why Quaker women's preaching
       survived and concludes that it was because they were from
       leading families and because marriage and ministry could be
       combined.

533   Labouchere, Rachel. *Abiah Darby, 1716-1793, of Coalbrook-
       dale: Wife of Abraham Darby II.* York: Sessions, 1988. Pp.
       316.
       Follows the diary of this notable Quaker woman, who made
       the first of many journeys as a minister in 1751.

534   Booth, Christopher C. "Ann Fothergill: The Mistress of
       Harpur Street," *Proceedings of the American Philosophical
       Society* 122 (1978): 340-54.

On the life of well-to-do Quakers in mid-eighteenth-century London.

535   Corfield, Kenneth. "Elizabeth Heyrick: Radical Quaker," in *Religion in the Lives*, pp. 41-67.
Heyrick (1769-1831) was a vigorous writer on behalf of abolitionism and a critic of social inequalities.

536   "Elizabeth Jacob of Limerick, 1675-1739," *JFHS* 11 (1914): 78-83.
The work of an Irish Quaker minister who made five preaching trips to England between 1701 and 1729.

537   Dickson, Mora. *The Powerful Bond: Hannah Kilham 1774-1832*. London: Dobson, 1980. Pp. 252.
Hair, P. E. H. "A Bibliographical Note on Hannah Kilham's Linguistic Work," *JFHS* 49 (1960): 165-68.
_____. "Hannah Kilham and the Seneca Language," *Notes and Queries* 229 (1984): 58-62.
Kilham was first a Methodist, then a Quaker, and did pioneering work as an educator and linguist in West Africa.

538   Malmgreen, Gail. "Anne Knight and the Radical Subculture," *Quaker History* 71 (Fall 1982): 100-13.
In her fifties Knight (1786-1862) became involved in the antislavery movement and later was an advocate for women's suffrage; for her, says Malmgreen, "every political question was at base a religious one" (108).

539   Macgregor, Margaret E. *Amelia Alderson Opie: Worldling and Friend*. Northampton, MA: Smith College Studies in Modern Languages 14, 1933. Pp. 146.
Menzies-Wilson, Jacobine and Lloyd, Helen. *Amelia: The Tale of a Plain Friend*. Oxford: Oxford, 1937. Pp. 299.
Opie (1769-1853) was a minor author and poet who became a Plain Friend in 1825, requiring a very different kind of life from what she had led before.

540   Mounfield, Arthur. "Dorothy Ripley," *PWHS* 7 (1910): 31-33.

"Dorothy Ripley, Unaccredited Missionary," *JFHS* 22 (1925): 33-51; 23 (1926): 12-21, 77-79.
Ripley (1767-1831) made several trips to the United States to witness against slavery and engage in other ministries.

541   Green, Joseph J. "Elizabeth Robson," *JFHS* 14 (1917): 75-78.
As a minister from 1810, Robson (1771-1843) traveled extensively and was an early visitor to asylums, workhouses, and prisons.

542   Jennings, Judith. "The Journal of Margaret Hoare Woods: 'Bow me in deep humility of soul . . .'," *Quaker History* 75:1 (1986): 26-34.
Shows how her eight-volume journal (1771-1821) reveals a more complex person than the published extracts do; she struggled with doubts, misgivings, and resentments as she sought to find her role as a middle-class Quaker woman.

Other Protestant Nonconformity

543   Mineka, Francis E. *The Dissidence of Dissent: The Monthly Repository, 1806-38.* Chapel Hill: North Carolina, 1944. Pp. 458.
On the Unitarian journal that supported causes relating to the condition of women (divorce law reform, etc.) and encouraged Harriet Martineau in her early journalistic career.

544   McLachlan, Herbert. "A Liverpool Lady's Journal a Century Ago," *TUHS* 11 (1955): 1-19.
Glimpses into the life of liberal Nonconformity through the diaries of Caroline Thornely (1822-80), begun in 1841.

545   Hempton, David and Hill, Myrtle. "Women and Protestant Minorities in Eighteenth-Century Ireland," in *Women in Early Modern Ireland*, pp. 197-211.
Studies the role of women in three religious communities, Methodists, Quakers, and Moravians; in each case early positions of influence were not sustained into the nineteenth century when the organizations became more formal.

Roman Catholicism

546   Leys, M. D. R. "The Rights of Women: An Eighteenth-Cen-
       tury Catholic 'Petition'," *Month* 23 (1960): 83-88.
       In the context of a public debate between liberal and conser-
       vative Catholics at the end of the century, which included the
       question of whether bishops should be elected by the laity, the
       conservative group produced a "petition" allegedly from Cath-
       olic women claiming their "rights" to vote on the grounds of
       their greater spirituality; Leys notes that "it is not possible that
       the arguments were meant to be taken seriously" (86).

547   Fletcher, John Rory. *The Story of the English Bridgettines of
       Syon Abbey.* Bristol: Burleigh, 1933. Pp. 172.
       A narrative of relocations and conflicts in the only existing
       religious house that survived the Reformation; established in
       1415, it was exiled to the continent at the time of the dissolu-
       tion of monasteries and relocated there several times; part of
       the community returned to England in 1809, and the rest came
       from Portugal in 1861.

548   Walsh, T. J. *Nano Nagle and the Presentation Sisters.* Dub-
       lin: Gill and Son, 1959. Pp. 427.
       Nagle (1718-84) was a pioneer in Catholic education in Ire-
       land, founder of charity schools and, in 1776, a sisterhood.

549   Savage, Roland Burke. *A Valiant Dublin Woman: The Story of
       George's Hill (1766-1940).* Dublin: Gill and Son, 1940. Pp.
       312.
       On the founder, Maria Teresa Mulally (1728-1803), and the
       work of Catholic education in Ireland.

550   Gibbons, Margaret. *Glimpses of Catholic Ireland in the 18th
       Century.* Dublin: Browne and Nolan, 1932. Pp. 386.
       A biography of bishop Patrick Delany (1747-1814) and a
       history of the Brigidine Order of teaching sisters, revived by
       Delany at the end of the century.

551   Fahey, Anthony. "Female Asceticism in the Catholic Church:

A Case Study of Nuns in Ireland in the Nineteenth Century."
Ph.D., Illinois, 1982. Pp. 191.
Examines the foundation and growth of female religious orders
and congregations in the first half of the century, in relation to
the development of organized asceticism in the Catholic
Church.

552   . "Nuns in the Catholic Church in Ireland in the
Nineteenth Century," in *Girls Don't Do Honours: Irish Women
in Education in the Nineteenth and Twentieth Centuries*, ed.
Mary Cullen. Dublin: Women's Education Bureau, 1987. Pp.
7-30.
Contends that despite dramatic growth (from 120 to over 8,000
in the course of the century) and important new ministries of
education and health care, the position of nuns which echoed
that of women in the home may have contributed to a feminization of religion in this period.

553 Clear, Caitríona. "The Limits of Female Autonomy: Nuns in
Nineteenth-Century Ireland," in *Women Surviving: Studies in
Irish Women's History in the Nineteenth and Twentieth Centuries*, ed. Maria Luddy and Cliona Murphy. Dublin: Poolbeg,
1990. Pp. 15-50.
Shows how convents were often directly subordinate to dioc-
esan bishops; nuns compromised frequently with church authorities because otherwise they might not have survived.

554 A Member of the Congregation. *The Life and Work of Mary
Aikenhead*. London: Longmans, Green, 1924. Pp. 476.
On the founder (1787-1858) of the Congregation of Irish Sis-
ters of Charity.

555 A Loreto Sister. *Joyful Mother of Children: Mother Frances
Mary Teresa Ball*. Dublin: Gill, 1961. Pp. 347.
Ball (1794-1861) was founder of the order known as the "Lo-
reto nuns."

Women and English Hymnody

556   For reference material, see:
        Claghorn, Gene, ed. *Women Composers & Hymnists: A Con-
        cise Biographical Dictionary.* Metuchen: Scarecrow, 1984.
        Pp. 272.
        Rogal, Samuel J., ed. *Sisters of Sacred Song: A Selected
        Listing of Women Hymnodists in Great Britain and America.*
        New York: Garland, 1981. Pp. 162.
        Julian, John, ed. *A Dictionary of Hymnology.* 1892; later
        revised editions.

557   Maison, Margaret. "'Thine, Only Thine!' Women Hymn
        Writers in Britain, 1760-1835," in *Religion in the Lives*, pp.
        11-40.
        On the emergence and contributions of such religious poets as
        Anne Steele, Mrs. Barbauld, Ann and Jane Taylor, Harriet
        Auber, and Mrs. Hemans, along with the themes they ex-
        plored.

558   Thomson, Ronald W. "Anne Steele, 1716-1778," *Baptist
        Quarterly* n.s. 21 (1966): 368-71.
        Dixon, Michael F. and Steele-Smith, Hugh F. "Anne Steele's
        Health: A Modern Diagnosis," *Baptist Quarterly* 32 (1988):
        351-56.
        Hymns by Anne Steele. London: Gospel Standard Baptist
        Trust, 1967. Pp. xxiii + 160.
        Studies of one of the first British women to publish hymns.

559   McKellar, Hugh D. "The First Denominational Hymnbook,"
        Hymn 31 (1980): 33-37.
        Credits the Countess of Huntingdon as the originator of the
        idea of having a denominational hymnbook; the one for her
        congregations was published in 1780.

560   Dickson, Thomas S. *Caroline Fry, A Story of Grace.* Lon-
        don: Thynne, 1908. Pp. 16.
        A brief tract in praise of her life (1787-1846) and work as
        writer of popular evangelical books and hymns.

561   Allchin, A. M. *Ann Griffiths*. Cardiff: Wales, 1976. Pp. 72.
       (Revised ed., *Ann Griffiths: The Furnace and the Fountain*,
       1987.)
       Griffiths (1776-1805) was a Welsh Methodist hymn writer.

562   Trinder, Peter W. *Mrs. Hemans*. Writers of Wales Series.
       Cardiff: Wales, 1984. Pp. 75.
       Hemans (1793-1835) was a Welsh poet and author.

Missions

563   Donaldson, Margaret. "'The Cultivation of the Heart and the
       Moulding of the Will . . .': The Missionary Contribution of
       the Society for Promoting Female Education in China,
       India, and the East," in *Women in the Church*, pp. 429-42.
       _____. "The Invisible Factor—19th Century Feminist
       Evangelical Concern for Human Rights," *Journal for the
       Study of Religion* 2:2 (1989): 3-15.
       Two articles on the Female Education Society, founded in
       London in 1834 for the education and evangelization of women
       in missionary lands; it sent missionary teacher-evangelists first
       to China and later to India; the second article focuses on ex-
       amples from its work in southern Africa.

564   Nair, Janaki. "Uncovering the Zenana: Visions of Indian
       Womanhood in Englishwomen's Writings, 1813-1940," *Jour-
       nal of Women's History* 2:1 (Spring 1990): 8-24.
       Studies the varying thematic representations of the zenana (the
       separate women's quarters), all of which reinforced the con-
       nections between patriarchy, imperialism, and capitalism.

565   Hall, Catherine. "Missionary Stories: Gender and Ethnicity in
       England in the 1830s and 1840s," in *White, Male and Middle
       Class: Explorations in Feminism and History*. London: Rout-
       ledge, 1992. Pp. 205-54.
       Uses the experience of Baptist missionaries in Jamaica, in-
       cluding that of missionary wives, to illustrate the racial and
       gender contradictions involved in missionary discourse and
       activity, where notions of equality were juxtaposed by the

language of hierarchy.

566   Dickson, Mora. *The Inseparable Grief: Margaret Cargill of Fiji*. London: Epworth, 1976. Pp. 174.
_____. *Beloved Partner: Mary Moffat of Kuruman*. London: Gollancz, 1974. Pp. 238.
Two studies of missionary wives: Cargill (1809-40), a Scottish Methodist, and Moffat (1795-1871), a pioneer missionary to southern Africa.

Individuals

567   *Anna Laetitia Barbauld (1743-1825)*
The daughter and wife of liberal Dissenting ministers and a writer of some note as a member of the "Bluestocking" circle, Barbauld is treated in Betsy Rodgers, *Georgian Chronicle: Mrs. Barbauld and Her Family* (London: Methuen, 1949).

568   *Anne Dutton (1692-1765)*
A prolific author, defender of Calvinist theology, and friend of George Whitefield, Dutton has received modest attention in Stephen J. Stein, "A Note on Anne Dutton, Eighteenth-Century Evangelical," *Church History* 44 (1975): 485-91. Older studies include John C. Whitebrook's *Ann Dutton: A Life and Bibliography* (London: Cannon, 1921) and "The Life and Works of Mrs. Ann Dutton," *TBHS* 7 (1921): 129-46, and Arthur Wallington, "Wesley and Ann Dutton," *PWHS* 11:2 (1917): 43-48.

569   *Mary Bosanquet Fletcher (1739-1815)*
One of Wesley's most important women preachers and wife of one of his closest colleagues, she has been largely ignored by scholars; even the quite old study, T. Alexander Seed's *John and Mary Fletcher, Typical Methodist Saints* (London: Charles H. Kelly, 1906), devotes only two chapters to her work.

570   *Elizabeth Fry (1780-1845)*
Best known as an early prison reformer and member of a prominent Quaker family, Fry has still not received substantial

study; much of the work on her depends heavily on her journals. The two best monographs are June Rose, *Elizabeth Fry: A Biography* (London: Macmillan, 1980) and John Kent, *Elizabeth Fry* (London: Batsford, 1962); Janet Whitney's *Elizabeth Fry: Quaker Heroine* (Boston: Little, Brown, 1936) is a popular biography. Some articles that explore aspects of her work include Robert Alan Cooper, "Jeremy Bentham, Elizabeth Fry, and English Prison Reform," *JHI* 42 (1981): 675-90; Arthur J. Eddington, "Elizabeth Fry: 'Heretic' or Seer?" *JFHS* 34 (1937): 19-26; and Henry Barton Jacobs, "Elizabeth Fry, Pastor Fliedner, and Florence Nightingale," *Annals of Medical History* 3 (1921): 17-25.

571   *Willielma Maxwell, Lady Glenorchy (1741-86)*
The Scottish counterpart to the work of the Countess of Huntingdon on behalf of the Evangelical Revival, she has received very limited study; see D. P. Thomson, *Lady Glenorchy and Her Churches* (Crieff, Scotland: The Research Unit, 1967) and E. Dorothy Graham, "The Contribution of Lady Glenorchy and her Circle to the Evangelical Revival" (B.D., Leeds, 1964).

572   *Selina Hastings, Countess of Huntingdon (1707-91)*
There is no good study of the most important, if controversial, woman of the Evangelical Revival; a substantial work by Edwin Welch will appear in 1995. The best is still the centennial volume edited by J. B. Figgis, *The Countess of Huntingdon and Her Connexion* (London: S. W. Partridge, 1891). Among the popular works on her are Gilbert W. Kirby, *The Elect Lady* (East Grinstead: Trustees of the Countess of Huntingdon's Connexion, 1972); Francis Fletcher Bretherton, *The Countess of Huntingdon* (London: Epworth, 1940); and Henrietta Keddie (Sarah Tytler, pseud.), *The Countess of Huntingdon and Her Circle* (London: Pitman, 1907). Perhaps because of the paucity of serious monographic study, the articles also tend to be general or of limited help; some of these include Mollie C. Davis, "The Countess of Huntingdon: A Leader in Missions for Social and Religious Reform," in *Women in New Worlds* 2: 162-75, 381-84; and "The Countess of Huntingdon

and Whitefield's Bethesda," *Georgia Historical Quarterly* 56
(1972): 72-82; Margaret Lane, "The Queen of the Methodists," *Brycheiniog* 15 (1971): 85-99; David Mitchell, "Queen
of the Methodists: Selina, Countess of Huntingdon," *History
Today* 15:12 (1965): 846-54; R. G. Martin, "Selina Countess
of Huntingdon," *TCHS* 15 (1946): 57-63; and S. E. Boyd
Smith, "The Effective Countess: Lady Huntingdon and the
1780 edition of *A Select Collection of Hymns*," *Hymn* 44:3
(1993): 26-32. Evelyn Lord's "'A Good Archbishop': The
Countess of Huntingdon," *Archives* 19 (October 1991): 423-
32, is a brief look at her life and work, drawing on materials
available at several archives.

573   *Anna Jameson (1794-1860)*
A writer, art historian, and social critic, Jameson also wrote
Sisters of Charity in 1855, calling for Protestant sisterhoods to
train women in nursing and social service; the only monograph
on her life is Clara Thomas, *Love and Work Enough: The Life
of Anna Jameson* (Toronto: Toronto, 1967). Other studies
include Sheridan Gilley, "Victorian Feminism and Catholic
Art: The Case of Mrs. Jameson," in *The Church and the Arts*,
ed. Diane Wood (SCH 29) (Oxford: Blackwell, 1992), pp.
381-91; and Adele M. Holcomb, "Anna Jameson (1794-1860):
Sacred Art and Social Vision," in *Women as Interpreters of the
Visual Arts, 1820-1979*, ed. Clara Richter Sherman and Adele
M. Holcomb (Westport, CT: Greenwood, 1981), pp. 93-121.

574   *Catharine Macaulay (1731-91)*
Within the context of Nonconformist radical political thought,
Macaulay was an historian and advocate for equal education
for women. For various dimensions of her life and work, see
Lynne E. Withey, "Catharine Macaulay and the Uses of Histo-
ry: Ancient Rights, Perfectionism, and Propaganda," *JBS* 16:1
(1976): 59-83; Lucy M. Donnelly, "The Celebrated Mrs.
Macaulay," *William and Mary Quarterly* 6 (1949): 173-207;
Florence and William Boos, "Catharine Macaulay: Historian
and Political Reformer," *UWS* 3:1 (1980): 49-65; Florence S.
Boos, "Catharine Macaulay's *Letters on Education* (1790): An
Early Feminist Polemic," *UMPWS* 2 (1976): 64-78; Bridget

and Christopher Hill, "Catharine Macaulay and the Seventeenth Century," *Welsh History Review* 3 (1967): 381-402;
Barbara Brandon Schnorrenberg, "The Brood Hen of Faction:
Mrs. Macaulay and Radical Politics, 1765-1775," *Albion* 11
(1979): 33-45; Claire Gilbride Fox, "Catharine Macaulay, an
Eighteenth-Century Clio," *Winterthur Portfolio* 4 (1968): 129-
42; and Mildred C. Beckwith, "Catharine Macaulay, Eighteenth-Century English Rebel" (Ph.D., Ohio State, 1953).

575   *Catherine McAuley (1781-1841)*
The founder of the Sisters of Mercy in Dublin in 1831, Mc-
Auley's life is explored in Roland Burke Savage, *Catherine
McAuley: The First Sister of Mercy* (Dublin: Gill, 1949) and
Bertrand M. Degnan, *Mercy unto Thousands: The Story of
Catherine McAuley* (Dublin: Browne and Nolan, 1958); see
also Mary C. Sullivan, "Catherine McAuley's Theological and
Literary Debt to Alonso Rodriguez: The 'Spirit of the Institute'
Parallels," *Recusant History* 20 (1990): 81-105.

576   *Judith Montefiore (c. 1784-1862)*
Sonia L. Lipman's "Judith Montefiore—First Lady of Anglo-
Jewry," *TJHSE* 21 (1962-67): 287-303, provides a glimpse
into the life of a notable Jewish family and Montefiore's activity as patron of charities within the Sephardic community.

577   *Hannah More (1745-1833)*
Assessments of More have been sharply divided; as the most
prominent woman among the Anglican Evangelicals at the turn
of the century, educator of poor children, and author of numerous tracts on piety and morality, she is seen both as a
reactionary defender of traditional structures and as an incisive
social critic.   A critical analysis of her educational work is
John McLeish, *Evangelical Religion and Popular Education: A
Modern Interpretation* (London: Methuen, 1969).   There is no
recent biography, and the existing studies are complimentary;
see Mary G. Jones, *Hannah More* (Cambridge: Cambridge,
1952); Mary Alden Hopkins, *Hannah More and Her Circle*
(London: Longmans, Green, 1947); Annette M. B. Meakin,
Hannah More: A Biographical Study (London: Smith, Elder,

1911); and Marion Harland (pseud.), *Hannah More* (London: Putnam's, 1900). Several articles from the 1980s are the more interesting because they discuss her work from different perspectives, especially the question of the engagement of Evangelicalism with popular culture; these include Beth Kowaleski-Wallace, "Hannah and Her Sister: Women and Evangelicalism in Early Nineteenth-Century England," *Nineteenth-Century Contexts* 12:2 (Fall 1988): 29-51; Shirley A. Mullen, "Women's History and Hannah More," *Fides et Historia* 19:1 (1987): 5-21; Susan Pedersen, "Hannah More Meets Simple Simon: Tracts, Chapbooks, and Popular Culture in Late Eighteenth-Century England," *JBS* 25:1 (1986): 84-113; Mitzi Myers, "Hannah More's Tracts for the Times: Social Fiction and Female Ideology," in *Fetter'd or Free? British Women Novelists, 1670-1815*, ed. Mary Anne Schofield and Cecilia Macheski (Athens, OH: Ohio State, 1986), pp. 264-84; Lynne Agress, "Hannah More: Female Messiah or Devil's Disciple?" *University of Portland Review* 32 (Fall 1980): 3-10; and David Lyle Jeffrey, "Beyond a Frivolous Faith: The Incisive Witness of Hannah More," *Reformed Journal* 37:3 (1987): 23-27. A dissertation by Charles H. Ford, "Hannah More: A Critical Biography" (Ph.D., Vanderbilt, 1992), argues for her relative success in putting forth feminist ideas when compared with the work of Mary Wollstonecraft. Some earlier articles include A. G. Newell, "Early Evangelical Fiction," *Evangelical Quarterly* 38 (1966): 3-21, 81-98; and Harry B. Weiss, "Hannah More's Cheap Repository Tracts in America," *Bulletin of the New York Public Library* 50 (1946): 539-49, 634-41.

578   *Joanna Southcott (1750-1814)*
      A prophet who put woman at the center of the ongoing "gospel story," wrote a large number of mystical and millenarian tracts, and established a dedicated following in the last two decades of her life, Southcott is a complex and puzzling figure. The local reference work compiled by Eugene Patrick Wright, *A Catalogue of the Joanna Southcott Collection at the University of Texas* (Austin: Texas, 1969), lists 411 items and gives brief annotations as well as a general introduction to the Southcottian movement. A detailed study of her life and

thought in the context of her social and intellectual setting is James K. Hopkins, *A Woman to Deliver Her People: Joanna Southcott and English Millenarianism in an Era of Revolution* (Austin: Texas, 1982). Two broader analyses of millenarianism give some attention to her impact and her influence: J. F. C. Harrison, *The Second Coming: Popular Millenarianism, 1780-1850* (London: Routledge & Kegan Paul, 1979), and W. H. Oliver, *Prophets and Millennialists: The Use of Biblical Prophecy in England from the 1790s to the 1840s* (Oxford: Oxford, 1978). Her legacy among her followers is explored in P. J. Tobin, "The Southcottians in England, 1782-1895" (M.A., Manchester, 1978). Roger Robins's "Anglican Prophetess: Joanna Southcott and the Gospel Story," *AEH* 61 (1992): 277-302, argues that she and other women like her should have "an enlarged place in modern narratives of the rise of feminist ideology" (280). Some older studies include Arthur W. Exell, *Joanna Southcott at Blockley and the Rock Cottage Relics* (Shipston-on-Stour: Blockley Antiquarian Soc., 1977); G. R. Balleine, *Past Finding Out: The Tragic Story of Joanna Southcott and her Successors* (London: SPCK, 1956); Ronald Matthews, *English Messiahs: Studies of Six English Religious Pretenders, 1656-1927* (London: Methuen, 1936), pp. 43-84; Rachel J. Fox, *Joanna Southcott's Place in History: A Forecast* (Plymouth: J. H. Keys, 1925); and Charles Lane, "Life of Joanna Southcott" and "Bibliography of Joanna Southcott," *Report and Transactions of the Devonshire Association for the Advancement of Science, Literature, and Art* 44 (1912): 732-56, 757-809.

579   *Marianne Thornton (1797-1887)*
      Eldest child of one of the members of the "Clapham Sect," Thornton's life is studied in the context of her Anglican family in E. M. Forster, *Marianne Thornton, A Domestic Biography, 1797-1887* (New York: Harcourt, Brace, 1956).

580   *Charlotte Elizabeth Tonna (1790-1846)*
      Zealous Protestant, editor of *The Christian Lady's Magazine* from 1834 to 1846, social critic, and author of some 130 titles, Tonna has only recently received some study; see Monica

Correa Fryckstedt's "Charlotte Elizabeth Tonna: A Forgotten
Evangelical Writer," *Studia Neophilologica* 52 (1980): 79-102,
and "Charlotte Elizabeth Tonna and *The Christian Lady's
Magazine*," *Victorian Periodicals Review* 14 (1981): 43-51;
Elizabeth Ann Kowaleski, "The Dark Night of Her Soul: The
Effects of Anglican Evangelicalism on the Careers of Charlotte
Elizabeth Tonna and George Eliot" (Ph.D., Columbia, 1981),
and "'The Heroine of Some Strange Romance': The *Personal
Reflections* of Charlotte Elizabeth Tonna," *TSWL* 1 (1982):
141-53; Joseph Kestner, "Charlotte Elizabeth Tonna's *The
Wrongs of Woman*: Female Industrial Protest," *TSWL* 2
(1983): 193-214; and Ivanka Kovacevic and S. Barbara Kanner, "Blue Book into Novel: The Forgotten Industrial Fiction
of Charlotte Elizabeth Tonna," *Nineteenth-Century Fiction* 25
(1970): 152-73.

581   *Mary Wollstonecraft (1759-97)*
Important as a feminist theorist and political thinker, Wollstonecraft has been extensively studied since the early 1970s;
the reference work edited by Janet M. Todd, *Mary Wollstonecraft: An Annotated Bibliography* (New York: Garland, 1976),
lists works by and about her written between 1788 and 1975,
with extensive annotations and a general introduction.
Monographs published since 1975 include Virginia Sapiro, *A
Vindication of Political Virtue: The Political Theory of Mary
Wollstonecraft* (Chicago: Chicago, 1992); Gary Kelly, *Revolutionary Feminism: The Mind and Career of Mary Wollstonecraft* (New York: St. Martin's, 1992); Jennifer Lorch, *Mary
Wollstonecraft: The Making of a Radical Feminist* (Oxford:
Berg, 1990); Moira Ferguson and Janet Todd, *Mary Woll-
stonecraft* (Boston: Twayne, 1984); Margaret Tims, *Mary
Wollstonecraft, A Social Pioneer* (London: Millington, 1976);
and Emily W. Sunstein, *A Different Face: The Life of Mary
Wollstonecraft* (New York: Harper & Row, 1975).

In contrast to earlier work, many recent articles have focused attention on dimensions of Wollstonecraft's religious
thought, either independently or comparatively; some of the
most suggestive include Patricia Howell Michaelson, "Religious Bases of Eighteenth-Century Feminism: Mary Wollstone-

craft and the Quakers," *Women's Studies* 22 (1992-93): 281-96; Mervyn Nicholson, "The Eleventh Commandment: Sex and Spirit in Wollstonecraft and Malthus," *JHI* 51 (1990): 401-21; Orrin N. C. Wang, "The Other Reasons: Female Alterity and Enlightenment Discourse in Mary Wollstonecraft's *A Vindication of the Rights of Woman*," *Yale Journal of Criticism* 5:1 (Fall 1991): 129-49; Melissa A. Butler, "Wollstonecraft versus Rousseau: Natural Religion and the Sex of Virtue and Reason," in *Man, God, and Nature in the Enlightenment* pp. 65-73; and Mary Wilson Carpenter, "Sibylline Apocalyptic: Mary Wollstonecraft's *Vindication of the Rights of Woman* and Job's Mother's Womb," *Literature and History* 12 (1986): 215-28. For other interesting investigations, see G. J. Barker-Benfield, "Mary Wollstonecraft: Eighteenth-Century Commonwealthwoman," *JHI* 50 (1989): 95-116; two articles by Regina Janes, "On the Reception of Mary Wollstonecraft's *A Vindication of the Rights of Woman*," *JHI* 39 (1978): 293-302, and "Mary, Mary, Quite Contrary, Or, Mary Astell and Mary Wollstonecraft Compared," *Studies in Eighteenth-Century Culture* 5 (1976): 121-39; and two by Moira Ferguson, "Mary Wollstonecraft and the Problematic of Slavery," *Feminist Review* 42 (Autumn, 1992): 82-102, and "The Discovery of Mary Wollstonecraft's *The Female Reader*," *Signs* 3 (1978): 945-57.

CHAPTER 5

1850-1914:
THE WOMEN'S MOVEMENT,
SOCIAL REFORM, AND SUFFRAGE

Bibliographies, Guides, and Anthologies

582   McGregor, Oliver Ross. "The Social Position of Women in England, 1850-1914: A Bibliography," *British Journal of Sociology* 6 (1955): 48-60.
An early bibliographic essay covering major primary and secondary materials on the subject.

583   Huff, Cynthia. *British Women's Diaries: A Descriptive Bibliography of Selected Nineteenth-Century Women's Manuscript Diaries.* New York: AMS, 1985. Pp. xxxv + 139.
Fifteen of the fifty-nine diarists presented are listed under the category "Religious," spanning the period 1808-94.

584   Barrow, Margaret. *Women, 1870-1928: A Select Guide to Printed and Archival Sources in the United Kingdom.* London: Mansell, 1981. Pp. 249.
An uneven collection of information, more useful for background and the location of resources than for any specific consideration of religion.

585   Bailey, Susan F. *Women and the British Empire: An Annotated Guide to the Sources.* New York: Garland, 1983. Pp. 185.
Contains chapters on wives of administrators, settlers, missionaries, and native women.

586   Sakala, Carol. *Women of South Asia: A Guide to Resources.*
       Millwood, NY: Kraus, 1980. Pp. 517.
       In a section on "the colonial experience" there are entries
       under "Christian 'women's work' and conversions" and under
       Christian missions.

587   Mitchell, Sally, ed. *Victorian Britain: An Encyclopedia.* New
       York: Garland, 1988. Pp. 986.
       In this large interdisciplinary resource there are numerous
       articles on individual women and on themes related to women.

588   *Wellesley Index to Victorian Periodicals, 1824-1900.*   Ed.
       Walter E. Houghton, et al. 5 vols. Toronto: Toronto, 1966-
       89.
       An indispensable resource for locating articles by individual
       authors or subject area.

589   Doughan, David and Sanchez, Denise, eds. *Feminist Periodi-
       cals, 1855-1984. An Annotated Bibliography of British, Irish,
       Commonwealth, and International Titles.* Brighton: Harvester,
       1987. Pp. 316.
       Some 920 entries, organized chronologically; especially helpful
       in its listings of suffrage, temperance, social reform, mission-
       ary, and contemporary Christian feminist journals.

590   Bell, Peter, comp. *Index to Biographies of Women in Boase's
       Modern English Biography.* Edinburgh, 1986. Unpag.
       Some 1,130 names drawn from Frederic Boase's six-volume
       work of British men and women who died between 1851 and
       1900, with dates and primary activity.

591   For documentary collections, each with limited attention to
       religious themes, see:
       Murray, Janet Horowitz, ed.   *Strong-Minded Women and
           Other Lost Voices from Nineteenth-Century England.* New
           York: Pantheon, 1982. Pp. 453.
       Hollis, Patricia, ed. *Women in Public, 1850-1900: Documents
           of the Victorian Women's Movement.* London: Allen and
           Unwin, 1979. Pp. 336.

Bauer, Carol and Ritt, Lawrence. *Free and Enobled: Source Readings in the Development of Victorian Feminism.* Oxford: Pergamon, 1979. Pp. 317.

592   Vicinus, Martha, ed. *Suffer and Be Still: Women in the Victorian Age.* Bloomington: Indiana, 1972. Pp. 239.
_____. *A Widening Sphere: Changing Roles of Victorian Women.* Bloomington: Indiana, 1977. Pp. 326.
Each collection contains ten essays, reflecting the range of scholarly interest in women's history at the time, though not directly on religious topics.

General Historical Studies

593   Shiman, Lilian Lewis. *Women and Leadership in Nineteenth-Century England.* New York: St. Martin's, 1992. Pp. 263.
In her study of the long process of emergence into leadership roles, Shiman sees an important connection between the claims made by early Methodist women and those made in the largely secular world a century later.

594   John, Angela, ed. *Our Mother's Land: Chapters in Welsh Women's History, 1830-1939.* Cardiff: Wales, 1991. Pp. 216.
Eight essays; of special interest for their attention to religious themes are the editor's "Beyond Paternalism: The Ironmaster's Wife in the Industrial Community;" Sian Rhiannon Williams, "The True 'Cymraes': Images of Women in Women's Nineteenth-Century Welsh Periodicals;" and Ceridwen Lloyd-Morgan, "From Temperance to Suffrage."

595   Thane, Pat. "Late Victorian Women," in *Later Victorian Britain, 1867-1900,* ed. T. R. Gourvish and Alan O'Day. Basingstoke: Macmillan, 1988. Pp. 175-208, 320-22.
Focuses mostly on opportunities for employment across a range of economic classes.

596   Mackey, Jane and Thane, Pat. "The Englishwoman," in *Englishness: Politics and Culture, 1880-1920,* ed. Robert Colls

and Philip Dodd. London: Croom Helm, 1986. Pp. 191-229.
Considers the adjustments of the "separate spheres" ideology
to fit the turn-of-the-century situation, and the role of the
Religious Tract Society and the scouting movement in promoting these, especially the notion of women's "civilizing
mission" in relation to the Empire.

597   Jalland, Pat. *Women, Marriage, and Politics, 1860-1914.*
       Oxford: Oxford, 1987. Pp. 366.
       Studies the lives of women in some fifty upper-class politi-
       cians' families.

598   _____. "Victorian Spinsters: Dutiful Daughters, Desperate
       Rebels, and the Transition to the New Women," in *Exploring
       Women's Past*, pp. 129-70.
       On the roles and responses of middle and upper-class single
       women in the period 1870-1914.

599   Trollope, Joanna. *Britannia's Daughters: Women of the Brit-
       ish Empire.* London: Hutchinson, 1983. Pp. 224.
       Covers several different activities; religion is of interest to the
       author in chapters on nurses and missionaries.

600   Harrison, Brian. *Peaceable Kingdom: Stability and Change in
       Modern Britain.* Oxford: Clarendon, 1982. Pp. 493.
       Eight essays probe the sources of social and political cohesion
       since the industrial revolution, with significant attention to the
       contributions of women and the role of religion, as well as to
       the themes of philanthropy and reform.

601   Dyhouse, Carol. *Girls Growing Up in Late Victorian and
       Edwardian England.* London: Routledge & Kegan Paul, 1981.
       Pp. 224.
       Studies the social construction of femininity, where service and
       self-sacrifice are undergirded by a sense of duty and religious
       conviction.

602   Longford, Elizabeth. *Eminent Victorian Women.* London:
       Weidenfeld and Nicolson, 1981. Pp. 256.

A counter to Lytton Strachey's *Eminent Victorians*, with relevant chapters on George Eliot, Florence Nightingale, Josephine Butler, and Annie Besant.

603   Rees, Barbara. *The Victorian Lady*. London: Gordon & Cremonesi, 1977. Pp. 164.
A look at high society from the vantage point of the middle- and upper-class woman; chapter XI, "Piety," discusses church-going, Sunday observance, and charitable activity.

604   Crow, Duncan. *The Victorian Woman*. London: Allen & Unwin, 1971. Pp. 351.
A social history, focusing on changing conditions for women in Britain and the United States.

605   Cuddeford, Gladys M. *Women and Society: From Victorian Times to the Present Day*. London: Hamish Hamilton, 1967. Pp. 120.
A survey of the position of women over more than a century.

606   Young, A. F. and Ashton, E. T. *British Social Work in the Nineteenth Century*. London: Routledge & Kegan Paul, 1956. Pp. 264.
A comprehensive overview of efforts of individuals and organizations to assist those in distress.

607   Grisewood, H., ed. *Ideas and Beliefs of the Victorians*. London: Sylvan, 1949.
Short presentations on a number of subjects, including two on the "emancipation of women," pp. 254-67.

608   Millett, Kate. "The Debate over Women: Ruskin versus Mill," *Victorian Studies* 14 (1970): 63-82.
Compares the two authors to obtain nearly the whole range of Victorian thought on women.

609   Sager, Eric W. "The Social Origins of Victorian Pacifism," *Victorian Studies* 23 (1980): 211-36.
Studies the London Peace Society, including the activities of

its women members.

Literary Studies

610   Wolff, Robert Lee. *Gains and Losses: Novels of Faith and Doubt in Victorian England.* New York: Garland, 1977. Pp. 537.
A sweeping introduction to Garland's reprint series of 121 Victorian religious novels, discussing the spectrum of religious positions from Roman Catholic through three expressions of Anglicanism, Dissent, and doubt; a number of women writers are included.

611   Rowbotham, Judith. *Good Girls Make Good Wives: Guidance for Girls in Victorian Fiction.* Oxford: Blackwell, 1989. Pp. 301.
An investigation of didactic fiction; in chapter 2, "Religion as a Control on Reality," Rowbotham show how "religion played a central role in placing the ideal of family and the hierarchic order of authority within it, at the center of society" (54).

612   Sanders, Valerie. *The Private Lives of Victorian Women: Autobiography in Nineteenth-Century England.* Oxford: Berg, 1989. Pp. 184.
Studies the problems faced by women in writing about themselves, which produced a distinctive form of women's autobiography; among the individuals studied are Charlotte Yonge, Annie Besant, Frances Power Cobbe, and Harriet Martineau.

613   Foster, Shirley. *Victorian Women's Fiction: Marriage, Freedom, and the Individual.* London: Croom Helm, 1985. Pp. 240.
The theme of women and marriage is considered in the writings of five novelists; images of femaleness, angelic womanhood, and the role of religion in shaping these views are discussed.

614   Hickok, Kathleen. *Representations of Women: Nineteenth-Century British Women's Poetry.* Westport, CT: Greenwood,

1984. Pp. 277.
Studies some thirty-five minor poets; the most popular subject was love, and through this theme Hickok pursues a number of religious dimensions.

615   Blake, Kathleen. *Love and the Women Question in Victorian Literature: The Art of Self-Postponement.* Brighton: Harvester, 1983. Pp. 254.
Explores the theme of deferment in women's writings, which in Christina Rossetti's poetry (chapter 1) is part of her religious self-understanding.

616   Qualls, Barry. *The Secular Pilgrims of Victorian Fiction.* Cambridge: Cambridge, 1982. Pp. 217.
Chapters on Charlotte Brontë and George Eliot, together with Carlyle and Dickens, consider the Romantic relocation of religious themes and questions to nature and the inner life.

617   Mitchell, Sally. *The Fallen Angel: Chastity, Class, and Women's Reading, 1865-1880.* Bowling Green: Bowling Green, 1981. Pp. 223.
This "portrait of the unchaste woman in fiction" (xv) shows how religion frequently framed the ideal or was presented as a solution to the problem.

618   Colby, Vineta. *The Singular Anomaly: Women Novelists of the Nineteenth Century.* New York: New York, 1970. Pp. 313.
Focuses on a group of lesser-known writers whose work had an ethical and didactic purpose.

619   Maison, Margaret M. *The Victorian Vision: Studies in the Religious Novel.* London: Sheed and Ward, 1961. Pp. 360 (also published as *Search Your Soul, Eustace: A Survey of the Religious Novel in the Victorian Age*).
Within this broad theme, Maison considers the work of a number of women writers of several religious persuasions.

620   _____. *John Oliver Hobbes: Her Life and Work.* London: Eighteen Nineties Society, 1976. Pp. 78.

A biography of Pearl Mary Teresa Craigie (1867-1906), novelist and playwright and convert from Nonconformity to Catholicism.

621   Wolff, Robert Lee.   "Some Erring Children in Children's Literature: The World of Victorian Religious Strife in Miniature," in *The Worlds of Victorian Fiction*, ed. Jerome H. Buckley. Cambridge: Harvard, 1975. Pp. 298-318.
Shows how children's literature reveals religious perspectives; some of the authors considered are Catherine Sinclair, Charlotte Yonge, and Harriet Mozley.

622   Avery, Gillian.   *Nineteenth-Century Children: Heroes and Heroines in English Children's Stories 1780-1900.* London: Hodder and Stoughton, 1965. Pp. 260.
Contains chapters on evangelical and high church fiction, primarily written by women.

623   Jay, Elisabeth.   "Doubt and the Victorian Woman," in *The Critical Spirit and the Will to Believe: Essays in Nineteenth-Century Literature and Religion*, ed. David Jasper and T. R. Wright. New York: St. Martin's, 1989. Pp. 88-103.
Explores the contention in much of the fiction of this period "that a capacity for sustained intellectual scepticism and femininity must prove mutually incompatible" (101), with reflections on such writers as Ruskin, Eliot, Patmore, Yonge, and Hardy.

624   Showalter, Elaine.   "Women Writers and the Double Standard," in *Woman in Sexist Society*, ed. Vivian Gornick and Barbara K. Moran. New York: Basic, 1971. Pp. 323-43.
On the conflict between the writers and society's understanding and expectations for women. The double standard here refers to the literary abilities of men and women; female novelists were often disparaged or dismissed and thus denied the freedom to explore and describe their own experience.

625   _____.   "Dinah Mulock Craik and the Tactics of Sentiment: A Case Study in Victorian Female Authorship," *Femi-*

nist Studies 2:2-3 (1975): 5-23.

Asserts that Craik (1826-87) understood the plight of the unmarried woman and presented a program of self-reliance and
self-development; she also affirmed the option of Anglican
sisterhoods for women.

626   Hewitt, Margaret. "Anthony Trollope: Historian and Sociol-
       ogist," *British Journal of Sociology* 14 (1963): 226-39.
       Trollope's novels are used as a source for examining the
       changing role of women in mid-Victorian Britain.

627   Cruse, Amy. *The Victorians and Their Books*. London: Allen
       & Unwin, 1935. Pp. 444.
       In this broad study, a consideration of the contributions of
       women to religious fiction, with particular attention to the
       works of Charlotte Yonge (pp. 42-64).

628   Williams, Merryn. *Margaret Oliphant: A Critical Biography*.
       Basingstoke: Macmillan, 1986. Pp. 217.
       Colby, Vineta and Robert A. *The Equivocal Virtue: Mrs.
       Oliphant and the Victorian Literary Market Place*. Ham-
       den, CT: Archon, 1966. Pp. 281.
       Two examples of work on Mrs. Oliphant (1828-97), whose
       novels often dealt with a religious context, both Anglican and
       Dissenting.

629   Examples of recent dissertations on religious themes taken up
       by women writers include:
       Jenkins, Ruth Y. "Reclaiming Myths of Power: Narrative
          Strategies of Nightingale, Brontë, Gaskell, and Eliot."
          Ph.D., SUNY at Stony Brook, 1988. Pp. 320.
       Melnyk, Julie Ann. "Faith of Our Mothers: Women's Reli-
          gious Utterance in Nineteenth-Century Britain." Ph.D.,
          Virginia, 1993. Pp. 369.
       Scheinberg, Cynthia. "Miriam's Daughters" Women's Poetry
          and Religious Identity in Victorian England." Ph.D., Rut-
          gers, 1992. Pp. 335.
       Scott, Rosemary. "Poetry and Piety: The Role of Verse in
          Mid-Victorian Sunday Reading." Ph.D., Open University,

1992. Pp. 461.

Works on Women and Religion, 1900-1913

630   Contemporary publications early in the century addressed
       unresolved questions concerning the appropriate role for wom-
       en in the church, implications of the women's movement for
       religious institutions, and suffrage. The following works pub-
       lished through 1913 are listed by year of publication:

Burstall, Sara Annie. *Christianity and Womanhood*. London:
    Charles H. Kelly, 1904. Pp. 22.

Hodgkin, Jonathan Backhouse. *Woman's Place in the Church*.
    London, 1907. Pp. 24.

Richardson, Jerusha Davidson (Mrs. Aubrey). *Women of the
    Church of England*. London: Chapman and Hall, 1907.
    Pp. 352.

Chappell, Jennie. *Women of Worth*. London: Partridge,
    1908. Pp. 158.

Gollock, Georgina A. *The Vocation of Women*. London:
    Longmans, Green, 1908. Pp. 32.

Pan-Anglican Papers. Being Problems for Consideration at
    the Pan-Anglican Congress, 1908. 2 vols., London: SPCK,
    1908.

Pan-Anglican Congress, 1908. Vol. IV, Section C: *The
    Church's Ministry*. London: SPCK, 1908. Pp. 310.

Bell, Maurice F. *The Church and Women's Suffrage*. Lon-
    don: Church League for Women's Suffrage, 1909. Pp. 8.

Dawson, E. C. *Heroines of Missionary Adventure*. London:
    Seeley, 1909. Pp. 340.

Thomas, Lloyd. *The Emancipation of Womanhood*. London:
    n.p., 1909. Pp. 10.

Weston, Agnes. *My Life Among the Bluejackets*. London: J.
    Nisbet, 1909. Pp. 329.

Coit, Stanton. *Woman in Church and State*. London: West
    London Ethical Society, 1910. Pp. 70.

Gun, J. E. *Christianity and Women: A Reply to Some Recent
    Skeptical Assertions*. London: Culley, 1910. Pp. 95.

Lennard, Vivian R. *Woman, Her Power, Influence, and Mis-
    sion*. London: Skeffington, 1910. Pp. 216.

Palmer, Margaret. *Mothers' Union Work—A Vocation*. London: Allenson, 1910. Pp. 89.

Baker, Hatty. *Women in the Ministry*. London: C. W. Daniel, 1911. Pp. 66.

Howard, Elizabeth Fox. *Woman in the Church and in Life*. Bannisdale, Malton, 1911. Pp. 15.

Simms, A. E. N. *St. Paul and the Woman Movement*. London: Church League for Women's Suffrage, 1911. Pp. 12.

Creighton, Louise. *Missions: Their Rise and Development*. London: Williams and Norgate, 1912. Pp. 256.

Gollock, Minna C. "The Share of Women in the Administration of Missions," *IRM* 1 (1912): 674-87.

Keating, Joseph. *Christianity and "Women's Rights."* London: Catholic Truth Society, 1912. Pp. 24.

McDougall, Eleanor. "The Influence of Christianity on the Position of Women," *IRM* 1 (1912): 435-51.

de Sélincourt, Agnes. "The Place of Women in the Modern National Movements of the East," *IRM* 1 (1912): 98-107.

The Religious Aspects of the Women's Movement. London: Collegium, 1912. Pp. 67.

Bishop of Kensington. *The Moral Issues Involved in the Women's Movement*. London: Church League for Women's Suffrage, 1913. Pp. 8.

Cohen, Percy. "Jews and Feminism," *Westminster Review* 180 (1913): 454-62.

DeBruin, Elizabeth. "Judaism and Womanhood," *Westminister Review* 180 (1913): 124-30.

Despard, Charlotte. *Theosophy and the Woman's Movement*. London: TPS, 1913. Pp. 55.

Fairfield, Zoe. *The Woman's Movement*. London: SCM, 1913. Pp. 31.

Hanson, Helen B. *From East to West: Women's Suffrage in Relation to Foreign Missions*. London: Church League for Women's Suffrage, 1913. Pp. 21.

Orchard, W. E. "The Motherhood of God," in *Sermons on God, Christ, and Man*. London: J. Clarke, 1913. Pp. 69-80.

Robinson, Sarah. *The Soldier's Friend: A Pioneer's Record*. London: T. Fisher Unwin, 1913. Pp. 313.

Rouse, Ruth. "Foreign Missions and the Women's Movement in the West," *IRM* 2 (1913): 148-64.

Spielmann, Gertrude E. "Woman's Place in the Synagogue," *Jewish Review* 4 (1913): 24-36.

Swanwick, Helena M. *The Future of the Women's Movement.* London: G. Bell and Sons, 1913. Pp. 208.

Clery, Arthur E. "The Religious Aspect of Women's Suffrage," *Irish Review* 3 (1913-14): 479-84.

Ideals and Images

631   Poovey, Mary. *Uneven Developments: The Ideological Work of Gender in Mid-Victorian England.* Chicago: Chicago, 1988. Pp. 282.
On the construction of gender and the debate that occurred over it, as seen in five areas: medicine, law, literature, education and work, and nursing. Poovey shows in these cases how the conceptualization of difference as a matter of gender has been able to endure while its artificialities have become increasingly visible.

632   Auerbach, Nina. *Woman and the Demon: The Life of a Victorian Myth.* Cambridge: Harvard, 1982. Pp. 255.
A wide-ranging study of the central myths of Victorian womanhood—the angel and the demon, the old maid, and the fallen woman—through art, fiction, and individual lives, in order to illumine the unofficial beliefs of a religiously troubled age.

633   Thomson, Patricia. *The Victorian Heroine, A Changing Ideal, 1837-1873.* London: Oxford, 1956. Pp. 178.
Investigates the interplay between the feminist movement and the Victorian novel, especially the gradual influence of the theme of emancipation on the latter.

634   Marsh, Jan. *Pre-Raphaelite Women: Images of Femininity.* New York: Harmony, 1987. Pp. 160.
Discusses the melding of religion and romanticism with feminine images, such as "holy virgins," "doves and mothers," and "medieval damozels."

635   Casteras, Susan P. *The Substance or the Shadow: Images of Victorian Womanhood*. New Haven: Yale Center for British Art, 1982. Pp. 103.
_____. *Images of Victorian Womanhood in English Art*. Rutherford, NJ: Fairleigh Dickinson, 1987. Pp. 191.
The first is a catalogue for a 1982 exhibition, with text and representative plates; the second is significantly enlarged, examining a full spectrum of images from the virginity of the nun to the degradation of the prostitute and including 147 figures and 12 color reproductions.

636   _____. "Virgin Vows: The Early Victorian Artists' Portrayal of Nuns and Novices," in *Religion in the Lives*, pp. 129-60; 12 plates [also in *Victorian Studies* 24 (1981): 157-84].
The establishment of Anglican sisterhoods in the 1840s helped to produce a genre of nun paintings reflecting characteristics of idealized womanhood; Casteras shows how these contributed to the conflict in society over images and roles of women.

637   Gorham, Deborah. "The Ideology of Femininity and Reading for Girls, 1850-1914," in *Lessons for Life: The Schooling of Girls and Women, 1850-1950*, ed. Felicity Hunt. Oxford: Blackwell, 1987. Pp. 39-59.
Sees three overlapping emphases in the literature for girls in this period: "the daughter at home," "the widening sphere," and "the school girl;" in the first two, religious writers like Charlotte Yonge and organizations such as the Religious Tract Society are prominent.

638   Gorsky, Susan. "The Gentle Doubters: Images of Women in English Women's Novels, 1840-1920," in *Images of Women in Fiction: Feminist Perspectives*, ed. Susan K. Cornillon. Bowling Green, OH: Bowling Green, 1972. Pp. 28-54.
Considers images that confirmed or challenged the stereotype of women as obedient, chaste, and pious.

639   Pope, Barbara Corrado. "Angels in the Devil's Workshop: Leisured and Charitable Women in Nineteenth-Century England and France," in *Becoming Visible: Women in European*

History, ed. Renate Bridenthal and Claudia Koonz. Boston: Houghton Mifflin, 1977. Pp. 296-324.
Suggests that the most acceptable way to challenge the inherent constrictions in the ideal of domesticity was to expand the opportunities within it, such as the emphasis on charitable activities after mid-century; eventually, with the professionalization of educational and charitable work, women gradually became subordinate in endeavors they had initiated.

"First Wave" Feminism

640   Levine, Philippa. *Feminist Lives in Victorian England: Private Roles and Public Commitment*. Oxford: Blackwell, 1990. Pp. 241.
A collective biography of feminism, covering roughly the latter half of the century, using some two hundred individuals, to demonstrate the interaction and overlap of private and public lives as well as the subtlety of the feminist agenda in undermining the dominant ideology regarding women; explores the connection between religion, family, and politics in the lives of these individuals.

641   _____. *Victorian Feminism, 1850-1900*. London: Hutchinson, 1987. Pp. 176.
On the creation of a domestic ideology for women and the several campaigns that challenged those values regarding education, political rights, employment, and marriage and morality.

642   Caine, Barbara. *Victorian Feminists*. Oxford: Oxford, 1992. Pp. 284.
Studies four prominent participants in the women's movement: Emily Davies, Frances Power Cobbe, Josephine Butler, and Millicent Garrett Fawcett; religious themes and issues are discussed, especially with the first three.

643   _____. "Feminism, Suffrage, and the Nineteenth-Century English Women's Movement," *WSIF* 5 (1982): 537-50.
Shows that a substantial part of the movement was conserva-

tive in its view of the role of women in society; this can be seen, Caine observes, if participants' concern for the private and domestic lives of women is recognized along with their interest in the public and the political.

644   Banks, Olive. *Becoming a Feminist: The Social Origins of "First Wave" Feminism.* Brighton: Wheatsheaf, 1986. Pp. 184.
Analyses some 116 persons, including 98 women, by generational periods; Banks notes "the wide variety of religious beliefs that appeared to be compatible with feminism" (15).

645   Forster, Margaret. *Significant Sisters: The Grassroots of Active Feminism, 1839-1939.* London: Secker and Warburg, 1984. Pp. 353.
Studies of eight women and the chief focus or interest of each, including Nightingale, Davies, and Butler.

646   Ramelson, Marian. *The Petticoat Rebellion: A Century of Struggle for Women's Rights.* London: Lawrence and Wishart, 1967. Pp. 208.
Kamm, Josephine. *Rapiers and Battleaxes: The Women's Movement and Its Aftermath.* London: Allen & Unwin, 1966. Pp. 240.
Two surveys of the women's movement from the eighteenth to the twentieth century.

647   Strachey, Ray. *The Cause: A Short History of the Women's Movement in Great Britain.* 1928; London: Virago, 1978. Pp. 429.
A classic on this subject, written by one who participated in the final two decades of the suffrage campaign.

648   Tabor, Margaret E. *Pioneer Women.* 1st and 2nd Series. London: Sheldon, 1925 and 1927. Pp. 123 each.
Each volume contains short studies of the life and contributions of four important nineteenth-century women, including Mary Carpenter, Elizabeth Fry, Octavia Hill, Agnes Jones, Hannah More, Florence Nightingale, and Mary Slessor.

Employment and Other Opportunities for Women

649   Alexander, Sally, ed. *Studies in the History of Feminism,
       1850s-1930s.* London: Dept. of Extra Mural Studies, U. of
       London, 1984. Pp. 74.
       Six articles on aspects of women's work in this period.

650   Vicinus, Martha. *Independent Women: Work and Community
       for Single Women, 1850-1920.* Chicago: Chicago, 1985. Pp.
       396.
       Studies how middle-class single women responded to the crisis
       of "redundancy" and "transformed this passive role into one of
       active spirituality and passionate social service" (5), through
       separate residential communities and institutions, including
       Anglican sisterhoods and deaconess houses, nursing communi-
       ties, educational institutions, and settlement houses.

651   Deacon, Alan and Hill, Michael. "The Problem of 'Surplus
       Women' in the Nineteenth Century: Secular and Religious
       Alternatives," in *A Sociological Yearbook of Religion in Brit-
       ain: 5,* ed. Michael Hill. London: SCM, 1972. Pp. 87-102.
       A charting of contemporary responses to this mid-century issue
       in terms of conservative/radical and secular/religious dichoto-
       mies: secular conservatives encouraged immigration, while
       secular radicals pushed for opportunities in education and the
       professions; religious conservatives supported the development
       of deaconess institutions, and religious radicals favored Angli-
       can sisterhoods with independence and autonomy.

652   Worsnop, Judith. "A Reevaluation of 'the Problem of Surplus
       Women' in 19th-Century England: The Case of the 1851
       Census," *WSIF* 13 (1990): 21-31.
       A review of the arguments offered by the several participants
       in the debate.

653   Summers, Anne. *Angels and Citizens: British Women as
       Military Nurses, 1854-1914.* London: Routledge & Kegan
       Paul, 1988. Pp. 371.
       _____. "Pride and Prejudice: Ladies and Nurses in the

Crimean War," *History Workshop* 16 (Autumn 1983): 33-56.
The story of the social transition from "women's mission" (seen as Christian pastoral activity) to an understanding of service in the secular national state, which also changed notions of women's participation in philanthropy. The article explores the conflicts produced over issues of class and religious party among the groups that came to Scutari.

Education

654   Kamm, Josephine. *Hope Deferred: Girls' Education in English History.* London: Methuen, 1965. Pp. 324.
Broad coverage, from the Anglo-Saxon period to contemporary issues.

655   Bryant, Margaret. *The Unexpected Revolution: A Study in the History of the Education of Women and Girls in the Nineteenth Century.* London: Institute of Education, 1979. Pp. 134.
Argues that the cause of women's education "was primarily a religious movement. . . . With few exceptions these women in all their diversity of belief and personality were sustained by religious faith and practice" (72-73); and concludes that on balance the religious interests worked in favor of women, as opposed to the development of new scientific beliefs which tended to weaken their case and exert pressure against it.

656   Burstyn, Joan N. *Victorian Education and the Ideal of Womanhood.* London: Croom Helm, 1980. Pp. 185.
Studies how the middle-class construction of the ideal of womanhood became the focus for a coalition of opponents of the higher education of women; their economic, physiological, and biblical arguments attempted to show that gender differences were either innate or essential for the continuation of a civilized society.

657   _____. "Religious Arguments Against the Higher Education for Women in England, 1840-1890," *Women's Studies* 1 (1972): 111-31.

Presents the case chiefly from clergy who saw education for women as a threat to traditional notions of subordination, to the faith itself, and to clerical power in the universities.

658   Sutherland, Gillian. "The Movement for the Higher Education of Women: Its Social and Intellectual Context, c. 1840-1880," in *Politics and Social Change in Modern Britain: Essays Presented to A. F. Thompson*, ed. P. J. Waller. Brighton: Harvester, 1987. Pp. 91-116.
A collective social and intellectual profile of those who created the first institutions of higher education for women.

659   Binfield, Clyde. *Belmont's Portias: Victorian Nonconformists and Middle-Class Education for Girls*. London: Dr. Williams's Trust, 1981. Pp. 35.
On the Nonconformist interest in education for girls, including the work of the Congregational minister Benjamin Parsons (1797-1855).

660   Simms, T. H. *Homerton College, 1695-1978*. Cambridge: Crampton, 1979. Pp. 109.
At first a Dissenting academy, then a theological college, Homerton eventually became an educational college and was restricted to women between 1896 and 1978.

661   Pike, Elsie and Curryer, Constance E. *The Story of Walthamstow Hall: A Century of Girls' Education*. London: Carey, 1938. Pp. 143.
Walthamstow Hall was founded in 1838 as a school for missionaries' daughters.

662   Grylls, Mary R. G. *Queen's College, 1848-1948*. London: Routledge, 1948. Pp. 133.
Birley, Robert. "Maurice and Education," *Theology* 76 (1973): 449-62.
This college for women was founded by F. D. Maurice, and clergy served as principals until the early twentieth century.

663   Tarrant, Dorothy. "Unitarians and Bedford College," *Trans-*

actions of the Unitarian Historical Society 9 (1947-50): 201-206.
Focuses on the founder, Elisabeth Jesser Reid, and other Unitarians connected with the establishment of the Ladies College in 1849.

664   Clarke, A. K. *History of the Cheltenham Ladies' College, 1853-1953*. London: Faber & Faber, 1953. Pp. 193.
Steadman, Florence C. *In the Days of Miss Beale: A Study of Her Work and Influence*. Cheltenham: Burrow, 1931. Pp. 194.
Raikes, Elizabeth. *Dorothea Beale of Cheltenham*. London: Constable, 1908. Pp. 432.
Beale (1831-1906) served as first principal of this Anglican school; it eventually developed a collegiate program after 1893, becoming St. Hilda's College, Oxford.

665   Dyhouse, Carol. "Miss Buss and Miss Beale: Gender and Authority in the History of Education," in *Lessons for Life: The Schooling of Girls and Women, 1850-1950*, pp. 22-38.
Kamm, Josephine. *How Different from Us: A Biography of Miss Buss and Miss Beale*. London: Bodley Head, 1958. Pp. 272.
Burstall, Sara A. *Frances Mary Buss, an Educational Pioneer*. London: SPCK, 1938. Pp. 94.
Buss (1827-94) founded two girls' schools in London; the comparative studies discuss the two leaders' contrasting personalities and styles, including their sense of mission and religious commitments.

666   Bradbrook, M. C. *"That Infidel Place": A Short History of Girton College, 1869-1969*. London: Chatto & Windus, 1969. Pp. 168.
Bennett, Daphne. *Emily Davies and the Liberation of Women, 1830-1921*. London: A. Deutsch, 1990. Pp. 279.
Stephen, Barbara. *Emily Davies and Girton College*. London: Constable, 1927; rept, 1976. Pp. 387.
Rosen, Andrew. "Emily Davies and the Women's Movement, 1862-1867," *JBS* 19 (1979): 101-21.

Davies was a moderate feminist, the daughter of a prominent Anglican Evangelical cleric, and founder of the first college for women at Cambridge.

667   Bailey, Gemma, ed. *Lady Margaret Hall: A Short History.* London: Oxford, 1923. Pp. 144.
       Battiscombe, Georgina. *Reluctant Pioneer: A Life of Elizabeth Wordsworth.* London: Constable, 1978. Pp. 320.
       Wordsworth (1840-1932) was the first principal of LMH, an Oxford college for women with close associations to the Church of England founded in 1879.

668   Griffin, Penny, ed. *St. Hugh's: One Hundred Years of Women's Education in Oxford.* Basingstoke: Macmillan, 1986. Pp. 339.
       St. Hugh's was the idea of Elizabeth Wordsworth, to provide education for women of moderate means.

669   Firth, Catherine B. *Constance Louisa Maynard, Mistress of Westfield College: A Family Portrait.* London: Allen and Unwin, 1949. Pp. 349.
       Vicinus, Martha. "'One Life to Stand Beside Me': Emotional Conflicts in First-Generation College Women in England," *Feminist Studies* 8 (1982): 603-28.
       One of the first students at Girton College, Maynard (1849-1935) began Westfield College in 1882 as a self-consciously Christian institution; Vicinus uses her as a test case for showing the difficulties of pioneering new relationships, new institutions, and new ambitions.

670   Freeman, Clifford B. *Mary Simpson of Boynton Vicarage: Teacher of Ploughboys and Critic of Methodism.* York: East Yorkshire Local History Soc., 1972. Pp. 44.
       Simpson (1820-84), a devout Anglican, founded a school for rural children and wrote against the influence of Methodism in one of its strongest areas.

671   For studies of other individuals involved in the education of women, see:

Ellsworth, Edward W. *Liberators of the Female Mind: The
    Shirreff Sisters, Educational Reform, and the Women's
    Movement.* Westport, CT: Greenwood, 1979. Pp. 345.

Wills, Stella. "The Anglo-Jewish Contribution to the Educa-
    tion Movement for Women in the Nineteenth Century,"
    TJHSE 17 (1951-52): 269-81.

Bingham, Caroline. "'Doing Something for Women': Mat-
    thew Vassar and Thomas Holloway," *History Today* 36:6
    (1986): 46-51.

McClelland, Vincent Alan. "Herbert Vaughan, The Cam-
    bridge Teachers' Training Syndicate, and the Public
    Schools, 1894-1899," *Paedagogica Historica* 15 (1975): 16-
    38.

Suffrage

672   Histories of the suffrage movement do not routinely refer to
       religious themes or to involvement of churches, but the
       movement itself is so crucial to the subject that a range of
       works should be listed in this bibliography; these include:

Pugh, Martin. *Women's Suffrage in Britain, 1867-1928.* Lon-
    don: Historical Association, 1980. Pp. 40.

Kent, Susan Kingsley. *Sex and Suffrage in Britain, 1860-
    1914.* Princeton: Princeton, 1987. Pp. 295.

Liddington, Jill and Norris, Jill. *One Hand Tied Behind Us:
    The Rise of the Women's Suffrage Movement.* London:
    Virago, 1978. Pp. 304.

Rosen, Andrew. *Rise Up, Women!: The Militant Campaign of
    the Women's Social and Political Union, 1903-1914.* Lon-
    don: Routledge & Kegan Paul, 1974. Pp. 312.

Fulford, Roger. *Votes for Women.* London: Faber and Faber,
    1957. Pp. 343.

Fawcett, Millicent Garrett. *Women's Suffrage: A Short Histo-
    ry of a Great Movement.* 1912; New York: Source Book,
    1970. Pp. 94.

Lewis, Jane, ed. *Before the Vote Was Won: Arguments for
    and Against Women's Suffrage.* London: Routledge &
    Kegan Paul, 1987. Pp. 497.

Harrison, Brian. *Separate Spheres: The Opposition to*

Women's Suffrage in Britain. London: Croom Helm, 1978. Pp. 274.

Riley, Linda Walker. "The Opposition to Women's Suffrage, 1867-1918." B. Litt., Oxford, 1977. Pp. 238.

Hamilton, Margaret. "Opposition to Woman Suffrage in England, 1865-1884: A Case Study of a Countermovement," *Victorians Institute Journal* 4 (1975): 59-73.

Blackwood, Eileen. "Opposition to Woman Suffrage in Edwardian Britain," *Ozark Historical Review* 9 (Spring 1980): 26-36.

Mason, Francis M. "The Newer Eve: The Catholic Women's Suffrage Society in England, 1911-1923," *Catholic Historical Review* 72 (1986): 620-38.

Leneman, Leah. "The Scottish Churches and 'Votes for Women'," *Scottish Church History Society Records* 24 (1991): 237-52.

Park, Jihang. "The British Suffrage Activists of 1913: An Analysis," *Past & Present* 120 (1988): 147-62.

Murphy, Cliona. *The Women's Suffrage Movement and Irish Society in the Early Twentieth Century.* Philadelphia: Temple, 1989. Pp. 233.

John Stuart Mill and *The Subjection of Women*

673   Mill's 1869 work is a classic example of a nineteenth-century liberal feminist argument; it has received renewed attention since 1970, with some debate among scholars about its importance and the merit of its contentions. For a coverage of material through 1978, with limited annotations, see:

Laine, Michael. *Bibliography of Works on John Stuart Mill.* Toronto: Toronto, 1982. Pp. 173.

674   A sample of other work includes:

Tulloch, Gail. *Mill and Sexual Equality.* Hertfordshire: Wheatsheaf, 1989. Pp. 212.

Aiken, Susan Hardy. "Scripture and Poetic Discourse in *The Subjection of Women*," *PMLA* 98 (1983): 353-73.

Collini, Stefan. "John Stuart Mill and the Subjection of Women," *History Today* 34:12 (1984): 34-39.

Shanley, Mary Lyndon. "Marital Slavery and Friendship: John Stuart Mill's *The Subjection of Women*," *Political Theory* 9 (1981): 229-47.

Caine, Barbara. "John Stuart Mill and the English Women's Movement," *Historical Studies* 18 (1978): 52-67.

Annas, Julia. "Mill and the Subjection of Women," *Philosophy* 52 (1977): 179-94.

Sexuality, Marriage, Family, and Birth Control

675   Dyhouse, Carol. *Feminism and the Family in England, 1880-1939*. Oxford: Blackwell, 1989. Pp. 204.
Feminist reflections on the family—especially, a critique of the patriarchal family as Victorians experienced it and the proposals for alternative models.

676   Lewis, Jane. *Women in England 1870-1950: Sexual Divisions and Social Change*. Brighton: Wheatsheaf, 1984. Pp. 240.
Studies gender roles, marriage and motherhood for working- and middle-class women.

677   Fee, Elizabeth. "The Sexual Politics of Victorian Sexual Anthropology," *Feminist Studies* 1:3-4 (1973): 23-39 [also in *Clio's Consciousness Raised*, ed. Mary S. Hartman and Lois W. Banner (New York: Harper & Row, 1974), pp. 86-102].
Considers the efforts of a generation of social anthropologists to discern the proper role of women by showing that the current patriarchal family is the result of evolution from savagery to civilization.

678   Rover, Constance. *Love, Morals, and the Feminists*. London: Routledge & Kegan Paul, 1970. Pp. 183.
On the interaction between feminism and issues of public morality having to do with sex; attention centers on the Mills, Josephine Butler, Annie Besant, Marie Stopes, and the Pankhursts.

679   Mort, Frank. *Dangerous Sexualities: Medico-Moral Politics in England Since 1830*. London: Routledge & Kegan Paul, 1987.

Pp. 280.
Explores the historical construction of sexuality and the jux-
taposition of conflicting moral languages, with special focus on
the impact of the medical profession, over four periods covering about a century; between 1860 and 1914, Mort argues,
"'feminine' and feminist appropriations of evangelical religious
morality proved especially important in providing women with
the voice to resist male professionals" (8).

680 _____. "Purity, Feminism, and the State: Sexuality and
Moral Politics, 1880-1914," in *Crises in the British State,
1880-1930*, ed. Mary Langan and Bill Schwartz. London:
Hutchinson, 1985. Pp. 209-25.
Analyses the conflict between purity feminists, here represented by the Anglican activist Ellice Hopkins, and the government over state regulation of sexual activity.

681 Jeffreys, Sheila. *The Spinster and Her Enemies: Feminism
and Sexuality, 1880-1930*. London: Pandora, 1985. Pp.
232.
_____. "'Free from All Uninvited Touch of Man': Wom-
en's Campaigns Around Sexuality, 1880-1914," *WSIF* 5
(1982): 629-45.
_____, ed. *The Sexuality Debates*. London: Routledge &
Kegan Paul, 1987. Pp. 632.
In a wide-ranging critique of the legacy of the late nineteenth
century with respect to sexuality, Jeffreys gives close attention
to the "social purity movement" and its religious foundations,
which is seen as an important part of the struggle against male
dominance; the third item is a collection of documents from
the period on this issue.

682 Cole, J. M. and Bacon, F. C. *Christian Guidance of the Social Instincts: A Survey of the Church's Work for Social Purity*.
London: Faith, 1928. Pp. 214.
On the Anglican activities on behalf of women and girls that
continued the interests of Josephine Butler and Ellice Hopkins.

683 Boyd, Kenneth M. *Scottish Church Attitudes to Sex, Mar-*

riage, and the Family, 1850-1914. Edinburgh: Donald, 1980. Pp. 401.

Explores the question of the Scottish churches' social and cultural influence through two themes: the control of sexual behavior through ecclesiastical discipline and the regulation of marriage, and family religion.

684   Studies of the development of and the debate over birth control, most of which consider the interests of the churches, include:

Banks, J. A. and Olive. *Feminism and Family Planning in Victorian England.* New York: Schocken, 1964. Pp. 142.

Banks, Joseph A. *Victorian Values: Secularism and the Size of Families.* London: Routledge & Kegan Paul, 1981. Pp. 203.

McLaren, Angus. *Birth Control in Nineteenth-Century England.* London: Croom Helm, 1978. Pp. 263.

Soloway, Richard A. *Birth Control and the Population Question in England, 1877-1930.* Chapel Hill: North Carolina, 1982. Pp. 418.

Fryer, Peter. *The Birth Controllers.* London: Secker & Warburg, 1965. Pp. 384.

685   Huff Cynthia.   "Chronicles of Confinement: Reactions to Childbirth in British Women's Diaries," *WSIF* 10 (1987): 63-68.

Studies fifty-eight manuscript diaries of primarily middle-class women.

686   Cominos, Peter T. "Late-Victorian Sexual Responsibility and the Social System," *IRSH* 8 (1963): 18-48, 216-50.

Concludes that "a comprehensive system of interlocking institutions consisting of Respectable celibacy and Respectable marriage on the one hand, and of celibacy and prostitution and marriage and prostitution on the other hand, were regulated by two systems of morality: firstly, the single standard of purity or continence, and secondly, the double standard of impurity and incontinence" (230); the result, Cominos states, was a pattern of immature relationships.

687   Caine, Barbara. "Women's 'Natural State': Marriage and the
        Nineteenth-Century Feminists," *Hecate* 3 (1977): 84-102.
        Contends that early feminists considered the subject of mar-
        riage within rather narrow limits; they accepted the view that
        marriage and career were mutually exclusive, and they did not
        take up the question of female sexuality—"Ultimately they
        accepted many of the broad stereotypes about the role of the
        family and the moral influence of women" (100).

Divorce and Other Legal Issues

688   Works on the history of legal rights for women, on family law
        and divorce, occasionally touch on religious issues and re-
        sponses of churches; for some useful studies, see the follow-
        ing:
        Stetson, Dorothy M. *A Woman's Issue: The Politics of Family
            Law Reform in England*. Westport, CT: Greenwood, 1982.
            Pp. 278.
        Holcombe, Lee. *Wives and Property: Reform of the Married
            Women's Property Law in Nineteenth-Century England*.
            Toronto: Toronto, 1983. Pp. 311.
        Crofts, Maud I. *Women Under English Law*. London: Na-
            tional Council of Women of Great Britain, 1925. Pp. 101.
        Reiss, Erna. *The Rights and Duties of Englishwomen*. Man-
            chester: Sherratt & Hughes, 1934. Pp. 269.
        St. John-Stevas, Norman. "Women in Public Law," in *A
            Century of Family Law, 1857-1957*, ed. R. H. Graveson
            and F. R. Crane. London: Sweet and Maxwell, 1957. Pp.
            256-88.
        Horstman, Allen. *Victorian Divorce*. New York: St. Mar-
            tin's, 1985. Pp. 196.
        McGregor, O. R. *Divorce in England, A Centenary Study*.
            London: Heinemann, 1957. Pp. 220.
        Shanley, Mary Lyndon. "'One Must Ride Behind': Married
            Women's Rights and the Divorce Act of 1857," *Victorian
            Studies* 25 (1982): 355-76.

Prostitution and the Victorian Crusade

689   Walkowitz, Judith R. *Prostitution and Victorian Society:*
       Women, Class, and the State. Cambridge: Cambridge,
       1980. Pp. 347.
       Walkowitz, Judith R. and Daniel J. "'We are not Beasts of
       the Field': Prostitution and the Poor in Plymouth and
       Southampton Under the Contagious Diseases Acts," *Femi-*
       nist Studies 1:3-4 (1973): 73-106.
       Studies of the Contagious Diseases Acts of 1864, 1866, and
       1869, their enforcement, and various forms of resistance to
       them as an instance of class and gender relations in Britain.

690   _____. "Male Vice and Feminist Virtue: Feminism and
       the Politics of Prostitution in Nineteenth-Century Britain,"
       History Workshop 13 (Spring 1982): 79-93.
       Shows how the attack on commercial sex by early feminists
       and its development into social purity campaigns, initially
       intended to protect women, also had the effect of encouraging
       the prerogatives of patriarchy and repressive legislation against
       working-class women.

691   Mahood, Linda. *The Magdalenes: Prostitution in the Nine-*
       teenth Century. New York: Routledge, 1990. Pp. 205.
       Explores the development of discourses relating to the problem
       of prostitution in Scotland—medical, philanthropic and pious
       (chiefly evangelical religion), and governmental—as well as the
       resistance to their proposals.

692   Littlewood, Barbara and Mahood, Linda. "Prostitutes, Mag-
       dalenes, and Wayward Girls: Dangerous Sexualities of Work-
       ing Class Women in Victorian Scotland," *Gender & History* 3
       (1991): 160-75.
       On the system of policing Glasgow women within a paternalist
       culture, but as an alternative to state regulation; includes the
       involvement of church leaders in the work.

693   Pearce, Samuel B. P. *An Ideal in the Working: The Story of*
       the Magdalen Hospital, 1758-1958. London: n.p., 1958. Pp.

100.
A brief bicentenary account of work for the recovery of prostitutes.

694   Luddy, Maria. "Prostitution and Rescue Work in Nineteenth-Century Ireland," in *Women Surviving*, pp. 51-84.
On the "Magdalen asylums," frequently run by religious organizations and on a model of repentance and spiritual regeneration; no serious consideration was given to the causes of prostitution, Luddy says.

695   Other monographic treatments of this topic include:
McHugh, Paul. *Prostitution and Victorian Social Reform.* New York: St. Martin's, 1980. Pp. 306.
Pearson, Michael. *The Age of Consent: Victorian Prostitution and Its Enemies.* Newton Abbot: David and Charles, 1972. Pp. 225.
Deacon, Richard. *The Private Life of Mr. Gladstone.* London: Muller, 1965. Pp. 189.
Nield, Keith, ed. *Prostitution in the Victorian Age: Debates on the Issue from Nineteenth-Century Critical Journals.* Westmead, Hants.: Gregg, 1973. Unpag.

696   Smith, F. B. "Ethics and Disease in the Later Nineteenth Century: The Contagious Diseases Acts," *Historical Studies* 15 (1971): 118-35.
Studies how a particular understanding of disease as "constitutional" led to support for the C. D. Acts, and how the religious-liberal opponents of the laws were eventually victorious.

697   L'Espérance, Jean. "Woman's Mission to Woman: Explorations in the Operation of the Double Standard and Female Solidarity in Nineteenth-Century England," *Histoire sociale—Social History* 12 (1979): 316-38.
_____. "The Work of the Ladies National Association for the Repeal of the Contagious Diseases Acts," *Bulletin of the Society for the Study of Labour History* 26 (Spring 1973): 13-15.
Two essays on different aspects of the campaign against the

C. D. Acts: the first explores the differences between a feminist approach emphasizing equality and solidarity among social classes and a non-feminist approach focusing on social purity and the moral superiority of women; the second discusses the LNA, its middle-class character, and the strong participation by Nonconformist women in its leadership.

698   Hamilton, Margaret. "Opposition to the Contagious Diseases Acts, 1864-1886," *Albion* 10 (1978): 14-27.
       Considers the reasons for this opposition and how it succeeded in bringing about repeal; support from churches was important, Hamilton concludes.

699   Gorham, Deborah. "The Maiden Tribute of Modern Babylon Re-examined: Child Prostitution and the Idea of Childhood in Late-Victorian England," *Victorian Studies* 21 (1978): 353-79.
       Robson, Ann. "The Significance of 'The Maiden Tribute of Modern Babylon'," *Victorian Periodicals Newsletter* 11 (1978): 51-57.
       Strauss, Sylvia. "Raising the Victorian Women's Consciousness: White Slavery and the Women's Movement," *UMPWS* 2 (1978): 13-31.
       These articles address the final act of the moral crusade against the C. D. Acts, which involved W. T. Stead's exposure of child prostitution and the ensuing storm of publicity in 1885-86; it united socialists, evangelicals, and suffragists as no other part of the campaign had done. The articles also explore the ambiguous results of the crusade for later issues relating to women.

700   Gartner, Lloyd P. "Anglo-Jewry and the Jewish International Traffic in Prostitution," *AJS Review* 78 (1982-83): 129-78.
       Bristow, Edward. "British Jewry and the Fight against the International White-Slave Traffic, 1885-1914," *Immigrants & Minorities* 2 (1983): 152-70.
       Explorations of efforts by the Jewish communities to combat traffic in prostitution.

701   Hughes, Peter E. "Cleanliness and Godliness: A Sociological
        Study of the Good Shepherd Convent Refuges for the Social
        Reformation and Christian Conversion of Prostitutes and Con-
        victed Women in Nineteenth-Century Britain." Ph.D., Brunel,
        1985. Pp. 510.
        How the commercial laundry business of this Roman Catholic
        order (established in England in 1840) became the central
        activity and main feature of its reform work and contributed
        symbolic support in the process of transformation from sin to
        salvation.

702   Barrett, Rosa M. *Ellice Hopkins*. London: Wells, Gardner,
        Darnton, 1907. Pp. 276.
        The Anglican leader of the "social purity" crusade, Hopkins
        (1836-1904) was a tireless advocate for a single standard of
        sexual morality.

Religious Critics

703   Budd, Susan. *Varieties of Unbelief: Atheists and Agnostics in
            English Society, 1850-1960*. London: Heinemann, 1977.
            Pp. 307.
        Royle, Edward. *Radicals, Secularists, and Republicans: Pop-
            ular Freethought in Britain, 1866-1915*. Manchester: Man-
            chester, 1980. Pp. 380.
        Smith, Warren S. *The London Heretics, 1870-1914*. London:
            Constable, 1967. Pp. 319.
        Few women participated in the secular or freethought move-
        ment; but secular societies often tried to recruit women, and
        some (notably Annie Besant) had leadership roles.   These
        studies include such material in their investigations.

704   Howard, Cecil. *Mary Kingsley*. London: Hutchinson, 1957.
        Pp. 231.
        A traveller and writer on Africa, Kingsley (1862-1900) was
        especially interested in native religion on its own terms.

705   Hardy, Dennis. *Alternative Communities in Nineteenth-Centu-
        ry England*. London: Longman, 1979. Pp. 268.

Treats four types of communities. One of the several sectarian communities, known as the New Forest Shakers, practiced community of goods and celibacy in the 1870s; it was led by a former traveling preacher, Mary Ann Girling, thought to be the female reincarnation of Christ. After her death in 1886, the community disbanded.

Women and Evangelicalism

706   Bebbington, David. "Evangelicals and the Role of Women, 1800-1930," *Christian Arena* 37:4 (1984): 19-21, 23.
Detailed footnoting provides guidance to sources in a brief and sweeping look at conflicting perspectives of evangelicals on this issue.

707   Anderson, Olive. "Women Preachers in Mid-Victorian Britain: Some Reflections on Feminism, Popular Religion and Social Change," *Historical Journal* 12 (1969): 467-84.
Follows the careers of some forty middle-class women in the 1860s who preached on invitation only, usually in large halls, and to respectable audiences. Their activity was connected to lay participation in the holiness movement and to its pre-millennial emphasis that stressed the importance of women preachers (from Acts 2:17-18), but Anderson suggests that the range of religious activity for women in this period may also have contributed to the eventual decline in the number of women preachers.

708   Cutt, Margaret N. *Ministering Angels: A Study of Nineteenth-Century Evangelical Writing for Children.* Wormley: Five Owls, 1979. Pp. 226.
Focuses on four writers in this exploration of tract tales published from the 1840s to the early twentieth century: Maria Louisa Charlesworth (1819-81); Charlotte Maria Tucker (1821-93); Sarah Smith ("Hesba Stretton," 1832-91); and Catherine A. Walton (1849-1939).

709   Dieter, Melvin E. *The Holiness Revival of the Nineteenth Century.* Metuchen, NJ: Scarecrow, 1980. Pp. 356.

A primarily American focus. Chapter IV deals with European dimensions; Dieter states that the English involvement was heavily dependent on the activities of the Palmers and the Smiths, two husband-wife teams.

710   Figgis, J. B. *Keswick from Within.* 1914; New York: Garland, 1985. Pp. 192.
      Nugent, S. M. "Women at Keswick," in *The Keswick Convention: Its Message, Its Method and Its Men,* ed. C. F. Harford. London: Marshall, 1907. Pp. 193-202.
      Brief recollections of the participation of women in the Keswick meetings from 1875 on.

711   Bett, Henry. *Dora Greenwell.* London: Epworth, 1950. Pp. 80.
      Maynard, Constance L. *Dora Greenwell: A Prophet for Our Own Times on the Battleground of Our Faith.* London: Allenson, n.d. Pp. 242.
      Greenwell (1821-82) was a religious writer and poet.

712   Taylor, Ina. *Victorian Sisters.* London: Weidenfeld and Nicolson, 1987. Pp. 218.
      A corporate and family biography (of the four daughters of the Rev. George B. Macdonald), showing the interaction between Wesleyanism and Victorian society in the latter half of the nineteenth century.

713   O'Rorke, L. E. *The Life and Friendships of Catherine Marsh.* London: Longmans, Green, 1917. Pp. 399.
      Marsh (1818-1912) was a religious writer, parish visitor, and philanthropist.

714   Thomson, D. P. *Women of the Scottish Church.* Galashiels: A. Walker, 1946. Nos. 1-3.
      Short studies of Jane Melville (1813-1900), a teacher; Elizabeth Clephane (1830-69), a hymnwriter; and Lady Grisell Baillie (1822-91), the first Scottish deaconess.

715   Magnusson, Mamie. *Out of Silence: The Woman's Guild,*

1887-1987. Edinburgh: St. Andrew, 1987. Pp. 144.
A centenary history of this Church of Scotland organization.

The Spirit of Reform

716   Boyd, Nancy. *Three Victorian Women Who Changed Their
       World: Josephine Butler, Octavia Hill, Florence Nightingale.*
       New York: Oxford, 1982. Pp. 276.
       A study of three pioneers of social reform, with special focus
       on the ways in which their religious views were connected to
       their activities.

717   Harrison, Brian.   "State Intervention and Moral Reform in
       Nineteenth-Century England," in *Pressure from Without in
       Early Victorian England*, ed. Patricia Hollis. London: Edward
       Arnold, 1974. Pp. 289-322.
       On the crusades for moral reform legislation and the conflicts
       that these efforts entailed.

718   _____. *Drink and the Victorians*. London: Faber and
          Faber, 1971. Pp. 510.
          _____. *Dictionary of British Temperance Biography.*
          Coventry: Society for the Study of Labour History, 1973.
          Pp. 139.
          _____. "The British Prohibitionists 1853-1872: A Bio-
          graphical Analysis," *IRSH* 15 (1970): 375-467.
       Aspects of the temperance movement, c. 1815-72; although
       women had only limited involvement, the question of the effect
       of drink on the home was an important issue.   In the 1970
       article Harrison states that "to a limited extent the . . . move-
       ment was in itself a feminist movement—defending the inter-
       ests of women and children against the selfishness of men"
       (402).

719   Shiman, Lilian Lewis.   "'Changes are Dangerous': Women
       and Temperance in Victorian England," in *Religion in the
       Lives*, pp. 193-215.
       Traces the stages of activities of temperance women from 1829
       to 1914; in the latter phase, Shiman asserts, large numbers of

women participated through "Gospel Temperance" work.

720   Fletcher, J. M. J. *Mrs. Wightman of Shrewsbury.* London:
       Longmans, Green, 1906. Pp. 300.
       A biography of the most prominent woman (1815-98) in the
       temperance cause, who attracted a number of Anglican clergy
       to her work.

721   Rendall, Jane. "'A Moral Engine'? Feminism, Liberalism and
       the *English Woman's Journal,*" in *Equal or Different,* pp. 112-
       38, 260-67.
       Looks at the individuals, the commitments, and the problems
       involved with this journal in its brief existence, 1858-64, in-
       cluding the various religious interests of the participants.

722   Kinnaird, Emily. *Reminiscences.* London: J. Murray, 1925.
       Pp. 199.
       Personal recollections of a YWCA worker, with discussion of
       other Christian institutional reformers as Ellen Ranyard and
       Catherine Marsh.

723   Summers, Anne. "Ministering Angels—Victorian Ladies and
       Nursing Reform," *History Today* 39:2 (1989): 31-37.
       Contends that by studying the careers of two early disciples of
       Florence Nightingale, Jane Shaw Stewart and Agnes Jones,
       one can see "the fervour of missionary Christianity, the ideal
       of reconciliation between social classes, and the glorification of
       the separate, and largely domestic, sphere of female action"
       (31).

Philanthropy

724   Lewis, Jane. *Women and Social Action in Victorian and Ed-
       wardian England.* Stanford: Stanford, 1991. Pp. 338.
       Studies the development from women's philanthropy to social
       action and the emergence of social work and social welfare
       policy through the lives of five major participants, including
       Octavia Hill and Beatrice Webb.

725   Parker, Julia. *Women and Welfare: Ten Victorian Women in Public Social Service.* London: Macmillan, 1989. Pp. 220.
        A group portrait of activists and/or writers, including a chapter on religious experiences, especially a sense of vocation.

726   Prochaska, F. "A Mother's Country: Mothers' Meetings and Family Welfare in Britain, 1850-1950," *History* 74 (1989): 379-99.
        Studies an important dimension of social service work which had the intent of building a common culture across social classes; it sharply declined during World War II, Prochaska notes, and never recovered its former influence.

727   Checkland, Olive. *Philanthropy in Victorian Scotland: Social Welfare and the Voluntary Principle.* Edinburgh: Donald, 1980. Pp. 416.
        A comprehensive study, including a discussion of "the philanthropy of piety."

728   Walton, Ronald G. *Women in Social Work.* London: Routledge & Kegan Paul, 1975. Pp. 308.
        On the development of the profession from 1860 to 1971; the themes of philanthropy and reform are prominent among the first generation of social workers.

729   Wood, Ethel M. *The Pilgrimage of Perseverance.* London: National Council of Social Service, 1949. Pp. 90.
        A broad history of women's organizations and what they have achieved.

730   Gerard, Jessica. "Lady Bountiful: Women of the Landed Classes and Rural Philanthropy," *Victorian Studies* 30 (1987): 183-210.
        On the marriage of paternalism, religion, and good works, through the ministrations of landed women.

731   Luddy, Maria. "Women and Charitable Organisations in Nineteenth-Century Ireland," *WSIF* 11 (1986): 301-305.
        Studies the work of philanthropic women in developing a

public role for women as active and effective social workers in Irish society; two aspects of interest are noted: the depth of religious feeling in the published materials, and the limited involvement of lay Catholic women—their role was taken over by the expanding religious orders for women.

732   Simey, Margaret B. *Charitable Effort in Liverpool in the Nineteenth Century*. Liverpool: Liverpool, 1951. Pp. 150.
A local study, with attention to the roles of nurses and home visitors and the work of Josephine Butler.

733   Prochaska, F. K. "Body and Soul: Bible Nurses and the Poor in Victorian London," *Historical Research* 60 (1987): 336-48.
Ducrocq, Françoise. "The London Biblewomen and Nurses Mission, 1857-1880: Class Relations/Women's Relations," in *Women and the Structure of Society*, ed. Barbara J. Harris and JoAnn McNamara. Durham: Duke, 1984. Pp. 98-107.
Platt, Elspeth. *The Story of the Ranyard Mission, 1857-1937*. London: Hodder and Stoughton, 1937. Pp. 128.
Selfe, Rose Emily. *Light Amid London Shadows*. London: J. M. Dent, 1906. Pp. 179.
Several studies of the district nursing and visitation program created by Ellen Ranyard (1810-79) as part of "women's mission to women" and conducted within the framework of Victorian domestic ideology.

734   Briggs, Asa and Macartney, Anne. *Toynbee Hall: The First Hundred Years*. London: Routledge & Kegan Paul, 1984. Pp. 208.
Picht, Werner. *Toynbee Hall and the English Settlement Movement*. London: G. Bell, 1914. Pp. 214.
Although Samuel Barnett receives the bulk of attention as the founder, glimpses of the work of his wife Henrietta are available in these studies as well.

735   James, Angela and Hills, Nina, eds. *Mrs. John Brown, 1847-1935*. London: J. Murray, 1937. Pp. 214.

Reflections on the work of a temperance and social purity activist in England and South Africa.

736   Rickards, E. C. *Felicia Skene of Oxford: A Memoir*. London: J. Murray, 1902. Pp. 392.
An Oxford Movement author, Skene (1821-99) also conducted programs on behalf of women prisoners and the poor.

737   McCrone, Kathleen E. "Feminism and Philanthropy in Victorian England: The Case of Louisa Twining," *Canadian Historical Association Historical Papers* (1976): 123-39.
Studies the connection between conservative religion and increasing opportunities for women.

Church of England

738   Heeney, Brian. *The Women's Movement in the Church of England: 1850-1930*. Oxford: Clarendon, 1988. Pp. 144.
_____. "The Beginnings of Church Feminism: Women and the Councils of the Church of England, 1897-1919," *JEH* 33 (1982): 88-109 (also in *Religion in the Lives*, pp. 260-84).
_____. "Women's Struggle for Professional Work and Status in the Church of England, 1900-1930," *Historical Journal* 26 (1983): 329-47.
The monograph is a beginning effort on the subject, cut short by the author's untimely death. It considers the nineteenth-century "context of subordination" (Part I) as the condition that produced "church feminism" (Part II); the bulk of the articles are included in the material in Part II.

739   Hillsman, Walter. "Women in Victorian Church Music: Their Social, Liturgical, and Performing Roles in Anglicanism," in *Women in the Church*, pp. 443-52.
Focuses on roles for women in parish settings, noting the contrasting periods of relative importance for singers and instrumentalists on the one hand and for organists on the other.

740   Harrison, Brian. "For Church, Queen and Family: The Girls'

Friendly Society, 1874-1920," *Past & Present* 61 (1973): 107-38.

One of three important Anglican family organizations, the G.F.S. was founded in 1874 and reached its peak of membership in 1913; Harrison suggests that it contributed to women's emancipation in several ways, but also notes that feminism was one of the factors eroding its foundations.

741   Reffold, A. E. *A Noble Army of Women: The Story of Marie Carlile and the Church Army Sisters.* London: Church Book Room, 1947. Pp. 40.

Rowan, Edgar. *Wilson Carlile and the Church Army.* London: Hodder and Stoughton, 1905. Pp. 487.

Like the Salvation Army, on which it was patterned, this Anglican organization conducted evangelistic work, adding social and welfare programs later; it recruited and employed a large number of women in nursing and social work.

742   Cropper, Margaret. *Shining Lights—Six Anglican Saints of the Nineteenth Century.* London: Darton, Longman and Todd, 1963. Pp. 192.

Three women are featured within the common theme of sanctity: Christina Rossetti, Mother Cecile of Grahamstown, and Mary (Mrs. John) Brown.

The Oxford Movement and Religious Orders for Women

743   Crumb, Lawrence N. *The Oxford Movement and Its Leaders: A Bibliography of Secondary and Lesser Primary Sources.* Metuchen, NJ: Scarecrow, 1988. Pp. 706. Supplement, 1993. Pp. 304.

Over 7500 entries in the two volumes, organized by year of publication; a few entries on individual women.

744   Reed, John Shelton. "A Female Movement: The Feminization of Nineteenth-Century Anglo-Catholicism," *AEH* 57 (1988): 199-238.

Considers the special appeal of Anglo-Catholicism to women because of its challenge to Victorian family ideology—especially its option of new and meaningful work for single women in a religious vocation; by 1900, Reed notes, there were dozens of sisterhoods, with some 2000-3000 women.

745   Chapman, Raymond. *Faith and Revolt: Studies in the Literary Influence of the Oxford Movement.* London: Weidenfeld and Nicolson, 1970. Pp. 328.
Within the larger topic, substantial discussion of the works of Christina Rossetti and Charlotte Yonge.

746   Sparrow-Simpson, W. J. *The History of the Anglo-Catholic Revival from 1845.* London: Allen & Unwin, 1932. Pp. 304.
Anson, Peter F. *The Call of the Cloister.* 1955; 4th ed., London: SPCK, 1964. Pp. 650.
Cameron, Allan T. *The Religious Communities of the Church of England.* London: Faith, 1918. Pp. 203.
Allchin, A. M. *The Silent Rebellion: The Anglican Religious Communities, 1845-1900.* London: SCM, 1958. Pp. 256.
_____. "Le développement de la vie religieuse communautaire dans l'Église d'Angleterre aux XIXe siècle," *Irénikon* 35 (1962): 49-64.
Sockman, Ralph. *The Revival of the Conventual Life in the Church of England in the Nineteenth Century.* New York: W. D. Gray, 1917. Pp. 229.
Weller, Reginald H. *Religious Orders in the Anglican Communion.* Milwaukee: Young Churchman, 1909. Pp. 38.
Each of these takes up the general topic of the revival of the religious life in the Church of England through the work of the Oxford Movement, and thus has some material on the establishment of religious orders for women.

747   Hill, Michael. *The Religious Order: A Study of Virtuoso Religion and Its Legitimation in the Nineteenth-Century Church of England.* London: Heinemann, 1973. Pp. 344.
Within the context of a sociological analysis of the character and role of the religious order in a larger institutional church, Hill considers the particular emergence of Anglican religious orders for men and women; he contends that sisterhoods "are

the first signs of incipient feminism among women of the middle class" (10) because of their degree of moral and organizational autonomy.

748   Mumm, Susan E. D. "'Lady Guerillas of Philanthropy': Anglican Sisterhoods in Victorian England." Ph.D., Sussex, 1993. Pp. 399.
Studies the growth of sisterhoods from their beginnings in 1845 to the existence of more than eighty by 1900, along with the opportunities these provided for women.

749   Denison, Keith Malcolm. "The Sisterhood Movement: A Study in the Conflicts of Ideals and Spiritual Disciplines in Nineteenth-Century Anglicanism." Ph.D., Cambridge, 1971. Pp. 380.
Considers the implications for spiritual theology of the teachings of the Oxford Movement leaders as they relate to religious orders for women, and argues that the pattern that developed was incompatible with the Anglican genius and resulted in isolation from the mainstream of Anglican life.

750   Williams, Thomas J. "The Beginnings of Anglican Sisterhoods," *HMPEC* 16 (1947): 350-72.
A general article on foundations in England and America, with sketches of the orders and their founders.

751   Williams, Thomas J. and Campbell, Allan W. *The Park Village Sisterhood*. London: SPCK, 1965. Pp. 155.
Norton, Sr. Ann Frances. "A History of the Community of St. Mary the Virgin, Wantage: Foundation and Early Development (1848-1858)." M.A., Durham, 1974. Pp. 135.
A Hundred Years of Blessing within an English Community. London: SPCK, 1946. Pp. 193.
Society of the Sisters of Bethany. *The Society of the Sisters of Bethany, 1866-1966*. Bournemouth, 1966. Pp. 23.
Sister Jean. *God Thorn*. Bognor Regis: New Horizon, 1981. Pp. 63.
Several studies of individual religious orders for women within the Church of England.

752   Anson, Peter F. *Building Up the Waste Places: The Revival of
       Monastic Life on Medieval Lines in the Post-Reformation
       Church of England*. Leighton Buzzard: Faith, 1973. Pp. 275.
       A history of the establishment of Anglican Benedictine com-
       munities on an enclosed model in the years 1856-1913; a
       community for women was founded in 1867 alongside one
       already created for men. Eventually one community of men
       and one of women went into the Roman Catholic Church.

753   Swinford, Frances K. "Women of the Oxford Movement,"
          Living Church 188:6 (February 5, 1984): 8-9.
       Peck, Winifred F. "The Ladies of the Oxford Movement,"
          Cornhill Magazine 148 (1933): 3-14.
       White, Rosemary A. "Women of the Oxford Movement,"
          Catholic World 162 (December 1945): 255-57.
       Short articles on the women whose lives in the Church of
       England were shaped by the ideals of the Oxford Movement.

754   For studies of individuals who became founders of communi-
       ties or role models in the Church, see:
       Warner, R. Townsend. *Marian Rebecca Hughes, Mother
          Foundress of the Society of the Holy and Undivided Trinity,
          Oxford*. London: Oxford, 1933. Pp. 32.
       *A Valiant Victorian: The Life and Times of Mother Emily
          Ayckbowm (1836-1900) of the Community of the Sisters of
          the Church*. London: Mowbray, 1964. Pp. 258.
       Mother Cecile in South Africa, 1883-1906. Compiled by a
          Sister of the Community. London: SPCK, 1930. Pp. 308.
       Manton, Jo. *Sister Dora: The Life of Dorothy Pattison*. Lon-
          don: Methuen, 1971. Pp. 380.
       Sister Felicity Mary. *Mother Millicent Mary of the Will of
          God: Mother Foundress of the Society of the Precious
          Blood, 1869-1956*. London: Macmillan, 1968. Pp. 163.

The Deaconess Movement in the Church of England

755   Grierson, Janet. *The Deaconess*. London: CIO, 1981. Pp.
       144.
       A compact but detailed history of the deaconess order from its

restoration in 1862 to the present, with an emphasis on the effort of women to claim a fuller role in the church's ministry; considers changes, conflicts, and continuing issues in view of the sharp increase in numbers in the 1970s.

756   Prelinger, Catherine M.   "The Female Diaconate in the Anglican Church: What Kind of Ministry for Women?" in *Religion in the Lives*, pp. 161-92.
A history of the movement to the early part of the twentieth century, including discussion of the difficulties of attracting persons after the first decade (there were barely two hundred by the end of the nineteenth century, compared to the much larger numbers in the religious orders).

757   Sister Joanna.   "The Deaconess Community of St. Andrew," *JEH* 12 (1961): 215-30.
Centenary reflections on the founding of the first community in 1861.

758   For earlier histories and reflections on this office, see:
Robinson, Cecilia.   *The Ministry of Deaconesses*.   London: Methuen, 1898; 2nd ed., 1914.   Pp. 241.
Sister Margaret.   *The Deaconess*.   London: Faith Press, 1919. Pp. 120.
The Order of Deaconesses in the Anglican Church.   London, 1911.   Pp. 23.

759   Grierson, Janet.   *Isabella Gilmore, Sister to William Morris*. London: SPCK, 1962.   Pp. 243.
Robinson, Elizabeth, ed.   *Deaconess Gilmore: Memories*. London: SPCK, 1924.   Pp. 55.
Gilmore (1842-1913) trained as a nurse following the death of her husband and soon thereafter was persuaded to begin a deaconess program in the diocese of Rochester.

Roman Catholicism

760   Beck, G. A., ed.   *The English Catholics, 1850-1950*.   London: Burns, Oates, 1950.

Two relevant essays: Edward Cruise's "Development of the Religious Orders," pp. 442-74, alternates his history between male and female orders; W. J. Battersby's "Educational Work of the Religious Orders of Women: 1850-1950," pp. 337-64, studies the remarkable growth in education of girls in the nineteenth century and its decline in the twentieth in the face of competition from state education.

761   O'Brien, Susan. *"Terra Incognita*: The Nun in Nineteenth-Century England," *Past & Present* 121 (1988): 110-40.
Focuses on three English congregations in order to illustrate the dramatic growth over the century (from two to approximately ninety communities, with 8,000-10,000 sisters in some six hundred convent houses); O'Brien observes that the new congregations tended to be active rather than cloistered and were shaped by the visions of their founders.

762   _____. "Lay Sisters and Good Mothers: Working-Class Women in English Convents, 1840-1910," in *Women in the Church*, pp. 453-65.
Compares the religious life and opportunities for service in congregations that divided their membership by class or status and those that did not.

763   _____. "Making Catholic Spaces: Women, Decor, and Devotion in the English Catholic Church, 1840-1900," in *The Church and the Arts*, pp. 449-64.
Studies the role of women in creating distinctive Catholic spaces for worship and prayer, through decoration, displays for the liturgical year, and the promotion of devotion to female saints.

764   Arnstein, Walter L. "The Great Victorian Convent Case," *History Today* 30:2 (1980): 46-50.
_____. *Protestant versus Catholic in Mid-Victorian England: Mr. Newdegate and the Nuns*. Columbia: Missouri, 1982. Pp. 271.
Studies in Victorian anti-Catholicism featuring an 1869 lawsuit that raised the question of "the propriety of convents as institu-

tions and the manner in which they ought to be treated by the laws of England" (220).

765   Steele, Francesca M. *The Convents of Great Britain*. London: Sands, 1902. Pp. 320.
A directory of more than ninety separate congregations of women, with brief sketches of each, its founding, locations, rule, dress, and the like.

766   Anon. *Sisters of the Cross and Passion: Origin and Progress of the Congregation*. Dublin: Dollard, 1960. Pp. 267.
A history of the order, founded in Manchester in 1850.

767   Nuns of Tyburn Convent. *Tyburn Hill of Glory*. London: Burns Oates, 1952. Pp. 167.
The story of a Benedictine community founded in France in 1897, moving to England in 1901.

768   There are a number of biographies of individual sisters, many of whom were founders of their communities; while often focusing on the theme of sanctity, they also contain information on struggle, vocation, and perseverance; these include:
Kerr, Amabel. *Sister Chatelain, or Forty Years' Work in Westminster*. London: Catholic Truth Soc., 1900. Pp. 140.
Kerr, Cecil. *Memoir of a Sister of Charity: Lady Etheldreda Fitzalan Howard*. London: Burns Oates and Washbourne, 1928. Pp. 113.
_____. *Teresa Helena Higginson: Servant of God, "The Spouse of the Crucified," 1844-1905*. London: Sands, 1927. Pp. 364.
Quinlan, Mary H. *Mabel Digby, Janet Erskine Stuart: Superiors General of the Society of the Sacred Heart, 1895-1914*. Privately Printed, 1982. Pp. 302.
Pollen, Anne. *Mother Mabel Digby: A Biography of the Superior General of the Society of the Sacred Heart, 1835-1911*. London: J. Murray, 1914. Pp. 404.
Monahan, Maud. *Life and Letters of Janet Erskine Stuart, Superior General of the Society of the Sacred Heart, 1857-*

1914. London: Longmans, Green, 1922. Pp. 524.

Hudson, George V. *Mother Genevieve Dupuis: Foundress of the English Congregation of the Sisters of Charity of St. Paul the Apostle, 1813-1903.* London: Sheed & Ward, 1929. Pp. 327.

S.M.C. *Steward of Souls: A Portrait of Mother Margaret Hallahan.* London: Longmans, Green, 1952. Pp. 181.

Memoir of Mother Mary Judith, Congregation of Our Lady of Sion, 1847-1932. By a Member of the Community. London: Longmans, Green, 1936. Pp. 196.

Dougherty, Patrick. *Mother Mary Potter, Foundress of the Little Company of Mary (1847-1913).* London: Sands, 1961. Pp. 304.

Winowska, Maria. *Pioneer of Unity: The Life of Caroline Sheppard, the First English Little Sister of the Poor.* London: Burns & Oates, 1969. Pp. 285.

Gilbert, John W. *Mother Mary Ignatius Sherrington: A Memoir.* London: Sands, 1915. Pp. 94.

Wells, Ruth Gilpin. *A Woman of Her Time and Ours: Mary Magdalen Taylor, SMG.* Charlotte, NC: Laney-Smith, 1988. Pp. 249.

Devas, Francis C. *Mother Mary Magdalen of the Sacred Heart (Fanny Margaret Taylor): Foundress of the Poor Servants of the Mother of God, 1832-1900.* London: Burns Oates & Washbourne, 1927. Pp. 385.

Bennett, Alice H. *Through an Anglican Sisterhood to Rome.* London: Longmans, Green, 1914. Pp. 203.

Mason, Margaret J. "Nuns and Vocations of the Unpublished Jerningham Letters," *Recusant History* 21 (1993): 503-55.

769   A few studies of lay Catholic women include:

McCarron, Mary. "Nineteenth-Century Liberal Catholicism: The Case of Charlotte Lady Blennerhassett (1843-1917)." Ph.D., Graduate Theological Union, 1989. Pp. 346.

Donovan, Grace. "An American Catholic in Victorian England: Louisa, Duchess of Leeds, and the Carroll Family Benefice," *Maryland Historical Magazine* 84 (1989): 223-34.

Elliott, Bernard. "Laura Phillipps De Lisle: A Nineteenth-

Century Catholic Lady," *Recusant History* 20 (1991): 371-79.

Roman Catholicism in Ireland

770   MacCurtain, Margaret and Ó Corráin, Donncha, eds. *Women in Irish Society: The Historical Dimension.* Dublin: Arlen House The Women's Press, 1979.
Of ten essays, two deal with religious topics; Joseph Lee's "Women and the Church Since the Famine," pp. 37-45, notes that after the famine the main options for women beyond the domestic were emigration or the religious life; Patricia Redlich's "Women and the Family," pp. 82-91, argues that stress on women over conflicting roles in modern society has been increased in the support of the Church for traditional domestic roles.

771   Inglis, Tom. *Moral Monopoly: The Catholic Church in Modern Irish Society.* Dublin: Gill and Macmillan, 1987.
Chapter 8, on the Irish mother, discusses the creation of the "ideal" Irish mother and the role of the Church in this development.

772   Clear, Caitríona. *Nuns in Nineteenth-Century Ireland.* Dublin: Gill and Macmillan, 1987. Pp. 214.
Explores the dramatic growth of women religious in the nineteenth century against the background of broader social and economic conditions for women; in 1900 there were 368 houses and 35 orders, compared to 1801 with eleven houses and six religious orders.

773   _____. "Walls within Walls—Nuns in 19th-Century Ireland," in *Gender in Irish Society,* ed. Chris Curtin, et al. Galway: Galway, 1987. Pp. 134-51.
Using annual entry registers from two convents in Limerick, Clear argues that class differences determined whether one became a choir nun or a lay sister.

774   Bolster, Evelyn. *The Sisters of Mercy in the Crimean War.*

Cork: Mercier, 1964. Pp. 338.

Gillgannon, M. M. "The Sisters of Mercy as Crimean War Nurses." Ph.D., Notre Dame, 1962. Pp. 447.

Hurley, Frank. "Kinsale Nuns in the Crimea: 1854-56," *Kinsale Historical Journal* 1 (1986): 31-34.

Murphy, J. J. W. "An Irish Sister of Mercy in the Crimean War," *Irish Sword* 5 (1961-62): 251-61.

These works explore the perspective of the Irish sisters, especially important in relation to the conflicts that occurred with Florence Nightingale in the Crimea.

775   Sr. Mary Pauline. *God Wills It! Centenary Story of the Sisters of St. Louis*. Dublin: Browne and Nolan, 1959. Pp. 320.
This French teaching order moved to Ireland in 1859, eventually establishing houses in other countries as well.

776   Biographies of individual women religious include:

Gildea, Denis. *Mother Mary Arsenius of Foxford*. London: Burns Oates & Washbourne, 1936. Pp. 198.

Gibbons, Margaret. *The Life of Margaret Aylward: Foundress of the Sisters of the Holy Faith*. London: Sands, 1928. Pp. 426.

Vidulich, Dorothy. *Peace Pays a Price: A Study of Margaret Anna Cusack, The Nun of Kenmare*. Rev. ed., Washington: Sisters of St. Joseph of Peace, 1990. Pp. 86.

Eagar, Irene ffrench. *Margaret Anna Cusack: One Woman's Campaign for Women's Rights*. 1970; Dublin: Arlen House The Women's Press, 1979. Pp. 250.

Cusack's (1829-99) story is one of religious pilgrimage, changing sense of vocation, vision, conflict with church hierarchy, persistence, disillusionment, and, ultimately, restoration of reputation in the 1970s.

777   O'Connor, Anne V. "Influences Affecting Girls' Secondary Education in Ireland, 1860-1910," *Archivium Hibernicum* 41 (1986): 83-98.
Considers the conflict between a French model stressing religion and preparation for marriage and an English model favoring a vocational or academic curriculum; the hierarchy favored

the first, but Catholic parents increasingly demanded the other, O'Connor declares.

778 _____. "Images of the Evil Woman in Irish Folklore: A Preliminary Study," *WSIF* 11 (1988): 281-85.
Suggests that such images occur in a context where there is an important religious emphasis in the tradition, and they are usually balanced by images of woman as good or saintly.

Nonconformity

779 Whitehorn, Constance M. *Women's Share in the Life and Work of the Church*. London: Presbyterian Historical Society of England, 1958. Pp. 16.
A brief overview of activities in the Presbyterian Church from the mid-nineteenth century, including missionary work and organizational life.

780 Price, A. Whigham. *The Ladies of Castlebrae: The Life of Dr. Agnes Smith Lewis and Dr. Margaret Dunlop Gibson.* London: Presbyterian Historical Society, 1964. Pp. 23.
_____. *The Ladies of Castlebrae.* London: Headline, 1985. Pp. 242.
Twin sisters and loyal to their Scottish Presbyterian heritage, they were private scholars and travelers who discovered a palimpsest that came to be called the Lewis Syriac Gospels.

781 Field-Bibb, Jacqueline. "Women and Ministry: The Presbyterian Church of England," *Heythrop Journal* 31 (1990): 150-64.
Studies the debate over ordination of women from its beginnings in 1884 to the first ordination in 1956.

782 Martindale, Hilda. *From One Generation to Another, 1839-1944*. London: Allen & Unwin, 1944. Pp. 208.
Personal and family memoirs, especially useful for the portrait of her Congregational mother, Louisa Spicer Martindale (1839-1914), who founded a Congregational Hall in her village with the stipulation that there be equality of the sexes in conducting services and in management of the hall.

783   Rose, Doris M. *Baptist Deaconesses.* London: Carey Kings-
        gate, 1954. Pp. 36.
        A brief account of the work from its beginnings in 1890.

784   Black, S. B., ed. *A Farningham Childhood.* Otford, Kent:
        Darenth Valley, 1988. Pp. 126.
        Part of the autobiography of the Baptist writer, Marianne
        Farningham (1834-1909), preceded by a contextual biography.

785   Stinchcombe, Owen. "Elizabeth Malleson (1828-1916) and
        Unitarianism," *TUHS* 20:1 (April, 1991): 56-61.
        Ruston, Alan. "Clementia Taylor (1810-1908)," *ibid.*: 62-68.
        Brief studies of notable Unitarians.

786   Davey, Cyril James and Thomas, Hugh. *Together Travel On:
        A History of Women's Work.* London: Cargate, 1984. Pp.
        23.
        An account of Methodist women's missionary activity from its
        beginnings in 1858 to the present.

787   Tyack, Lena. *Caroline Meta Wiseman.* London: Charles H.
        Kelly, 1915. Pp. 183.
        Wiseman (1834-1912) was secretary of the Women's Auxiliary
        of the Wesleyan Methodist Society and one of the first women
        elected to a local school board in 1871.

788   Moore, Robert. *Pit-Men, Preachers and Politics: The Effects
        of Methodism in a Durham Mining Community.* Cambridge:
        Cambridge, 1974. Pp. 292.
        A fine regional study, c. 1870-1930; few references to women,
        but they helpfully enlarge one's understanding of this particular
        religious culture.

789   Smith, Henry. *Ministering Women: The Story of the Work of
        the Sisters Connected with the United Methodist Deaconess
        Institute, Together with Some Account of the Origin and Histo-
        ry of the Institute.* London: Crombie, [1913]. Pp. 205.
        Instituted in 1891, the Methodist deaconess program prepared
        women to serve as evangelists, home visitors for the poor and

the sick, missionaries, and special agents—in other words, to
fill in the gaps in the existing system.

790   Parr, James T. *The Angel of Blackfriars; or, The Sister with
      the Shining Face.* London: Hammond, 1914. Pp. 108.
      A biography of Emma Davis (1859-1911), the first Primitive
      Methodist deaconess.

791   Isichei, Elizabeth. *Victorian Quakers.* Oxford: Oxford, 1970.
      Pp. 326.
      Widely acclaimed as a denominational study; while Isichei
      gives only limited attention to the position of women, the work
      of many Quaker women is discussed extensively in the chapter
      on philanthropy.

792   For studies of individual Quaker women, see:
      Abel, Trudi. "Needles and Penury in 19th Century London:
         The Diary of a Poor Quaker Seamstress," *Quaker History*
         75:2 (1986): 102-14.
      Scott, Richenda. *Elizabeth Cadbury, 1858-1951.* London:
         Harrop, 1955. Pp. 200.
      Whitney, Janet. *Geraldine S. Cadbury, 1865-1941: A Biogra-
         phy.* London: Harrop, 1948. Pp. 200.
      Cadbury, M. Christabel. *The Story of a Nightingale Nurse
         and Kindred Papers.* London: Headley, 1939. Pp. 40.
      Tod, Robert J. N. *Caroline Fox, Quaker Blue-Stocking, 1819-
         1871.* York: Sessions, 1980. Pp. 76.
      Harris, Wilson. *Caroline Fox.* London: Constable, 1944.
         Pp. 358.
      Fox, Hubert, ed. *Marion Fox, Quaker: A Selection of Her
         Letters.* London: Allen & Unwin, 1951. Pp. 188.
      Brown, Beatrice Curtis, ed. *Isabel Fry, 1869-1958: Portrait
         of a Great Teacher.* London: Arthur Barker, 1960. Pp.
         166.
      Jones, Enid Huws. *Margery Fry: The Essential Amateur.*
         London: Oxford, 1966. Pp. 256.
      Hobhouse, Rosa. *Mary Hughes: Her Life for the Dispos-
         sessed.* London: Rockliff, 1949. Pp. 124.
      Tod, R. J. N. *Caroline Emelia Stephen, Quaker Mystic,*

1834-1909. Birmingham: n.p., 1978. Pp. 71.

Greenwood, Ormerod. "Elizabeth Bevan Tonjoroff (1847-1907)," *JFHS* 49:1 (1959): 7-23.

Salvation Army

793   Moyles, R. G. *A Bibliography of Salvation Army Literature in English (1865-1987)*. Lewiston, NY: Edwin Mellen, 1988. Pp. 209.
A comprehensive listing of literature by and about the Salvation Army, with no annotations; no separate classification for materials on women, but much is to be found throughout, including in the section on biography.

794   Sandall, Robert, et al. *The History of the Salvation Army*. 7 vols.; London, 1947-86.
The standard history of the denomination.

795   Search, Pamela. *Happy Warriors: The Story of the Social Work of the Salvation Army*. London: Arco, 1956. Pp. 173.
Focuses on the beginnings and on work at the time of writing.

796   Watson, Bernard. *A Hundred Years' War: The Salvation Army 1865-1965*. London: Hodder & Stoughton, 1964. Pp. 318.
Stories of individual service, not a history of the denomination.

797   Richards, Miriam M. *Workers Together*. London: Salvation Army, 1970. Pp. 56.
Focuses on Catherine Booth and the role of women in the work of the Salvation Army.

798   Bishop, Edward. *Blood and Fire! The Story of General William Booth and the Salvation Army*. London: Longmans, 1964. Pp. 114.
A popular history; despite the title, there is much attention to the contributions of Catherine Booth.

799   Larsson, Flora. *My Best Men Are Women*. London: Hodder and Stoughton, 1974. Pp. 189.

Vignettes of women officers and their work, from Catherine Booth to the present.

800   Unsworth, Madge. *Maiden Tribute: A Study in Voluntary Social Service.* London: Salvationist Pub., 1949. Pp. 168. On the Army's work with girls and young women.

801   Higginbotham, Ann R. "Respectable Sinners: Salvation Army Rescue Work with Unmarried Mothers, 1884-1914," in *Religion in the Lives*, pp. 216-33. On the activities of the Women's Social Services, which prefigured later developments in social work.

802   Ball, Gillian. "Practical Religion: A Study of the Salvation Army's Social Services for Women, 1884-1914." Ph.D., Leicester, 1987. Pp. 311. A study of the relation between theory and practice, including analysis of 1500 cases of women served.

803   Clarke, Douglas. "Female Ministry in the Salvation Army," *Expository Times* 95 (1984): 232-35. A brief exploration of Catherine Booth's principle of equality and its establishment in the Army.

804   Walker, Pamela J. "Pulling the Devil's Kingdom Down: Gender and Popular Culture in the Salvation Army, 1865-1895." Ph.D., Rutgers, 1992. Pp. 313. Considers the cultural conflicts involved in the Army's use of working-class urban culture, many of which involved gender issues.

805   Booth Tucker, Frederick. *The Consul: A Sketch of Emma Booth Tucker.* New York: Salvation Army, 1903. Pp. 192. Daughter of the founders, Booth Tucker (1860-1903) worked in India and the United States.

806   Booth, Bramwell. *Echoes and Memories.* London: Salvationist Publishing, 1925. Pp. 223. Although an autobiography, it contains some discussion of his

mother's ideas and influence on the development of roles for women in the Army.

Spiritualism

807   For general histories of the movement, with some attention to the role of women in it, see:

Brandon, Ruth. *The Spiritualists: The Passion for the Occult in the Nineteenth and Twentieth Centuries*. London: Weidenfeld and Nicolson, 1983. Pp. 308.

Oppenheim, Janet. *The Other World: Spiritualism and Psychic Research in England, 1850-1914*. Cambridge: Cambridge, 1985. Pp. 503.

Nelson, Geoffrey K. *Spiritualism and Society*. London: Routledge, 1969. Pp. 307.

Barrow, Logie. *Independent Spirits: Spiritualism and English Plebeians, 1850-1910*. London: Routledge & Kegan Paul, 1986. Pp. 338.

Porter, Katherine H. *Through a Glass Darkly: Spiritualism in the Browning Circle*. Lawrence: Kansas, 1958. Pp. 160.

808   Owen, Alex. *The Darkened Room: Women, Power and Spiritualism in Late Victorian England*. London: Virago, 1989. Pp. 314.

_____. "Women and Nineteenth-century Spiritualism: Strategies in the Subversion of Femininity," in *Disciplines of Faith*, pp. 130-53.

Owen studies the role of women as mediums, healers, and believers during the golden age of English spiritualism and shows how traditional understandings of womanhood were subverted and transformed without being seen as a challenge to the patriarchal order.

809   Walker, Mary. "Between Fiction and Madness: The Relationship of Women to the Supernatural in Late Victorian Britain," in *That Gentle Strength: Historical Perspectives on Women in Christianity*, ed. Lynda L. Coon, et al. Charlottesville: Virginia, 1990. Pp. 230-42.

Suggests that the Victorian ideal of womanhood helps to explain why more women than men reported supernatural occurrences and why the Society for Psychic Research tried so hard to de-emphasize those contributions.

810   Dickerson, Vanessa D. "A Spirit of Her Own: Nineteenth-Century Feminine Explorations of Spirituality," in *That Gentle Strength*, pp. 243-58.
Looks at the writings of several women and concludes that "through spiritualism, mesmerism, and supernaturalism, the Victorian woman probed the nature and extent of her spirituality and discovered expression, freedom, and power" (256).

811   Skultans, Vieda. "Mediums, Controls and Eminent Men," in *Women's Religious Experience*, ed. Pat Holden.   London: Croom Helm, 1983. Pp. 15-26.
Explores the careers of some nineteenth-century mediums to confirm the contention that "the typical spiritualist experience involves a female medium and a male spirit or control" (17).

812   Hall, Trevor H. *The Spiritualists: The Story of Florence Cook and William Crookes*. London: Duckworth, 1962. Pp. 188.
A study in parapsychology and scientific investigation.

813   Walkowitz, Judith R. "Science and the Seance: Transgressions of Gender and Genre in Late Victorian London," *Representations* 22 (Spring 1988): 3-29.
The story of Georgina Weldon's activities as a spiritualist and her legal battles against medical doctors who accused her of madness.

814   Aspinwall, Bernard. "Social Catholicism and Health: Dr. and Mrs. Thomas Low Nichols in Britain," in *The Church and Healing* (SCH 19), ed. W. J. Sheils.   Oxford: Blackwell, 1982. Pp. 249-70.
Americans who settled in England in 1861, the Nicholses were interested in the relationship between spiritualism and health, including the health education of women.

Theosophy

815   Campbell, Bruce F. *Ancient Wisdom Revived: A History of the Theosophical Movement*. Berkeley: California, 1980. Pp. 249.
A balanced consideration of both contributions and problems in the course of a century's history; the work of major women leaders is discussed in connection with the development of the movement.

816   Dixon, Joy. "Gender, Politics, and Culture in the New Age: Theosophy in England, 1880-1935." Ph.D., Rutgers, 1993. Pp. 364.
Explores the transformative vision of Theosophy that attracted women in significant numbers by the early twentieth century.

817   Burfield, Diana. "Theosophy and Feminism: Some Explorations in Nineteenth-Century Biography," in *Women's Religious Experience*, pp. 27-56.
A study of the appeal of Theosophy to women, with brief biographies of three prominent individuals: Anna Kingsford (1846-88), Isabelle de Steiger (1836-1927), and Isabel Cooper-Oakley (1854-1914).

Judaism

818   Kuzmack, Linda Gordon. *Woman's Cause: The Jewish Woman's Movement in England and the United States, 1881-1933*. Columbus: Ohio State, 1990. Pp. 280.
On the creation of a distinctly Jewish feminism, which challenged traditional Judaism and established links with secular women's organizations.

819   Burman, Rickie. "Women in Jewish Religious Life: Manchester 1880-1930," in *Disciplines of Faith*, pp. 37-55.
_____. "The Jewish Woman as Breadwinner: The Changing Value of Women's Work in a Manchester Immigrant Community," *Oral History* 10:2 (1982): 27-39.
_____. "'She Looketh Well to the Ways of Her House-

hold': The Changing Role of Jewish Women in Religious
Life, c. 1880-1930," in *Religion in the Lives*, pp. 234-59.
Burman studies the impact of immigration on the role of wom-
en in the Jewish community, as domestic religious activity
assumed greater prominence and the traditional male activities
of scholarship and piety were less valued.

Missions

820   Melman, Billie. *Women's Orients: Englishwomen and the
      Middle East, 1718-1918: Sexuality, Religion, and Work.* Lon-
      don: Macmillan, 1992. Pp. 417.
      Melman presents the perspectives of women travelers as they
      wrote about their experiences as pilgrims, tourists, missionar-
      ies, and ethnographers, together with the changes in these
      views over two hundred years. The section on religion focus-
      es on the dual impact of the evangelical construction of femi-
      ninity and the revival of millenarian evangelicalism on women
      in mission work in the Middle East.

821   Bowie, Fiona, et al. *Women and Missions: Past and Present.
      Anthropological and Historical Perceptions.* London: Berg,
      1992. Pp. 279.
      Thirteen essays address two broad themes: the experience of
      women missionaries in the nineteenth century and the impact
      of Christian missions on women. Bowie's introduction is
      followed by four essays on the first theme, two of which focus
      on recruitment for missionary service. The eight essays on the
      second theme take up large topics (such as education, family,
      and the issue of empowerment) in the context of the mission-
      ary encounter with women in a particular country.

822   Studies of particular denominations or women's missionary
      organizations include:
      Findlay, G. G. and Holdsworth, W. W. *The History of the
          Wesleyan Methodist Missionary Society.* 5 vols., London:
          Epworth, 1921-24.
      Hellier, Anna M. *Workers Together: The Story of the Wom-
          en's Auxiliary of the Wesleyan Methodist Missionary Soci-*

ety. London: Cargate, 1931. Pp. 64.

Dewey, Margaret. *The Messengers: A Concise History of the United Society for the Propagation of the Gospel.* London: Mowbray, 1975. Pp. 158.

Humphrey, Ellen F. *Ministries of Women During Fifty Years in Connection with the S.P.G.* London: SPG, 1915. Pp. 83.

Hewitt, Gordon. *The Problems of Success: A History of the Church Missionary Society 1910-1942.* 2 vols., London: SCM, 1971-77.

Jubilee, 1867-1917: Fifty Years' Work among Women in the Far East. London: Carey, 1917. Pp. 51. [Baptist]

Hewat, Elizabeth G. K. *Vision and Achievement, 1796-1956.* Edinburgh: T. Nelson, 1960. Pp. 308. [Church of Scotland]

Swan, Annie S. *Seed Time and Harvest: The Story of the Hundred Years Work of the Women's Foreign Mission of the Church of Scotland.* London: Nelson, 1937. Pp. 159.

823   Potter, Sarah Caroline. "The Social Origins and Recruitment of English Protestant Missionaries in the Nineteenth Century." Ph.D., London, 1974. Pp. 274.
A sociological study dealing with four missionary societies in the context of broader changes in the culture; one chapter on women shows how they participated in the shift in emphasis from salvation to service in the last part of the century, but they did on the mission field essentially what they had done at home.

824   The work of women in missions in China is explored in:
Barr, Pat. *To China with Love: The Lives and Times of Protestant Missionaries in China, 1860-1900.* New York: Doubleday, 1973. Pp. 210.

Thompson, Phyllis. *Each to Her Post: Six Women of the China Inland Mission.* London: Hodder and Stoughton, 1982. Pp. 158.

Platt, W. J. *Three Women: Mildred Cable, Francesca French, Evangeline French.* London: Hodder and Stoughton, 1964. Pp. 219.

825   The role of women in missions in Africa is studied in:
        Gaitskell, Deborah L. "Female Mission Initiatives: Black and
            White Women in Three Witwatersrand Churches, 1903-
            1939." Ph.D., London, 1981. Pp. 391.
        Pirouet, M. Louise. "Women Missionaries of the Church
            Missionary Society in Uganda 1896-1920," in *Missionary
            Ideologies in the Imperialist Era: 1880-1920*, ed. Torben
            Christenson and William R. Hutchison. Aarhus: Aros,
            1982. Pp. 231-40.
        Oliver, Caroline. *Western Women in Colonial Africa*. West-
            port, CT: Greenwood, 1982.
        Chapters 4 and 5 discuss the work of Mary Slessor (1848-
        1915) in Nigeria and of Mother Kevin (1875-1957), an Irish
        Franciscan, in Uganda.

826   The work of women in missions in India is told in:
        Pollock, J. C. *Shadows Fall Apart: The Story of the Zenana
            Bible and Medical Mission*. London: Hodder and Stough-
            ton, 1958. Pp. 221.
        Tinling, Christine I. *India's Womanhood: Forty Years' Work
            at Ludhiana*. London: Lutterworth, 1935. Pp. 119.
        Balfour, Margaret I. and Young, Ruth. *The Work of Medical
            Women in India*. London: Oxford, 1929. Pp. 201.
        Forbes, Geraldine H. "In Search of the 'Pure' Heathen: Mis-
            sionary Women in Nineteenth-Century India," *Economic
            and Political Weekly* 21:17 (1986): 2-8.
        Robinson, A. M. "Women to Women: The Work of the
            C.E.Z.M.S.," *East and West Review* 1 (1935): 165-71.

827   Biographical studies of individual women missionaries include:
        M.L.H. *Sister Xavier Berkeley (1861-1944), Sister of Charity
            of St. Vincent de Paul: Fifty-four Years a Missionary in
            China*. London: Burns Oates, 1949. Pp. 257.
        Rice, Clara C. *Mary Bird: The Friend of the Persians*. Lon-
            don: CMS, 1920. Pp. 14.
        Houghton, Frank. *Amy Carmichael of Dohnavur*. London:
            SPCK, 1953. Pp. 390.
        Saunders, Una M. *Mary Dobson: Musician, Writer, and Mis-
            sionary*. London: A. & C. Black, 1926. Pp. 191.

Livingstone, W. P. *Christina Forsyth of Fingoland: The Story of the Loneliest Woman in Africa.* London: Hodder and Stoughton, 1918. Pp. 236.

Healey, Edna. *Wives of Fame.* London: Sidgwick & Jackson, 1986. Pp. 210 [includes Mary Livingstone (1821-62)].

Carus-Wilson, Mary. *A Woman's Life for Kashmir: Irene Petrie.* Chicago: Fleming H. Revell, 1901. Pp. 343.

Buchan, James. *The Expendable Mary Slessor.* Edinburgh: Saint Andrews, 1980. Pp. 253.

Christian, Carol and Plummer, Gladys. *God and One Redhead: Mary Slessor of Calabar.* London: Hodder and Stoughton, 1970. Pp. 190.

Livingstone, William P. *Mary Slessor of Calabar, Pioneer Missionary.* London: Hodder and Stoughton, 1916. Pp. 347.

Cable, Mildred and French, Francesca. *A Woman Who Laughed, Henrietta Soltau.* London: China Inland Mission, 1934. Pp. 240.

Scott, Mrs. Henry E. *A Saint in Kenya: A Life of Marion Scott Stevenson.* London: Hodder and Stoughton, 1932. Pp. 320.

Guinness, Joy. *Mrs. Howard Taylor, Her Web of Time.* London: China Inland Mission, 1949. Pp. 369.

Pollock, J. C. *Hudson Taylor and Maria: Pioneers in China.* London: Hodder & Stoughton, 1962. Pp. 223.

Cale, Patricia S. "A British Missionary in Egypt: Mary Louisa Whately," *Vitae Scholasticae* 3 (1984): 131-43.

Women and the Ecumenical Movement

828   Rouse, Ruth. *The World's Student Christian Federation.* London: SCM, 1948. Pp. 332.
       A history of its first thirty years, to 1924, with insights into the relation of various national women's movements and religion.

829   Tatlow, Tissington. *The Story of the Student Christian Movement of Great Britain and Ireland.* London: SCM, 1933. Pp. 944.

From its founding in the late nineteenth century to 1933; no specific attention to the role of women in the organization, but many references to specific individuals and their contributions.

830   Rowland, Wilmina M. *The Contribution of Ruth Rouse to the World's Student Christian Federation.* M.A., Yale, 1937. Pp. 281.

Franzén, Ruth. "The Legacy of Ruth Rouse," *International Bulletin of Missionary Research* 17 (1993): 154-58.

From 1897 to 1925 Rouse (1892-1956) worked for the WSCF as traveling secretary, publicist, author, leader, and contact person for other ecumenical organizations, before going on to even wider ecumenical work.

Women's Contribution to Hymnody

831   Grierson, Janet. *Frances Ridley Havergal: Worcestershire Hymnwriter.* Bromsgrove: Havergal Society, 1979. Pp. 197.

An Anglican Evangelical, Havergal (1836-79) was a popular author as well as hymnwriter.

832   Leaver, Robin A. *Catherine Winkworth: The Influence of Her Translations on English Hymnody.* St. Louis: Concordia, 1978. Pp. 198.

Shaen, Margaret J., ed. *Memorials of Two Sisters: Susanna and Catherine Winkworth.* London: Longmans, Green, 1908. Pp. 341.

Higginson, J. Vincent. "Catherine Winkworth and the Choral Book of England," *Hymn* 25 (1974): 9-14.

Catherine Winkworth (1827-78) translated a number of German hymns into English.

Wives of Ministers

833   Moore, Katharine. *Victorian Wives.* London: Allison and Busby, 1974. Pp. 208.

Provides glimpses of a number of ministerial wives from several denominations.

834   Clive, Mary. *Caroline Clive: From the Diary and Family
       Papers of Mrs. Archer Clive (1801-73)*. London: Bodley
       Head, 1949. Pp. 287.
       Uses Clive's diary (1841-47) to view the life of a parish rec-
       tor's wife.

835   Rickards, E. C. *Zoe Thomson of Bishopthorpe and her
       Friends*. London: J. Murray, 1916. Pp. 196.
       Thomson (d. 1913) was the wife of the bishop of Gloucester
       and Bristol, later archbishop of York.

Individuals

836   *Queen Victoria (1819-1901)*
       Her name shapes her age as no other monarch's does, but her
       person and her religious views and interests have not been as
       accessible as most other aspects of her reign.   Some recent
       studies that explore these dimensions are Dorothy Thompson,
       Queen Victoria: Gender and Power (London: Virago, 1990);
       Giles St. Aubyn, *Queen Victoria: A Portrait* (New York:
       Atheneum, 1992); and Stanley Weintraub, *Victoria: An Inti-
       mate Biography* (New York: Dutton, 1987).   Older works
       include Elizabeth Longford's *Victoria, R.I.* [London, 1964;
       also published as *Queen Victoria: Born to Succeed* (New York:
       Harper & Row, 1965)] and "Queen Victoria's Religious Life,"
       Wiseman Review 236 (1962): 107-26; and Walter Walsh's
       heroic narrative, *The Religious Life and Influence of Queen
       Victoria* (London: Swan Sonnenschein, 1902).   Useful articles
       are Walter L. Arnstein, "Queen Victoria and Religion," in
       Religion in the Lives, pp. 88-128; John Wolffe, "The End of
       Victorian Values? Women, Religion, and the Death of Queen
       Victoria," in *Women in the Church*, pp. 481-503; and Dudley
       W. R. Bahlman, "The Queen, Mr. Gladstone, and Church
       Patronage," *Victorian Studies* 3 (1960): 349-80.

837   *Annie Besant (1847-1933)*
       Spiritual pilgrim and notorious woman in the late nineteenth
       century, best known for her involvement in theosophy, Besant
       has more often been remembered by her followers than by

others; a listing of her writings is provided in Theodore Besterman, *A Bibliography of Annie Besant* (London: Theosophical Society, 1924). Recent studies exploring her life and
thought include Anne Taylor, *Annie Besant: A Biography*
(Oxford: Oxford, 1992); Catherine L. Wessinger, *Annie Bes-
ant and Progressive Messianism (1847-1933)* (Lewiston, NY:
Edwin Mellen, 1988); and Rosemary Dinnage, *Annie Besant*
(Harmondsworth: Penguin, 1986). Older works include the
detailed two-volume study by Arthur H. Nethercot, *The First
Five Lives of Annie Besant* and *The Last Four Lives of Annie
Besant* (London: Hart-Davis, 1961-63); Theodore Besterman,
Mrs. Annie Besant, A Modern Prophet (London: Kegan Paul,
Trench, Trubner, 1934); Gertrude M. Williams, *The Passion-
ate Pilgrim: A Life of Annie Besant* (New York: Coward-Mc-
Cann, 1931); and Geoffrey West, *The Life of Annie Besant*
(London: Howe, 1929). An investigation of her involvement
in the birth control debate in 1877, including three texts from
the period, is S. Chandrasekhar, *"A Dirty Filthy Book": The
Writings of Charles Knowlton and Annie Besant on Reproduc-
tive Physiology and Birth Control, and an Account of the
Bradlaugh-Besant Trial* (Berkeley: California, 1981).

838   *Barbara Bodichon (1827-91)*
        A writer and educator, Bodichon came from a Unitarian back-
        ground; the two main studies of her are Sheila Herstein, *A
        Mid-Victorian Feminist, Barbara Leigh Smith Bodichon* (New
        Haven: Yale, 1985), and Hester Burton, *Barbara Bodichon,
        1827-1891* (London: J. Murray, 1949).

839   *Catherine Booth (1829-90)*
        Booth's tract, "Female Ministry" (1859), is an important doc-
        ument in the history of the discussion of the ministry of
        women as well as being foundational for the Salvation Army's
        later inclusion of women at all levels of its work. But apart
        from references to her in general histories of the organization,
        there are few studies of her life and work; the best is by her
        granddaughter, Catherine Bramwell-Booth, *Catherine Booth:
        The Story of Her Loves* (London: Hodder and Stoughton,
        1970). Two articles that focus on the tract are Norman H.

Murdoch's "Female Ministry in the Thought of Catherine Booth," *Church History* 53 (1984): 348-62, and Roger Green's "Settled Views: Catherine Booth and Female Ministry," *Methodist History* 31 (1993): 131-47. An early admiring work is W. T. Stead, *Life of Mrs. Booth, The Founder of the Salvation Army* (London: Fleming H. Revell, 1900); and Cyril Barnes, *Words of Catherine Booth* (London: Salvationist Pub., 1981) is a brief and enthusiastic biography.

840   *Angela Burdett Coutts (1814-1906)*
A notable Victorian philanthropist and devoted Anglican, her life is studied in Diana Orton's *Made of Gold: A Biography of Angela Burdett Coutts* (London: H. Hamilton, 1980) and "Angela Burdett-Coutts," *History Today* 25 (1975): 271-78; see also Edna Healey, *Lady Unknown: The Life of Angela Burdett-Coutts* (London: Sidgwick & Jackson, 1978), and a personal biography by a distant relative, Clara Burdett Patterson, *Angela Burdett-Coutts and the Victorians* (London: J. Murray, 1953).

841   *Josephine Butler (1828-1906)*
Butler's two-decade crusade against the Contagious Diseases Acts until their repeal in 1886 made her a formidable figure in her lifetime, but her legacy has been less clear to later generations; the most detailed study, Glen Petrie's *A Singular Iniquity: The Campaigns of Josephine Butler* (London: Macmillan, 1971), focuses on that long activity.   Joseph Williamson's *Josephine Butler—The Forgotten Saint* (Leighton Buzzard: Faith, 1977) and L. Hay-Cooper's *Josephine Butler and Her Work for Social Purity* (London: SPCK, 1922) aimed to recover her memory for two different generations; two other narratives are Enid Moberly Bell, *Josephine Butler: Flame of Fire* (London: Constable, 1962), and A. S. G. Butler, *Portrait of Josephine Butler* (London: Faber and Faber, 1954).   Millicent G. Fawcett and Emily Mary Turner's *Josephine Butler: Her Work and Principles, and Their Meaning for the Twentieth Century* (London: Association for Moral and Social Hygiene, 1927) celebrated the centenary of her birth, as did Fawcett's "Josephine Butler," *Contemporary Review* 133 (1928): 442-46.

Useful but brief explorations in anthologies are Alison Mil-
bank, "Josephine Butler: Christianity, Feminism and Social
Action," in *Disciplines of Faith*, pp. 154-64; Pat Thane, "Josephine Butler," in *Founders of the Welfare State*, ed. Paul Barker (London: Heinemann, 1984), pp. 17-23; and Brian Harrison, "Josephine Butler," in *Eminently Victorian*, ed. John F.
C. Harrison, et al. (London: BBC, 1974), pp. 85-94. See also
V. M. Crawford, "Josephine Butler 1828-1906," *Month* 151
(1928): 311-16 and Anna Garlin Spencer, "Josephine Butler
and the English Crusade," *Forum* 49 (1913): 703-16; 50
(1913): 77-81, for older analyses.

842   *Mary Carpenter (1807-77)*
Carpenter's Unitarian family background gave her a strong
sense of religious vocation, which she exercised in the establishment of schools for poor children and an interest in prison
reform; the only extended study is Jo Manton's *Mary Carpenter and the Children of the Streets* (London: Heinemann,
1976). For other investigations of her activities, see Ruby J.
Saywell, *Mary Carpenter of Bristol* (Bristol: Historical Asso.,
1964); R. J. W. Selleck, "Mary Carpenter: A Confident and
Contradictory Reformer," *History of Education* 14 (1985):
101-15; N. C. Sargant, "Mary Carpenter of Bristol (1807-
1877) and her Connection with India through Ram Mohan
Roy, K. C. Sen, and the National Indian Association," *India
Church History Review* 12 (1978): 121-33; Margaret May,
"Innocence and Experience: The Evolution of the Concept of
Juvenile Delinquency in the Mid-Nineteenth Century," *Victo-
rian Studies* 17 (1973-74): 7-29; and Harriet Warm Schupf,
"Single Women and Social Reform in Mid-Nineteenth Century
England: The Case of Mary Carpenter," *Victorian Studies* 17
(1973-74): 301-17.

843   *Frances Power Cobbe (1822-1904)*
Cobbe was an essayist and moral philosopher who wrote on
behalf of women's causes and joined the antivivisection
movement near the end of her life; her interest in religious
questions is explored in Carol P. Bauer, "The Role of Religion
in the Creation of a Philosophy of Feminism: The Case of

Frances Power Cobbe," *Anima* 10 (Fall 1983): 59-70. Bauer
has also written two articles with Lawrence Ritt on Cobbe's
pioneering work against wife-beating: "'A Husband Is a Beat-
ing Animal': Frances Power Cobbe Confronts the Wife-Abuse
Problem in Victorian England," *IJWS* 6 (1983): 99-118, and
"Wife Abuse, Late Victorian Feminists and the Legacy of
Frances Power Cobbe," *IJWS* 6 (1983): 195-207. For consideration of Cobbe's activity on the issue of experimentation
with animals, see Richard D. French, *Antivivisection and
Medical Science in Victorian England* (Princeton: Princeton,
1975) and Daniel A. Dombrowski, "The Jesuits and the Zoo-
philists, Again," *Irish Theological Quarterly* 51 (1985): 232-
41.

844   *Cornelia Connelly (1809-79)*
Connelly moved from American Episcopalianism to Roman
Catholicism and from wife and mother to founder of a reli-
gious order for women in England; her life and legacy have
mostly been studied by members of her order. See Caritas
McCarthy's *The Spirituality of Cornelia Connelly: In God, For
God, With God* (Lewiston, NY: Edwin Mellen, 1986) and
"Cornelia and Pierce Connelly: New Perspectives on Their
Early Lives," *Records of the American Catholic Historical
Society of Philadelphia* 72:3-4 (1961): 92-105; Mother Marie
Thérèse, *Cornelia Connelly: A Study in Fidelity* (London:
Burns & Oates, 1963); Juliana Wadham, *The Case of Cornelia
Connelly* (London: Collins, 1956); and *The Life of Cornelia
Connelly, 1809-1879: Foundress of the Society of the Holy
Child Jesus* (London: Longmans, Green, 1922), by a member
of the Society.

845   *Charlotte Despard (1844-1939)*
Best known as an Irish political activist and writer, Despard is
described in her biographies as having engaged in a serious
spiritual quest, which ended with her conversion to Catholicism; see Margaret Mulvihill, *Charlotte Despard: A Biography*
(London: Pandora, 1989) and Andro Linklater, *An Unhusband-
ed Life: Charlotte Despard, Suffragette, Socialist, and Sinn
Feiner* (London: Hutchinson, 1980).

846   *George Eliot (1819-80)*
It would be impossible to list all of the relevant works dealing
with this major Victorian novelist, whose writings often included religious themes and issues; for assistance with the range of
studies on her, see the following reference works, each with
extended annotations: Constance Marie Fulmer, ed., *George
Eliot: A Reference Guide* (Boston: G. K. Hill, 1977) and
George Levine, ed., *An Annotated Critical Bibliography of
George Eliot* (Brighton: Harvester, 1988). Gordon S. Haight's
George Eliot: A Biography (Oxford: Oxford, 1968) is a comprehensive study giving significant attention to her religious
views and development; and Valerie Dodd's *George Eliot: An
Intellectual Life* (Basingstoke: Macmillan, 1990) is a careful
exploration of her thought. Jennifer Uglow's *George Eliot*
(New York: Pantheon, 1987) is a biographical and literary
investigation of the mission of a woman writer. The influence
of the young Mary Ann Evans's interest in millennial prophecy
on the later novels is studied in Mary Wilson Carpenter,
*George Eliot and the Landscape of Time: Narrative Form and
Protestant Apocalyptic History* (Chapel Hill: North Carolina,
1986). Some suggestive articles on the subject of religion in
Eliot's work include Elaine J. Lawless, "The Silencing of the
Preacher Woman: The Muted Message of George Eliot's
Adam Bede," *Women's Studies* 18 (1990): 249-68; Katherine
M. Sorenson, "Evangelical Doctrine and George Eliot's Narra-
tor in *Middlemarch*," *Victorian Newsletter* 74 (Fall 1988): 18-
26; and Kathleen Watson, "Dinah Morris and Mrs. Evans: A
Comparative Study of Methodist Diction," *Review of English
Studies* n.s. 22 (1971): 282-94. One recent dissertation is
Kimberly V. Adams, "Gender, Religion, and George Eliot's
Narratives of Development" (Ph.D., Harvard, 1989).

847   *Millicent Garrett Fawcett (1847-1929)*
Fawcett was a leader in the suffrage cause and active in nearly
every aspect of the women's movement at the turn of the
century; two biographical studies are David Rubinstein, *A
Different World for Women: The Life of Millicent Garrett
Fawcett* (London: Harvester Wheatsheaf, 1991) and Ray Strachey, *Millicent Garrett Fawcett* (London: J. Murray, 1931).

848   *Elizabeth Gaskell (1810-65)*
       A Unitarian from the north of England, Gaskell's novels pres-
       ent a picture of Dissent and stress the importance of family
       and the centrality of religion. Reference works include Jeffrey
       Welch, ed., *Elizabeth Gaskell: An Annotated Bibliography,*
       1929-1975 (New York: Garland, 1977) and Robert L. Selig,
       ed., *Elizabeth Gaskell: A Reference Guide* (Boston: G. K.
       Hall, 1977); each contains extensive annotations.   Recent
       analyses include Patsy Stoneman, *Elizabeth Gaskell* (Blooming-
       ton: Indiana, 1987); Tessa Brodetsky, *Elizabeth Gaskell*
       (Leamington Spa: Berg, 1986); Coral Lansbury's *Elizabeth*
       Gaskell (Boston: Twayne, 1984) and *Elizabeth Gaskell: The*
       Novel of Social Crisis (London: Paul Elek, 1975); Monica
       Correa Fryckstedt, *Elizabeth Gaskell's Mary Barton and Ruth:*
       A Challenge to Christian England (Stockholm: Almqvist and
       Wiksell, 1982); Enid L. Duthie, *The Themes of Elizabeth*
       Gaskell (Totowa, NJ: Rowman and Littlefield, 1980); Angus
       Easson, *Elizabeth Gaskell* (London: Routledge & Kegan Paul,
       1979); Winifred Gerin, *Elizabeth Gaskell: A Biography* (Ox-
       ford: Clarendon, 1976); and W. A. Craik, *Elizabeth Gaskell*
       and the English Provincial Novel (London: Methuen, 1975).
       Joanne Thompson's "Faith of Our Mothers: Elizabeth Gas-
       kell's 'Lizzie Leigh'," *Victorian Newsletter* 78 (Fall 1990): 22-
       26, shows how Gaskell presents the mother as the interpreter
       of God's will, reversing Milton's famous line.

849   *Beatrice Hankey (1858-1933)*
       The life of this little-known temperance worker is explored in
       Charles E. Raven and Rachel F. Heath, *One Called Help: The*
       Life and Work of Beatrice Hankey (London: Hodder and
       Stoughton, 1937).

850   *Octavia Hill (1838-1912)*
       Hill's life revolved around religion, charitable work, and
       education; her major program involved the rehabilitation of the
       poor through settlement in rehabilitated housing, and another
       interest led to the formation of the National Trust, as a way of
       preserving large tracts of land for the people. Gillian Darley's
       Octavia Hill: A Life (London: Constable, 1990) is a full-scale

study, the first in some decades; older works include William Thomson Hill's *Octavia Hill: Pioneer of the National Trust and Housing Reformer* (London: Hutchinson, 1956) and E. Moberly Bell's *Octavia Hill: A Biography* (London: Constable, 1942). The works edited by C. Edmund Maurice, *Life of Octavia Hill, As Told in Her Letters* (London: Macmillan, 1913) and Emily S. Maurice, *Octavia Hill: Early Ideals* (London: Allen & Unwin, 1928) are actually companion pieces of material toward a biography by her brother-in-law and sister. Relevant articles are Alan S. Watts, "Octavia Hill and the Influence of Dickens," *History Today* 24 (May 1974): 348-53, and Anthony S. Wohl, "Octavia Hill and *Homes of the London Poor*," *JBS* 10:2 (1970-71): 105-31, who concludes "that her efforts touched only a handful and that her overall effect was as harmful as it was beneficial" (130).

851   *Eliza Lynn Linton (1822-98)*
Novelist, journalist, and vigorous antifeminist, Linton's religious journey went from Christian zeal to rejection of orthodox Christianity to agnosticism, with a brief period in spiritualism. Nancy Fix Anderson's *Woman Against Woman in Victorian England: A Life of Eliza Lynn Linton* (Bloomington: Indiana, 1987) is a psychological study; her article, "Autobiographical Fantasies of a Female Anti-Feminist: Eliza Lynn Linton as Christopher Kirkland and Theodora Desanges," *Dickens Studies Annual* 14 (1985): 287-301, contends that her rejection of Christianity supports her identification with maleness, for she considered the doctrines of Christianity essentially feminine. Herbert Van Thal's *Eliza Lynn Linton: The Girl of the Period* (London: Allen & Unwin, 1979) focuses on her novels and correspondence. George Somes Layard was her literary executor; his *Mrs. Lynn Linton: Her Life, Letters, and Opinions* (London: Methuen, 1901) includes discussion of the major developments in her religious views, albeit somewhat defensively.

852   *Harriet Martineau (1802-76)*
Martineau moved from childhood Unitarianism to philosophy and freethought; she wrote widely on issues related to women

as well as on a range of other subjects. Recent intellectual biographies include Gillian Thomas, *Harriet Martineau* (Boston: Twayne, 1985) and Valerie Kossew Pichanick, *Harriet Martineau: The Woman and Her Work, 1802-76* (Ann Arbor: Michigan, 1981); the latter's article, "An Abominable Submission: Harriet Martineau's Views on the Role and Place of Women," *Woman's Studies* 5 (1977): 13-32, addresses the range of her feminist interests and her limited influence during her lifetime. Another recent study is Valerie Sanders, *Reason over Passion: Harriet Martineau and the Victorian Novel* (Sussex: Harvester, 1986). Robert K. Webb's *Harriet Martineau, A Radical Victorian* (London: Heinemann, 1960) is a substantial biography set against the background of Victorian radicalism; Vera Wheatley's *The Life and Work of Harriet Martineau* (London: William Clowes, 1957) makes much use of her autobiography and unpublished letters. Older and not entirely reliable works include John Cranstoun Nevill's *Harriet Martineau* (London: F. Muller, 1943) and Theodora Bosanquet's *Harriet Martineau: An Essay in Comprehension* (London: Etchells & Macdonald, 1927). Mitzi Myers considers her theological reflections in "Harriet Martineau's *Autobiography*: The Making of a Female Philosopher," in *Women's Autobiography: Essays in Criticism*, pp. 53-70; Betty Fladeland's larger study of antislavery advocates, *Abolitionists and Working-Class Problems in the Age of Industrialization* (Baton Rouge: LSU, 1984), includes a chapter on Martineau's involvement in this issue (pp. 74-92); and Janet Courtney's *Freethinkers of the Nineteenth Century* (London: Chapman & Hall, 1920) discusses Martineau's religious and philosophical ideas as one of seven examples (pp. 198-239).

853   *Florence Nightingale (1820-1910)*
       Best known for her work in establishing nursing as a profession, Nightingale's interests and activities were broad and far-reaching; she also had pronounced views on religious themes and questions. The reference work compiled by W. J. Bishop and Sue Goldie, *A Bio-bibliography of Florence Nightingale* (London: Dawsons of Pall Mall, 1962), contains a complete annotated list of her writings and a list of works about her

from 1854 to 1962. Edward T. Cook's two-volume *Life of Florence Nightingale* (London: Macmillan, 1913) was the first substantial and the official biography; Cecil Woodham-Smith's *Florence Nightingale, 1820-1910* (London: Constable, 1950) sought for a broader picture than Cook, but is less probing on her religious thought. Some other biographies include Elspeth Huxley, *Florence Nightingale* (London: Weidenfeld and Nicolson, 1975); Margaret L. Goldsmith, *Florence Nightingale: The Woman and the Legend* (London: Hodder and Stoughton, 1937); Rosalind Nash, *A Sketch of the Life of Florence Nightingale* (London: SPCK, 1937); and I. B. O'Malley, *Florence Nightingale, 1820-1856: A Study of Her Life Down to the End of the Crimean War* (London: Butterworth, 1931). A contentious study, F. B. Smith's *Florence Nightingale: Reputation and Power* (New York: St. Martin's, 1982) focuses on her public life (c. 1850s-1870s) and portrays her as caught up in a power game and possessing an unrelenting drive to dominate and control.

Several recent articles explore aspects of her religious life and thought, including George P. Landow, "Aggressive (Re)-interpretations of the Female Sage: Florence Nightingale's *Cassandra*," in *Victorian Sages and Cultural Discourse*, pp. 32-45; Elaine Showalter, "Florence Nightingale's Feminist Complaint: Women, Religion, and *Suggestions for Thought*," *Signs* 6 (1981): 395-412; and JoAnn G. Widerquist's "The Spirituality of Florence Nightingale," *Nursing Research* 41 (1992): 49-58, and "Florence Nightingale's Calling," *Second Opinion* 17:3 (January 1992): 108-21. A volume edited by Vern Bullough, et al., *Florence Nightingale and Her Era: A Collection of New Scholarship* (New York: Garland, 1990), contains two papers relevant to the larger topic: Mary P. Tarbox, "A Fierce Tenderness: Florence Nightingale Encounters the Sisters of Mercy," pp. 274-87; and JoAnn G. Widerquist, "Dearest Rev'd Mother," pp. 288-308. For somewhat wider analyses, see Evelyn L. Pugh, "Florence Nightingale and J. S. Mill Debate Women's Rights," *JBS* 21 (Spring 1982): 118-38, and Donald R. Allen, "Florence Nightingale: Toward a Psychohistorical Interpretation," *Journal of Interdisciplinary History* 6 (1975): 23-45.

Some older materials that take up Nightingale's religious thought or interests include Richard Rees's "Florence Nightingale's Philosophy," in *For Love or Money: Studies in Personality and Essence* (London: Secker & Warburg, 1960), pp. 23-57, and "Two Women Mystics," *Twentieth Century* 164 (August 1958): 101-12, citing affinities with Simone Weil; J. C. Mantripp, "Florence Nightingale and Religion," *London Quarterly and Holborn Review* 157 (1932): 318-25; Litton Strachey, *Eminent Victorians* (1918; Harmondsworth: Penguin, 1971), pp. 111-61; Shane Leslie, "Forgotten Passages in the Life of Florence Nightingale," *Dublin Review* 161 (1917): 179-98; and Wm. G. Tarrant, *Florence Nightingale as a Religious Thinker* (London: British & Foreign Unitarian Association, [1914]), which, despite being a tract, is a serious analysis.

854   *Phoebe Palmer (1807-74)*
Recent studies of this American Methodist evangelist give some attention to her four-year ministry in England; see Harold E. Raser, *Phoebe Palmer: Her Life and Thought* (Lewiston, NY: Edwin Mellen, 1987) and Charles Edward White, *The Beauty of Holiness: Phoebe Palmer as Theologian, Revivalist, Feminist, and Humanitarian* (Grand Rapids: Zondervan, 1986).

855   *Jessie Penn-Lewis (1861-1927)*
A limited study of this Welsh evangelist, compiled from diaries and notes, is Mary N. Garrard, *Mrs. Penn-Lewis: A Memoir* (London: Overcomer Book Room, 1931).

856   *Maude Petre (1863-1942)*
From a distinguished Roman Catholic family, Petre became a member of a religious order but eventually left it and became identified with the Catholic Modernists, especially through her association with one of its leading figures, George Tyrrell; her works exploring aspects of Catholic Modernism are important historical and theological studies in her time. Two recent intellectual biographies are Ellen Leonard's *Unresting Transformation: The Theology and Spirituality of Maude Petre* (Lanham, MD: University Press of America, 1991) and Clyde F.

Crews's *English Catholic Modernism: Maude Petre's Way of Faith* (Notre Dame: Notre Dame, 1984); the latter's article, "Maude Petre's Modernism," *America* 144:19 (May 16, 1981): 403-406, addresses the question of the church's relation to modern culture. Other essays include Charles J. Healy, "Maude Petre: Her Life and Significance," *Recusant History* 15 (1979-81): 23-42; Robert Hamilton, "Faith and Knowledge: The Autobiography of Maude Petre," *Downside Review* 85 (1967): 148-59; and James A. Walker, "Maude Petre (1863-1942): A Memorial Tribute," *Hibbert Journal* 41 (1942-43): 340-46.

857   *Christina Rossetti (1830-94)*
Attention to Rossetti's poetry has increased as her place in the literature of the period has been reassessed and as scholars have been more willing to take up the religious ground of her work and see her as an important representative of the aesthetic of the Tractarian movement. Two reference works are R. W. Crump, ed., *Christina Rossetti: A Reference Guide* (Boston: G. K. Hall, 1976) and Nilda Jiménez, comp., *The Bible and the Poetry of Christine Rossetti: A Concordance* (Westport, CT: Greenwood, 1979). The process of reassessment is seen in the following recent studies: Kathleen Jones, *Learning not to be First: The Life of Christina Rossetti* (Gloucestershire: Windrush, 1991); Katherine J. Mayberry, *Christina Rossetti and the Poetry of Discovery* (Baton Rouge: Louisiana State, 1989); Anthony W. Harrison, *Christina Rossetti in Context* (Chapel Hill: North Carolina, 1988); David A. Kent, ed., *The Achievement of Christina Rossetti* (Ithaca: Cornell, 1988), several essays of which address religious themes in her work; and Edna Kotin Charles, *Christina Rossetti: Critical Perspectives, 1862-1982* (London: Associated University Presses, 1985). Dolores Rosenblum's *Christina Rossetti: The Poetry of Endurance* (Carbondale: Southern Illinois, 1986) and "Christina Rossetti: The Inward Pose," in *Shakespeare's Sisters*, pp. 82-98, explore the construction of an aesthetic of renunciation in her work. Georgina Battiscombe's *Christina Rossetti: A Divided Life* (London: Constable, 1981) is a biography, while Ralph A. Bellas's *Christina Rossetti* (Boston: Twayne, 1977)

studies her prose and poetry and sees her work as "nourishing
hope in an age of weakening faith" (117). A recent compara-
tive study is Mary E. Finn, *Writing the Incommensurable:
Kierkegaard, Rossetti, and Hopkins* (University Park, PA:
Pennsylvania State, 1992); and a recent dissertation is Virginia
G. Sickbert, "Dissident Voices in Christina Rossetti's Poetry,"
(Ph.D., SUNY at Stony Brook, 1990).

Articles that address religious themes in Rossetti's writings
include Joel Westerholm, "'I Magnify Mine Office': Christina
Rossetti's Authoritative Voice in her Devotional Prose," *Victo-
rian Newsletter* 84 (Fall 1993): 11-17; Janet Galligani Casey,
"The Potential of Sisterhood: Christina Rossetti's *Goblin Mar-
ket*," *Victorian Poetry* 29 (1991): 63-78; Antony H. Harrison,
"Christina Rossetti and the Sage Discourse of Feminist High
Anglicanism," in *Victorian Sages and Cultural Discourse*, pp.
87-104; Diane D'Amico, "Christina Rossetti's *Christian Year*:
Comfort for 'the weary heart'," *Victorian Newsletter* 72 (Fall
1987): 36-42; Linda E. Marshall, "What the Dead Are Doing
Underground: Hades and Heaven in the Writings of Christina
Rossetti," *ibid.*: 55-60; and Jerome McGann's "The Religious
Poetry of Christina Rossetti," *Critical Inquiry* 10 (1983): 127-
44, and "Christina Rossetti's Poems: A New Edition and a
Revaluation," *Victorian Studies* 23 (1979-80): 237-54.

858   *Olive Schreiner (1855-1920)*
        Schreiner's best known novel is *The Story of an African Farm*
        (1883), which reflects her sense of the moral crises of her time
        involving race and gender.   Joyce Avrech Berkman's two
        studies, *The Healing Imagination of Olive Schreiner: Beyond
        South African Colonialism* (Amherst: Massachusetts, 1989) and
        Olive Schreiner: Feminism on the Frontier (Montreal: Eden,
        1979), explore her many efforts to deal with these; in the latter
        she claims that "though she jettisoned Christian theology, she
        retained much of the ethics of a Christian missionary family
        throughout her life" (49). Biographies include Ruth First and
        Ann Scott, *Olive Schreiner* (London: A. Deutsch, 1980); D.
        L. Hobman, *Olive Schreiner* (London: Watts, 1955); and S. C.
        Cronwright Schreiner, *The Life of Olive Schreiner* (1924; New
        York: Haskell House, 1973).   Liz Stanley's *Feminism and*

Friendship: Two Essays on Olive Schreiner (Manchester: Manchester, 1985) investigates the networks of friendships among feminists in this period and offers a critique of her husband's biography. Marion V. Friedmann's *Olive Schreiner: A Study in Latent Meanings* (Johannesburg: Witwatersrand, 1955) is a brief psychological approach. Reflections on *African Farm* provides an occasion for a review of her life and work in Claudia Roth Pierpont, "A Woman's Place," *New Yorker* (January 27, 1992), pp. 69-83.

859   *Priscilla Lydia Sellon (1821-76)*
       Sellon founded the Anglican Sisters of Mercy in 1848 and was important in the effort to establish sisterhoods in the Church of England; her story and the history of her community are told in Thomas Jay Williams, *Priscilla Lydia Sellon: The Restorer after Three Centuries of the Religious Life in the English Church* (1950; London: SPCK, 1965). Sean Gill's "The Power of Christian Ladyhood: Priscilla Lydia Sellon and the Creation of Anglican Sisterhoods," in *Modern Religious Rebels*, ed. Stuart Mews (London: Epworth, 1993), pp. 144-65, is an effort at reassessment, identifying some of the contradictions in her person and work.

860   *Hannah Whitall Smith (1832-1911)*
       The wife of an American holiness evangelist who became well known in her own right, Smith was prominent in the Brighton/Keswick conventions in the last quarter of the century; her granddaughter, Ray Strachey, wrote *Quaker Grandmother, Hannah Whitall Smith* (New York: Fleming H. Revell, 1914) and edited *Religious Fanaticism: Extracts from the Papers of Hannah Whitall Smith* (London: Faber & Gwyer, 1928). A recent dissertation is Roberta J. Stewart, "'Being a Child in the Father's House': The Life of Faith in the Published Works of Hannah Whitall Smith" (Ph.D., Drew, 1990).

861   *Mary E. Sumner (1828-1921)*
       The founder of the Anglican organization called the Mothers' Union, Sumner has received only limited attention, most of that from the society. An enthusiastic narrative published soon

after her death is Mary Porter and Mary Woodward, *Mary Sumner: Her Life and Work* (Winchester: Warren & Son, 1921), which includes a memoir of her life and a short history of the Mothers' Union; the biographical part by Mary Porter has appeared under the same title in several editions. Joyce Coombs's *George and Mary Sumner, Their Life and Times* (London: Sumner, 1965) is a family history, but offers insights into Sumner's work. Two institutional histories provide a wider look at her legacy: Olive Parker, *For the Family's Sake: A History of the Mothers' Union, 1876-1976* (Folkstone: Bailey and Swinfen, 1975); and Violet B. Lancaster, *A Short History of the Mothers' Union* (London: Mothers' Union, 1958).

862   *Mary Augusta (Mrs. Humphry) Ward (1851-1920)*
Author of the greatest religious cause célèbre in late Victorian England, *Robert Elsmere*, Ward's life and works can be studied for the perspective they offer on the struggles of religious faith at the end of the century. John Sutherland's *Mrs. Humphry Ward: Eminent Victorian, Pre-eminent Edwardian* (Oxford: Clarendon, 1990) is a critical biography, with attention to her own changing religious views. Esther M. G. Smith's *Mrs. Humphry Ward* (Boston: Twayne, 1980) provides an introduction to her novels. Other studies include William S. Peterson, *Victorian Heretic: Mrs. Humphry Ward's "Robert Elsmere"* (Leicester: Leicester, 1976); Enid Huws Jones, *Mrs. Humphry Ward* (London: Heinemann, 1973); and Janet Penrose Trevelyan, *The Life of Mrs. Humphry Ward* (London: Constable, 1923), a "life and letters" by her daughter.

863   *Charlotte Yonge (1823-1901)*
Yonge's novels and editing of magazines embodied the spirit of the Oxford Movement and contributed much to its popularity in the second half of the century; interest in her has revived with the interest in the writings of women. Her importance to the spread of the Oxford Movement is explored in Barbara Dennis, *Charlotte Yonge (1823-1901), Novelist of the Oxford Movement* (Lewiston, NY: Edwin Mellen, 1992); an earlier article, "The Two Voices of Charlotte Yonge," *Durham*

University Journal 65 (1972-73): 181-88, studies the tensions with her culture, especially her inability to deal with religious doubt.   Studies of her novels include Catherine Sandbach-Dahlstrom, *Be Good Sweet Maid. Charlotte Yonge's Fiction: A Study in Dogmatic Purpose and Fictional Form* (Stockholm: Almqvist & Wiksell, 1984); two dissertations: Barbara Mason, "Charlotte Mary Yonge's View of the Proper Roles for Women in the Nineteenth Century" (Ph.D., Indiana, 1984), and Virginia Thompson Bemis, "The Novels of Charlotte Yonge: A Critical Introduction" (Ph.D., Michigan State, 1980); and a collection of papers edited by Georgina Battiscombe and Marghanita Laski, *A Chaplet for Charlotte Yonge* (London: Cresset, 1965).   Biographical studies are offered by Georgina Battiscombe, *Charlotte Mary Yonge: The Story of an Uneventful Life* (London: Constable, 1943); Margaret Mare and Alicia C. Percival, *Victorian Best-Seller: The World of Charlotte M. Yonge* (London: Harrap, 1948); Ethel Romanes, *Charlotte Mary Yonge: An Appreciation* (London: Mowbray, 1908); and Christabel Coleridge, *Charlotte Mary Yonge: Her Life and Letters* (London: Macmillan, 1903). For relevant articles, see Elliott Engel, "Heir of the Oxford Movement: Charlotte Mary Yonge's *The Heir of Redclyffe*," *Etudes Anglaises* 33 (1980): 132-41; June Sturrock, "A Personal View of Women's Education 1838-1900: Charlotte Yonge's Novels," *Victorians Institute Journal* 7 (1979): 7-18; David Brownell, "The Two Worlds of Charlotte Yonge," in *The Worlds of Victorian Fiction*, pp. 165-78; S. Addleshaw, "The High Church Movement in Victorian Fiction: Charlotte M. Yonge," *Church Quarterly Review* 120 (1935): 54-73; and Sarah Bailey, "Charlotte Mary Yonge," *Cornhill Magazine* 150 (1934): 188-98.

Others

864   Balfour, Lady Frances. *Lady Victoria Campbell: A Memoir.*
       London: Hodder and Stoughton, 1912. Pp. 364.
       Covers the religious and charitable interests of this Scottish Presbyterian (1854-1910), but tends to hagiography.

865   Notestein, Wallace. "Lucy Lyttleton (Lady Frederick Caven-

dish)," in *English Folk*, pp. 23-50.
Deals with the important role of religion in her life (1841-
1925).

866   Lee, Amice. *Laurels and Rosemary. The Life of William and
       Mary Howitt*. London: Oxford, 1955. Pp. 350.
       Woodring, Carl R.   *Victorian Samplers: William and Mary
       Howitt*. Lawrence: Kansas, 1952. Pp. 252.
       Authors of more than 180 books on a number of subjects, the
       Howitts (1792-1879 and 1799-1888, respectively) engaged in a
       remarkable religious pilgrimage, from identification with the
       Quakers to Unitarianism to spiritualism and, finally (in Mary's
       case), Roman Catholicism.

867   Stocks, Mary D. *Eleanor Rathbone. A Biography*. London:
       V. Gollancz, 1949. Pp. 376.
       A suffrage activist, Rathbone (1872-1946) came from a long-
       standing Unitarian family from Liverpool.

868   Oldfield, Sybil. *Spinsters of This Parish: The Life and Times
       of F. M. Mayor and Mary Sheepshanks*. London: Virago,
       1984. Pp. 328.
       A story of contrasting lives, one of action and one of contem-
       plation, but each focused on the theme of fellowship and rec-
       onciliation; both were daughters of Anglican clerics.

869   Bruce, Mary Louisa. *Anna Swanwick*. London: T. Fisher
       Unwin, 1903. Pp. 263.
       A Unitarian, Swanwick (1813-99) was a translator and an
       active supporter of women's education and suffrage.

870   Mackerness, E. D. "Frances Parthenope, Lady Verney (1819-
       1890)," *Journal of Modern History* 30 (1958): 131-36.
       A defense of the literary contributions of Florence Nightin-
       gale's elder sister, with some discussion of her religious
       views.

CHAPTER 6

1914 TO THE PRESENT: RETRENCHMENT, SECULARIZATION, AND WOMEN'S MINISTRIES

Bibliographies and Guides

871   Evans, Mary and Morgan, David, eds. *Work on Women: A Guide to the Literature.* London: Tavistock, 1979. Pp. 83.
Organized by institutional structures that directly affect the pattern of women's lives; helpful for the context outside of religion.

872   *Women in Scotland: An Annotated Bibliography.* Edinburgh: Open University in Scotland, 1988. Pp. 65.
Broad coverage, but only limited sections on religion and on missions.

873   Bridges, Hugh, comp. *Feminist Theology and Women Priests. An Introduction and Annotated Bibliography.* Dublin: SCM, 1977. Pp. 82.
A contemporary focus, with references to relevant groups and periodicals.

874   Mitchell, Carol. "The 20th Century Witch in England and the United States: An Annotated Bibliography," *Bulletin of Bibliography* 39 (1982): 69-83.
More on the U.S. than on England; the bulk of studies deal with beliefs rather than with the persons involved.

875   Banks, Olive. *The Biographical Dictionary of British Femi-*

nists. Vol. Two: A Supplement, 1900-1945. New York: New York, 1990. Pp. 241.
Some overlap in time with volume one, but here the focus is on persons whose main activities took place in the twentieth century; 74 entries.

876   Lehmann, Stephen and Sartori, Eva, eds. *Women's Studies in Western Europe: A Resource Guide.* Chicago: American Library Asso., 1986. Pp. 129.
See especially Virginia Clark, "The Kern Factor: Women's Publishing in Western Europe," pp. 5-86, and Rita Pankhurst, "Collection Development and Women's Heritage: The Case of the Fawcett Library," pp. 107-23.

877   Cowley, Ruth. *What about Women: Information Sources for Women's Studies.* N.p.: Fanfare, [1984]. Pp. 103.
A directory of organizations and suggestions for developing a resource collection.

878   Cohen, Lesley, ed. *Women's Organisations in Great Britain 1985/86.* London: Women's National Commission, 1985. Pp. 73.
A long but incomplete list, frequently updated.

General Historical Studies

879   Brittain, Vera. *Lady into Woman: A History of Women from Victoria to Elizabeth II.* London: Macmillan, 1953. Pp. 256.
Deals with politics, education, employment, sexual morality, the struggle of married women, and women and war; no special discussion of religion, but it is noted as it is involved with other topics.

880   Lang, Elsie M. *British Women in the Twentieth Century.* London: T. Werner Laurie, 1929. Pp. 284.
On activities, education, the suffrage issue, and professions and careers open to women; some discussion of the debate over ordination of women and the work of the few women ministers by this date.

881   Adam, Ruth. *A Woman's Place, 1910-1975*. London: Chatto and Windus, 1975. Pp. 224.
        A somewhat jaunty social history, with attention to attitudes of churches on matters such as work, sexuality, marriage, and divorce.

882   Cecil, Robert. *Life in Edwardian England*. London: Batsford, 1969. Pp. 211.
        A broad social history; see especially chapter 8, "The State of Morals and the Rights of Women."

883   Crow, Duncan. *The Edwardian Woman*. London: Allen & Unwin, 1978. Pp. 231.
        From the monarchy down, with particular studies intended to provide portraits of the age.

884   Smith, Harold L., ed. *British Feminism in the Twentieth Century*. London: Elgar, 1990. Pp. 214.
        Eleven essays on various dimensions of continuation, decline, and renewal in the feminist movement. Especially useful for background are Susan Kingsley Kent's "Gender Reconstruction after the First World War" and Martin Pugh's "Domesticity and the Decline of Feminism, 1930-1950."

885   Pugh, Martin. *Women and the Women's Movement in Britain, 1914-1959*. Basingstoke: Macmillan, 1992. Pp. 347.
        Covers wars, politics, a new cult of domesticity and the decline of the women's movement, and changing notions of feminism and emancipation.

886   Alberti, Johanna. *Beyond Suffrage: Feminists in War and Peace, 1914-28*. London: Macmillan, 1989. Pp. 249.
        A composite biography of fourteen suffragists, their experiences and activities, as issues expand "beyond suffrage" to include equal pay, birth control, and advocacy of an equal sexual moral standard. Among those included are Maude Royden, Eleanor Rathbone, Evelyn Sharp, Corbett Ashby, and Ray Strachey.

887   Kent, Susan Kingsley.   "The Politics of Sexual Difference:
       World War I and the Demise of British Feminism," *JBS* 27
       (1988): 232-53.
       Considers an important cultural shift and explores the reasons
       why "feminism as a distinct political and social movement no
       longer existed" by 1930 (232).

888   Lewis, Jane.   "Beyond Suffrage: English Feminism in the
       1920s," *Maryland Historian* 6 (1975): 1-17.
       Explores the conflict between equalitarian feminists, who
       supported the principle of equal opportunity, and "new femi-
       nists," who advocated special legislation to address women's
       special needs in order to achieve real equality.

889   Harrison, Brian.   *Prudent Revolutionaries: Portraits of British
       Feminists Between the Wars*.   Oxford: Clarendon, 1987.   Pp.
       362.
       Biographical studies of fourteen inter-war feminists in order to
       present a collective picture of the movement; religion is in the
       background but relevant, as in his conclusion that these leaders
       "drew on deep reserves of patriotism and religion. . . . Like
       so many modern British reforming movements, feminism owed
       much to evangelicalism, and in its early years much also to
       nonconformity" (320).

890   Branson, Noreen.   *Britain in the Nineteen Twenties*.   London:
          Weidenfeld and Nicolson, 1975.   Pp. 274.
       Branson, Noreen and Heinemann, Margot.   *Britain in the
          Nineteen Thirties*.   London: Weidenfeld and Nicolson,
          1971.   Pp. 358.
       Each volume gives major attention to social and economic
       history.

891   Lewis, Jane.   *Women in Britain Since 1945*.   Oxford: Black-
       well, 1992.   Pp. 149.
       Surveys themes of family, sexuality, work, relation to the
       state, and roles in society; includes discussion of changes in
       the Church of England's views of sexuality and divorce.

892   Wilson, Elizabeth. *Only Halfway to Paradise: Women in
        Postwar Britain, 1945-1968*. London: Tavistock, 1980. Pp.
        233.
        A cultural history of the years prior to the emergence of the
        contemporary women's movement.

893   Hastings, Adrian. *A History of English Christianity 1920-
        1990*. London: Collins, 1991. Pp. 720.
        A comprehensive overview, with consideration of the position
        of women in church and society and the issue of women's
        ordination.

Reflections on Women and Society

894   Several approaches to dimensions of social change and their
        implications for women and the larger society, most of these in
        the first half of the century, include:
        Gollancz, Victor, ed. *The Making of Women: Oxford Essays
            in Feminism*. London: Allen & Unwin, 1917. Pp. 217.
        Hartley, Catherine Gasquoine. *Women's Wild Oats: Essays on
            the Refixing of Moral Standards*. London: T. W. Laurie,
            1919. Pp. 256.
        Gates, Evelyn, ed. *The Woman's Year Book, 1923-24*. Lon-
            don: Women Publishers, 1924. Pp. 697.
        Holtby, Winifred. *Women and a Changing Civilisation*. Lon-
            don: Bodley Head, 1934. Pp. 213.
        Goldsmith, Margaret L. *Women and the Future*. London:
            Drummond, 1946. Pp. 137.
        Klein, Viola. *The Feminine Character: History of an Ideolo-
            gy*. New York: International Universities, 1949. Pp. 228.
        Borrowdale, Anne. *A Woman's Work: Changing Christian
            Attitudes*. London: SPCK, 1989. Pp. 104.
        Some recent reflections on vocation and service, from the
        perspective of women's experience.

Works on Women and Religion, 1914-1930

895   In this transitional era, the themes shift from suffrage to an
        articulation of Christian feminism to a consideration of dimen-

sions of women's ministry, including the particular issue of ordination to the priesthood of the Church of England. The following works are listed by year of publication:

Christitch, Elizabeth. "Catholic Women and the Vote," *Franciscan Annals and Tertiary Record* 38 (1914): 129-35.

Catholic Social Guild Pamphlets. 3rd Series, London: Catholic Truth Society, 1914.

Dukes, Edwin J. *Our Sister Phoebe, Deacon of the Church*. London: J. Clarke, 1915. Pp. 63.

Fairfield, Zoe, ed. *Some Aspects of the Women's Movement*. London: SCM, 1915. Pp. 239.

Fletcher, Margaret. *Christian Feminism: A Charter of Rights and Duties*. London: P. S. King, 1915. Pp. 88.

Cohu, J. R. "Should Women 'Speak' in Church?" *Contemporary Review* 110 (1916): 474-81.

Gollock, Minna C. and G. A. *Half Done: Some Thoughts for Women*. London: United Council for Missionary Education, 1916. Pp. 60.

Lee, John. *The Church & Women*. London: Longmans, Green, 1916. Pp. 32.

Pinchard, Arnold. *Women and the Priesthood*. London: Soc. of S.S. Peter & Paul, 1916. Pp. 15.

Royden, Agnes Maude, ed. *Downward Paths: An Inquiry into the Causes Which Contribute to the Making of a Prostitute*. London: Bell, 1916. Pp. 200.

Tuker, M. A. R. "Women Preachers," *Nineteenth Century* 80 (1916): 1267-78.

"The Ministry of Women and the Tradition of the Church," *English Church Review* 7 (1916): 451-56.

Bardsley, Cyril C. B., ed. *Women and Church Work*. London: Longmans, Green, 1917. Pp. 116.

Goudge, H. L., et al. *The Place of Women in the Church*. London: R. Scott, 1917. Pp. 204.

Oldroyd, A. E. "The Place of Women in the Church," *English Church Review* 8 (1917): 399-403.

Sawbridge, Laura Helen. *The Vision and the Mission of Womanhood in the Empire and Beyond*. London: Wells Gardner, Darton, 1917. Pp. 406.

Streeter, B. H. and Picton-Turbervill, Edith. *Woman and the*

Church. London: T. Fisher Unwin, 1917. Pp. 112. [Picton-Turbervill's essays are also published in *Nineteenth Century* 80 (September and November 1916) and as *Should Women Be Priests and Ministers?* (London: Society for the Equal Ministry of Men and Women in the Church, 1953). Pp. 52. Athelstan Riley's "Male and Female Created He Them," *Nineteenth Century* 80 (1916): 836-40, is a critique of this position and is followed by a reply from Picton-Turbervill.]

Cohen, Chapman. *Woman and Christianity.* London: Pioneer, 1919. Pp. 96.

Penn-Lewis, Jessie. *The Magna Charta of Woman.* 1919; Minneapolis: Bethany Fellowship, 1975. Pp. 103.

Picton-Turbervill, Edith. *Christ and Woman's Power.* London: Morgan & Scott, 1919. Pp. 158.

The Ministry of Women. London: SPCK, 1919 (for Lambeth Conference of 1920). Pp. 320.

Hardman, Oscar. *The Anglican Deaconess.* London: SPCK, 1921. Pp. 32.

"Women's Work," in *Proceedings of the Fifth Ecumenical Methodist Conference, 1921.* London: Methodist Publishing House, 1921. Pp. 241-68.

Royden, A. Maude. *Women at the World's Crossroads.* New York: Women's Press, 1922. Pp. 139.

Chilvers, Ethel E. *The Ministry of Women and Their Message of Victory.* London: Stanley Martin, 1923. Pp. 128.

Smith, Charles Ryder. *The Biblical Doctrine of Womanhood in Its Historical Evolution.* London: Epworth, 1923. Pp. 128.

Rodgers, E. "In the Image of God," *Modern Churchman* 13 (1923-24): 242-50.

Wilkinson, J. R. "Women and the Priesthood," *Modern Churchman* 13 (1923-24): 383-92.

C.O.P.E.C. Commission Reports, vol. IV. *The Relation of the Sexes.* London: Longmans, Green, 1924. Pp. 215.

Royden, A. Maude. *The Church and Woman.* London: J. Clarke, 1924. Pp. 255.

Lamps of Hope. London: C.E.Z.M.S., 1925. Pp. 70.

Through Deep Waters: The Story of the Years 1924-25 in the

Work of the Church of England Zenana Missionary Society.
London: C.E.Z.M.S., 1926. Pp. 139.

Allen, R. Wilberforce. "Women and the Church," in *Methodism and Modern World Problems*. London: Methuen, 1926. Pp. 49-58.

Raven, Charles. *Women and Holy Orders*. London: Hodder and Stoughton, 1928. Pp. 128 [American ed., *Women and the Ministry* (Garden City: Doubleday, 1929)].

Smith, Charles Ryder. "The Ministry of Women," in *Methodism: Its Present Responsibilities*. Methodist Church Congress, 1929. London: Epworth, 1929. Pp. 49-56.

Soltau, Irene. *The Free-Woman: Some Inferences from the Thought of Jesus Christ in Relation to the Problems of Personality and Womanhood*. London: SCM, 1929. Pp. 208.

Women and the Church

896   Bacon, F. D. *Women in the Church*. London: Lutterworth, 1946. Pp. 146.
Sweeping coverage from the early church to the present, with more attention to recent developments and issues in the forms of women's ministry; important because of its even tone and serious investigation in its time.

897   Chamberlain, Elsie. "The World in Which We Worship," in *In Her Own Right*, ed. The Six Point Group. London: Harrap, 1968. Pp. 121-32.
One of ten essays on problems facing women fifty years after suffrage; the church is seen as one of the last bastions of male entrenchment.

898   King, Ursula. "The Role of Women in Today's Society: Reflections from a Christian Point of View," *Month* 10 (1977): 268-72.
Compares the situation of women in society with that in the church.

899   Langley, Myrtle. "'The Best Men's Club in the World': Atti-

tudes to Women in the British Churches," in *Religion, State, and Society in Modern Britain*, ed. Paul Badham. Lewiston, NY: Edwin Mellen, 1989. Pp. 293-320.

_____. "Extended Data Sheet on the Position of Women in Church and Society," *Epworth Review* 14:1 (1987): 21-33.

Langley offers contemporary surveys of the situation for women, with statistics and indications of important issues.

900   Nason-Clark, Nancy. "Clerical Attitudes towards Appropriate Roles for Women in Church and Society: An Empirical Investigation of Anglican, Methodist, and Baptist Clergy in Southern England." Ph.D., London School of Economics and Political Science, 1984.

_____. "Ordaining Women as Priests: Religious vs. Sexist Explanations for Clerical Attitudes," *Sociological Analysis* 48 (1987): 259-73.

Nason-Clark discerns clerical attitudes from a survey and personal interviews; the article focuses on Anglicans and concludes that a conservative sex role ideology is more of a determiner of one's position on the question than are scriptural and theological beliefs.

901   Maitland, Sara. *A Map of the New Country: Women and Christianity*. London: Routledge & Kegan Paul, 1983. Pp. 218.

A consideration of the challenges raised for the churches in "the women's issue" by one who identifies herself as an Anglo-Catholic and a feminist.

902   Furlong, Monica, ed. *Feminine in the Church*. London: SPCK, 1984. Pp. 194.

Twelve essays on issues from ordination to inclusive language in the liturgy, growing out of the work of the Movement for the Ordination of Women, established in 1979.

903   Britton, Margaret. *The Single Woman in the Family of God*. London: Epworth, 1982. Pp. 118.

Contends that the church has no theological foundation for the

Christian single life today; the model of the church as a family, for example, can distort the place of the single person in the church, Britton contends.

904   Lees, Shirley, ed. *The Role of Women*. Leicester: Inter-Varsity, 1984. Pp. 224.
        Keay, Kathy, ed. *Men, Women and God*. Basingstoke: Marshall Pickering, 1987. Pp. 304.
        Storkey, Elaine. "The Future for Women," in *In Search of Christianity*, ed. Tony Moss. London: Firethorn, 1986. Pp. 220-31.
        These works take the issue from the difference of views among evangelical Christians, that is, those committed to submit to Scripture as their guide on matters of faith and practice.

905   Holloway, Richard, ed. *Who Needs Feminism? Male Responses to Sexism in the Church*. London: SPCK, 1991. Pp. 164.
        Several essays offer additional perspectives in the conversation.

Ministries of Women

906   Bliss, Kathleen. *The Service and Status of Women in the Churches*. London: SCM, 1952. Pp. 208.
        The author was Secretary of the Board of Education in the Church of England from 1958 to 1966; this important benchmark book presented data gleaned from a World Council of Churches inquiry to more than fifty countries, and the British material is interwoven with that from other countries. The conclusion points to several issues needing further attention: how to enlarge the services that women could perform, how to attend to growing frustration among some at the reluctance to make "the modern woman" a Christian type of womanhood, and how to encourage Christians to give thought to the present place of women in society.

907   Thomson, D. P., ed. *Women in the Pulpit: Sermons and Addresses by Representative Women Preachers*. London: J.

Clarke, 1944. Pp. 192.
Thomson calls this "the first representative collection of sermons by women preachers to be issued in this country" (xi);
there are twenty-three selections.

908   *Women in the Church.* London: Society for the Ministry of
       Women in the Church, n.d. Unpag.
       Short articles, together with an essay by K. M. Baxter on "The
       Case for the Ordination of Women to the Priesthood."

909   *The Place of Women in the Church.* Edinburgh: Saint An-
       drew, 1959. Pp. 40.
       Thomson, D. P., ed. *Women Ministers in Scotland: Personal
       Records of Experience and Discovery.* Crieff: St. Ninian's,
       1965. Pp. 16.
       The first is a Church of Scotland study document, chiefly on
       the question of ordination, with a narrative of events relating
       to this issue from 1929-58; the second is a short tract on the
       issue of ordination of women in the Church of Scotland raised
       in 1963, containing statements from women ministers in two
       other Scottish churches.

910   Lehman, Edward C. *Women Clergy in England: Sexism,
       Modern Consciousness, and Church Viability.* Lewiston, NY:
       Edwin Mellen, 1987. Pp. 210.
       The report of a survey of attitudes to women in ministry on
       the part of lay members in four Protestant denominations:
       Anglican, Baptist, Methodist, and United Reformed.

911   Matthews, Ruth. "On Ministry and Ordination," in *The Expe-
       rience of Ordination,* ed. Kenneth Wilson. London: Epworth,
       1979. Pp. 127-47.
       Reflections of a Baptist minister.

912   Jarvis, Peter. "Men and Women Ministers of Religion,"
       Modern Churchman n.s. 22 (1979): 149-58.
       The report of a 1974 survey of Baptist, Methodist, and United
       Reformed ministers; Jarvis suggests that the Anglican Church
       has little to fear from ordaining women, since those entering

the priesthood would likely be of similar social and educational background and exhibit a similar range of attitudes as the men.

913   "Women in the Church," *St. Mark's Review* 104 (Dec. 1980): 1-53.
       Eight articles, chiefly from an Australian perspective; articles connecting the theme to English history are Margaret Rodgers, "Deaconesses and the Diaconate," pp. 38-47, and Doug Clark, "Female Ministry in the Salvation Army," pp. 48-53.

914   Tanner, Mary. "The Ministry of Women: An Anglican Reflection," *One in Christ* 21 (1985): 284-93.
       Reflections on the development of women's ministries in the Church of England since 1840 are built on a consideration of the nature of ministry and the nature of men and women created in God's image.

915   Matchett, Freda. "The Ministry of Women," in *Strategist for the Spirit: Leslie Hunter, Bishop of Sheffield, 1939-1962*, ed. Gordon Hewitt. Oxford: Becket, 1985. Pp. 184-94.
       Describes the structure of pastoral and missionary deployment developed by Hunter, which had places for women within it.

916   Dunkley, Sylvia. "Women Magistrates, Ministers, and Municipal Councillors in the West Riding of Yorkshire, 1918-1939." Ph.D., Sheffield, 1991.
       Within a larger study of professional roles, see chaps. 6 and 7 for a discussion of women ministers.

917   Oldham, J. H. *Florence Allshorn and the Story of St. Julian's*. New York: Harper and Row, 1951. Pp. 168.
       Brown, Eleanor. "The Legacy of Florence Allshorn," *International Bulletin of Missionary Research* 8 (1984): 24-28.
       Allshorn (1897-1950) was a missionary, trainer of missionaries, and organizer of a religious community of women.

918   Robbins, Keith. "Church and Politics: Dorothy Buxton and the German Church Struggle," in *Church Society and Politics* (SCH 12), ed. Derek Baker. Oxford: Blackwell, 1975. Pp.

419-33.
From 1933-39 Buxton worked to make the condition of the
Confessing Church in Germany better known to an English
audience.

919   Ridler, Anne. *Olive Willis and Downe House: An Adventure
        in Education.* London: J. Murray, 1967. Pp. 205.
        Willis (1877-1964) established a school for girls; Ridler ob-
        serves that "religion was at the root of all that Olive taught"
        (62).

920   Arnold, Dorothy M. *Dorothy Kerin—Called by Christ to
        Heal.* London: Hodder and Stoughton, 1965. Pp. 235.
        Kerin (1889-1963) engaged in a ministry of healing.

921   For autobiographical reflections on involvements in church and
        ministry, see:
        Canham, Elizabeth. *Pilgrimage to Priesthood.* London:
            SPCK, 1983. Pp. 113.
        Essex, Rosamund. *Woman in a Man's World.* London: Shel-
            don, 1977. Pp. 178.
        Kroll, Una. *Flesh of My Flesh.* London: Darton, Longman &
            Todd, 1977. Pp. 112.
        _____. "Beyond the Issue of Ordination," *Ecumenical
            Review* 40 (1988): 57-65.
        Higson, Jessie E. *The Story of a Beginning: An Account of
            Pioneer Work for Moral Welfare.* London: SPCK, 1965.
            Pp. 168.

Women and Spirituality

922   Garcia, Jo and Maitland, Sara, eds. *Walking on the Water:
            Women Talk about Spirituality.* London: Virago, 1983.
            Pp. 214.
        Hurcombe, Linda, ed. *Sex and God: Some Varieties of Wom-
            en's Religious Experience.* London: Routledge & Kegan
            Paul, 1987. Pp. 296.
        These volumes of essays connect feminist perspectives to
        issues of religious faith.

923   Byrne, Lavinia. *Women Before God*. London: SPCK, 1988.
        Pp. 111.
        _____, ed. *The Hidden Tradition: Women's Spiritual Writings Rediscovered*. London: SPCK, 1991. Pp. 198.
        Byrne explores how the distinctive experience of women's development can shape their spirituality; the second volume contains brief selections on various topics.

924   King, Ursula. *Women and Spirituality: Voices of Protest and Promise*. London: Macmillan, 1989. Pp. 273.
        A cross-cultural and interreligious analysis of a broad sweep of literature.

925   Rees, Bridget. "Wandering in the Wilderness: A Feminist Reflects on Education in Spirituality," in *Can Spirituality Be Taught?*, ed. Jill Robson and David Lonsdale. London: ACATE, 1987. Pp. 51-60.
        Michael, Christine. "The Religious Experience of Women," *MC* n.s. 33:3 (1991): 28-34.
        These two essays explore difficulties and possibilities in women's religious experience.

Construction of a Feminist Theology

926   Dowell, Susan and Hurcombe, Linda. *Dispossessed Daughters of Eve: Faith and Feminism*. London: SCM, 1981. Pp. 148.
        Langley, Myrtle. *Equal Woman: A Christian Feminist Perspective*. Basingstoke: Marshalls, 1983. Pp. 191.
        These early ventures are mainly interested in establishing the possibility of a Christian feminism, amid the split between religious opposition to feminism and a secular feminism alienated from institutional religion.

927   Hebblethwaite, Margaret. *Motherhood and God*. London: Chapman, 1984. Pp. 117.
        Reflections on the connection between mothering and reconciliation and on analogies from experience that can lead to calling God Mother. "Finding God in Motherhood: Release or

Trap?" *New Blackfriars* 65 (1984): 372-84, extends the discussion, with a critical review by Mary Pepper and a reply from Hebblethwaite.

928   Lewis, Alan E., ed. *The Motherhood of God*. Edinburgh: Saint Andrew, 1984. Pp. 71.
A controversial report to the Church of Scotland by a study group that was itself divided over the appropriateness of addressing God as Mother.

929   Oddie, William. *What Will Happen to God? Feminism and the Reconstruction of Christian Belief*. London: SPCK, 1984. Pp. 159.
A sharp attack on feminist theology that tends to see it as only one thing, bringing with it a "new imperialism."

930   Storkey, Elaine. *What's Right with Feminism*. London: SPCK, 1985. Pp. 186.
Attempts to establish the case for a biblically Christian feminism as an alternative to secular feminist and more liberal Christian responses.

931   Strachan, Elspeth and Gordon. *Freeing the Feminine*. Dunbar: Labarum, 1985. Pp. 208.
Reflections on the dominance of masculine attitudes, images, and structures in church and society.

932   Hampson, Daphne. "The Challenge of Feminism to Christianity," *Theology* 88 (1985): 341-50.
_____. "Women, Ordination, and the Christian Church," in *Speaking of Faith*, ed. Diana Eck and Devaki Jain. New Delhi: Kali for Women, 1986. Pp. 129-38.
_____ and Ruether, Rosemary Radford. "Is There a Place for Feminists in a Christian Church?" *New Blackfriars* 68 (1987): 7-24.
_____. *Theology and Feminism*. Oxford: Blackwell, 1990. Pp. 188.
A series of articulations of a post-Christian feminism based on the conviction that Christianity is a historical religion bound to

a sexist past. The dialogue with Ruether pursues the question
of whether one can be both a feminist and a Christian.

933   Tanner, Mary. *Christian Feminism: A Challenge to the
       Churches*. Loughborough, 1986. Pp. 14.
       Loades, Ann. *Searching for Lost Coins: Explorations in
       Christianity and Feminism*. London: SPCK, 1987. Pp.
       118.
       Hayter, Mary. *The New Eve in Christ: The Use and Abuse of
       the Bible in the Debate about Women in the Church*. Lon-
       don: SPCK, 1987. Pp. 190.
       Furlong, Monica, ed. *Mirror to the Church: Reflections on
       Sexism*. London: SPCK, 1988. Pp. 135.
       These four volumes from the latter 1980s, while exploring
       challenges to theology and church, build on the possibilities for
       Christianity that can draw upon the perspective of women's
       experience.

934   Grey, Mary. *Redeeming the Dream: Feminism, Redemption,
       and Christian Tradition*. London: SPCK, 1989. Pp. 209.
       Hannaford, Robert. "Women and the Human Paradigm," *New
       Blackfriars* 70 (1989): 226-33.
       Say, Elizabeth A. *Evidence on Her Own Behalf: Women's
       Narrative as Theological Voice*. Savage, MD: Rowman &
       Littlefield, 1990. Pp. 151.
       Fortune-Wood, Janet. "The Relationship between Christology
       and the Position of Women in the Church of England from
       a Feminist Theological Perspective." Ph.D., Exeter, 1991.
       Pp. 467.
       Further feminist explorations into specific theological ques-
       tions. Grey takes up issues of redemption and atonement;
       Hannaford is concerned with human nature; Say looks for
       narratives that genuinely reflect women's experience, finding
       these in novels as a form of moral argument; and Fortune-
       Wood argues that a christology informed by feminist theology
       could create a more inclusive understanding of the church.

935   Graham, Elaine and Walton, Heather. "Fiddling While Rome
       Burns: Feminism, Theology and Theological Education,"

British Journal of Theological Education 3:2 (Spring 1990):
12-17.
A conversation about the impact of feminist theology on theological education.

Church of England

936   Foss, David. "M.O.W. Then: The Church of England and the
       Ordination of Women before 1939," *CR* 335 (Christmas
       1986): 11-21.
       On the tentative beginnings of the proposal for ordination of
       women after 1914, with a review of the arguments offered on
       each side.

937   Bellamy, V. Nelle. "Participation of Women in the Public
       Life of the Church from Lambeth Conference, 1867-1978,"
       HMPEC 51 (1982): 81-98 [also in *Triumph over Silence*, pp.
       229-60].
       Examines Lambeth resolutions on the role of women and
       discusses the activities of women in leadership positions in the
       Church of England and the Episcopal Church in the United
       States.

938   Welsby, Paul A. *A History of the Church of England, 1945-
       1980.* New York: Oxford, 1984. Pp. 300.
       A largely institutional focus; the discussion of women in the
       Church centers on the ordination question in the 1960s and
       1970s.

939   *The Lambeth Conferences (1867-1948).* The Reports of the
       1920, 1930, and 1948 conferences with Selected Resolutions
       from the Conferences of 1867, 1878, 1897, and 1908. Lon-
       don: SPCK, 1948. Pp. 303.
       The 1920 and 1930 Conferences are especially important for
       questions of the ministry of women, with 1920 somewhat
       encouraging and 1930 limiting ministry to that of the deacon-
       ess.

940   *Women in the Church.* London: Church Assembly, 1948. Pp.

12.
An account of the record of the Central Council for Women's
Church Work from 1930 to 1948.

941   Marshall, H. S., ed. *Pastoralia for Women*. London: SPCK,
       1934. Pp. 154.
       Seven essays on aspects of church work available to women,
       following the limitations imposed by the 1930 Lambeth Con-
       ference, such as social work, teaching, youth work, and evan-
       gelization.

942   Rogers, M. I. *The Ministry of Women*. London: SPCK,
       1939. Pp. 16.
       Discusses opportunities for lay work and as deaconess, but
       also strongly complains against the exclusion of women from
       the priesthood.

943   *Women's Work in the Church*. Being the Report of a Com-
       mittee Appointed by the Archbishops of Canterbury and York
       in 1942. London: Church Assembly, 1943. Pp. 40.
       Contends that the Church should give women positions of
       comparable responsibility and leadership as are available in
       social, professional, and civil services.

944   Ady, Cecilia M. *The Role of Women in the Church*. London:
       Church Assembly, 1948. Pp. 86.
       An effort to show that there are many opportunities for wom-
       en's service in the Church.

945   Roxburgh, Margaret J. *Women's Work in the Church of Eng-
       land*. London: Anglican Group for the Ordination of Women,
       1958. Pp. 27.
       A brief review of a century of activity and discussion.

946   Hall, M. Penelope and Howes, Ismene V. *The Church in
       Social Work: A Study of Moral Welfare Work Undertaken by
       the Church of England*. London: Routledge & Kegan Paul,
       1965. Pp. 306.
       From its beginnings as "rescue work" to Church-sponsored

welfare work, primarily done by women.

947   Baldwin, Joyce. *Women Likewise*. London: Falcon, 1973.
       Pp. 32.
       Reviews opportunities for ministries for women in the Church;
       intended as an encouragement to women, without being an
       argument for ordination.

948   Maitland, Sara. "A Case History of Structural Oppression," in
       All Are Called: Towards a Theology of the Laity, ed. Patrick
       Rodger and the Working Group of the General Synod Board of
       Education. London: CIO, 1985. Pp. 18-21.
       Notes the contradictions in the Church's consideration of
       women and urges attention to the need for full human dignity
       in the Church.

949   Dawson, Rosemary. *And All That Is Unseen: A New Look at
       Women's Work*. London: Church House, 1986. Pp. 62.
       This report of the Industrial and Economic Affairs Committee
       of the General Synod Board for Social Responsibility is a
       broad analysis of the details of women's work at the present,
       with a challenge to the Church to rethink its theology and
       reshape practice in light of this.

950   *"Servants of the Lord": Roles of Women and Men in the
       Church of England*. Report of a Working Group appointed by
       the Standing Committee of the General Synod of the Church of
       England. London: General Synod, 1986. Pp. 115.
       Attempts a factual analysis of the current situation across the
       full range of Church life, followed by recommendations for
       addressing issues of sexism and clericalism.

951   Fullalove, Brenda H. "The Ministry of Women in the Church
       of England, 1919-70: Studies in the Debates and Reports of
       the Convocations and of the Assembly." M. Phil., Man-
       chester, 1986. Pp. 435.
       _____. "Women's Ministry in the C of E (1919-70),"
       Modern Churchman n.s. 29:2 (1987): 35-44; 29:3 (1987):
       41-50.

Fullalove traces issues related women's work in the Church, as these were considered by its decision-making bodies, and concludes that the position of women in professional ministry did not change significantly in this period.

Ordination of Women in the Church of England: 1930 to 1960

This question began to be put with some vigor near the end of the suffrage debate. Though dampened considerably by the decision of the 1930 Lambeth Conference, advocates continued over the next thirty years to present their case; but the views of opponents seemed to carry more force. The character of the conversation is seen through the chronological presentation of materials:

952   *Women and Priesthood*. London: Longmans, Green, 1930. Pp. 38.
       A report to the Lambeth Conference by persons who cannot see any objection in principle to the ordination of women to the priesthood; it urges greater recognition of the ministry of women deacons and a statement that the exclusion of women from the priesthood is a disciplinary rule, not an expression of an inherent incapacity in womanhood.

953   Roberts, Ursula. "Women and Priesthood," *Nineteenth Century* 108 (1930): 236-42.
       _____. "Women and Lambeth," *Contemporary Review* 139 (1931): 336-42.
       Roberts, Ursula and Cecil, Lord Hugh. "The Ordination of Women to the Priesthood," *Church Quarterly Review* 117 (1933): 1-24.
       Roberts argues that priesthood is a human function, not to be limited to males, and urges taking the teachings of Jesus regarding those to be his followers. In a debate with her view, Cecil claims that the Bible and the history of the church consistently exclude women from the priesthood, and he emphasizes the differences between men and women as affecting "their whole nature" (23).

954   Acres, E. Louie. *Some Questions and Answers Concerning
       Women and Priesthood.* London: Allenson, [1931]. Pp. 96.
       Takes up the arguments of those opposed to ordination of
       women and refutes them.

955   Underhill, Evelyn. "The Ideals of the Ministry of Women," in
       Mixed Pasture. London: Methuen, 1933. Pp. 113-22.
       Mackenzie, Kenneth D. *Women and the Liturgical Ministry.*
       London: Mowbray, 1934. Pp. 43.
       Two arguments that appeal to Catholic order and the special
       character of women's ministry to object to ordination of wom-
       en.

956   *The Ministry of Women.* Report of the Archbishops' Com-
       mission, 1935. London: Church Assembly, 1935. Pp. 90.
       Although not favoring admission to the priesthood for women,
       this report recommends enlarging opportunities for deaconesses
       and lay women workers.

957   Williams, N. P. "Deaconesses and 'Holy Orders'," (1938), in
       N. P. Williams, ed. E. W. Kemp. London: SPCK, 1954. Pp.
       185-201.
       Contends that deaconesses are not in "holy orders" because
       that has to do with the conduct of public worship; for women
       to do this is against the mind of the church and the laws of
       nature, Williams contends.

958   Smythe, P. R. *The Ordination of Women.* London: Skeffing-
       ton, 1939. Pp. 240.
       A theological approach to the question, concluding with a case
       in favor; contains a good bibliography on the discussion of the
       issue since 1910.

959   Acres, E. Louie. "The Chung Hua Sheng Kung Hui and the
       Ministry of Women," *IRM* 28 (1939): 116-23.
       Paton, David M. "Chinese Deaconess," *Theology* 31 (1978):
       263-71.
       On the Chinese Anglican case. Acres wonders if the mission
       field could be a guide in the question of the ministry of women

and notes that Chinese responses to a survey support the admission of women to full orders; Paton recounts the story of the ordination of the deaconess Lei Tim-oi by Bishop Ronald Hall to the priesthood in 1944 and the debate that followed.

960   Riley, Harold. *Can Women Be Ordained?* London: CLA, 1946. Pp. 12.

Kirk, Kenneth E. "The Ordination of Women," (1948), in *Beauty and Bands and Other Papers.* London: Hodder and Stoughton, 1955. Pp. 177-88.

Lewis, C. S. "Priestesses in the Church?" (1948), in *Undeceptions*, ed. Walter Hooper. London: G. Bles, 1971. Pp. 191-96.

The Chinese case sparked new discussion, with these opponents appealing to the need for order and headship and asserting the need for a male priesthood to speak on behalf of God.

961   Howard, Robert W. *Should Women Be Priests?* Oxford: Blackwell, 1949. Pp. 49.

Three sermons before the University of Oxford exploring history and recent policy and considering fears expressed by opponents; Howard urges an end to fears and a move to permit ordination of women.

962   Bailey, Sherwin. "Women and the Church's Lay Ministry," *Theology* 57 (1954): 322-30.

Thrall, M. E. "The Ordination of Women to the Priesthood," *ibid.*: 330-35.

Correspondence follows in succeeding issues, November 1954-March 1955.

_____. *The Ordination of Women to the Priesthood: A Study of the Biblical Evidence.* London: SCM, 1958. Pp. 115.

In companion articles Bailey argues for a model of partnership rather than subordination, and Thrall takes a biblical approach to claim that "the Christian priesthood should be representative of redeemed humanity, of a priestly people consisting of both men and women" (334); Thrall's monograph takes the same theme to greater theological analysis.

963   Blomfield, F. Cruttwell. *Wonderful Order*. London: SPCK, 1955. Pp. 43.
      Appeals to a universal hierarchal order, complete with both unity and distinction in the vocation of men and women, with priesthood being the vocation of men.

964   Lace, O. Jessie. *The Ordination of Women to the Historic Ministry of the Church*. London: Anglican Group for the Ordination of Women to the Historic Ministry of the Church, 1958. Pp. 14.
      Women and Holy Orders. London: Anglican Group for the Ordination of Women to the Historic Ministry of the Church, n.d. Pp. 16.
      Mascall, E. L. *Women in the Priesthood of the Church*. London: Church Union, 1958. Pp. 39.
      The beginnings of the pamphlet war for the mind of the Church, supported by organizations on either side of the issue; the first two offer arguments in favor, and the third presents arguments against.

Ordination of Women in the Church of England: Since 1960

      Around 1960 the character of the discussion began to shift, with more active interest by Church assemblies in the issue and a greater willingness to re-think the entire question. Again, the development can be seen in a basic chronological presentation of the publications:

965   *The Ordination of Women*. London: Society for the Ministry of Women in the Church, 1961. Pp. 8.
      An introduction to the question, showing the lines of discussion in several denominations.

966   Howard, Christian. "The Ordination of Women," in *Living in Faith: A Call to the Church*, ed. Kathleen Jones. Oxford: Oxford, 1980. Pp. 109-20.
      A brief narrative of the history of the debate from 1962 to 1978, with the views of each side presented.

967   *Gender and Ministry.* A Report Prepared for the Church
      Assembly by the Central Advisory Council and for the Minis-
      try. London: CIO, 1962. Pp. 31.
      Urges a full re-consideration of women's ministry in view of
      changes in society and the needs of the Church.

968   *Women and Holy Orders.* Report of a Commission appointed
      by the Archbishops of Canterbury and York. London: CIO,
      1966. Pp. 134.
      From the 1962 Church Assembly, a report of evidence and
      arguments on the question, not to advise the Church on what
      to do. The cases both for and against are presented, as well as
      that of a third view, that no theological argument against ordi-
      nation is conclusive, but that other reasons relating to church
      union, tradition, and potential controversy are sufficient to
      continue present practice.

969   *Women & Holy Orders.* London: Anglican Group for the
      Ordination of Women to the Historic Ministry of the Church,
      1966. Pp. 16.
      Takes up traditional objections as well as the more recent ones
      in the third view and offers refutations of each.

970   *Women in Ministry: A Study.* Report of the Working Party Set
      Up Jointly by the Ministry Committee of the Advisory Council
      for the Church's Ministry and the Council for Women's Minis-
      try in the Church. London: CIO, 1968. Pp. 75.
      A report on how the Church of England currently uses women
      in its total ministry.

971   *Women and the Ordained Ministry: A Report.* Anglican-
      Methodist Commission on Women and Holy Orders. London:
      SPCK, 1968. Pp. 14.
      Studies how the issue affects re-union discussions going on at
      the time, e.g., if the Methodist Church did ordain women and
      the Church of England would not.

972   *The Present and the Future—Women's Ministry in the Church
      of England.* London: Anglican Group for the Ordination of

Women to the Historic Ministry of the Church, 1972. Pp. 30.
The report of a one-day conference, considering the current
situation and potential next steps in the discussion.

973 *The Ordination of Women to the Priesthood.* A Consultative
Document Presented by the Advisory Council for the Church's
Ministry. Oxford: Church Army, 1972. Pp. 87.
Recognizing fundamental disagreements and strong feelings on
each side, the report nonetheless concludes that it is time for
full and open consideration of the issue.

974 *Report of the Lambeth Conference, 1978.* London: CIO,
1978. Pp. 127.
The first such Conference after the American Episcopal
Church's ordinations of women; its resolutions on the question
recognize member churches' autonomy and affirm commitment
to the unity of the Anglican Communion.

975 *The Ordination of Women to the Priesthood: A Second Report
by the House of Bishops.* London: General Synod of the
Church of England, 1988. Pp. 140.
Characterizes the conversation over the previous decade and
considers four central issues: priesthood and the representation
of God in Christ, the question of headship, ecumenical implications, and sources of authority. Three parties in the Church
are noted: supporters, opponents, and those who believe that
ordination of women to the priesthood is not opportune at this
time.

976 Chapman, Jennifer. *The Last Bastion: Women Priests—The
Case For and Against.* London: Methuen, 1989. Pp. 166.
Chapman's interviews with people on both sides provide the
basis of the narrative.

977 Field-Bibb, Jacqueline S. *Women Towards Priesthood: Ministerial Politics and Feminist Praxis.* Cambridge: Cambridge,
1991. Pp. 369.
A study in the relation between sexuality, self identity, and
institution, as the issue of ordination of women is debated in

three English churches: Methodist, Anglican, and Roman Catholic.

A. Arguments against the Ordination of Women

978   Arguments from both the Catholic and Evangelical wings of the Church are included in the following materials, much of it part of the pamphlet war:

Richardson, Alan. "Women and the Priesthood," in *Lambeth Essays on Ministry* (for Lambeth Conference 1968), ed. Archbishop of Canterbury. London: SPCK, 1969. Pp. 75-78.

Flockton, Sue. *Why Not Ordain Women?* London: CLA, 1972. Pp. 5.

Mascall, Eric. *Women Priests?* London: CLA, 1972. Pp. 26.

Dicken, Hélène. *Women and the Apostolic Ministry.* London: CLA, n.d. Pp. 9.

Bruce, Michael and Duffield, G. E., eds. *Why Not? Priesthood and the Ministry of Women.* Abingdon: Marcham, 1972. Pp. 144. Ten essays.

Saward, John. *The Case against the Ordination of Women.* London: CLA, 1972. Pp. 20.

_____. *Christ and His Bride.* London: CLA, 1977. Pp. 16.

Women in the Priesthood? Reflections of a Group of Theologians. London: CLA, 1973. Pp. 14.

Newman, Maurice. *The Apostolate, the Ministry, and the Sexes.* London: CLA, 1974. Pp. 17.

Brett, Winifred and Watson, Vera. *Women Priests Impossible?* London: L.A.L., n.d. [c. 1974]. Pp. 19.

Carter, Douglas. *Debating the Ordination of Women.* London: CLA, 1974. Pp. 8.

Demant, V. A. *Why the Christian Priesthood Is Male.* London: CLA, 1977. Pp. 21 [first appeared as a supplementary essay in *Women and Holy Orders*, 1966].

Moore, Peter, ed. *Man, Woman, and Priesthood.* London: SPCK, 1978. Pp. 181. [Nine essays]

Powell, Douglas. *The Ordination of Women and the End of*

Man. London: CLA, 1978. Pp. 45.

Rowell, Geoffrey. "Anglican Anxieties: The Ministry of the Church and the Ordination of Women," *Contemporary Review* 249 (1986): 178-83.

Vasey, Michael. "Ordaining Women—Can We Do Better?" *Anvil* 4:1 (1987): 23-37.

Round, W. D. "Does the Priesthood Exclude Womanhood?" *Churchman* 102 (1988): 30-43.

Baker, Tony. "Men, Women, and the Presbyterate: Does Scripture Speak Clearly?" *Churchman* 104 (1990): 43-50.

B. Arguments on Behalf of the Ordination of Women

979   Edwards, Ruth B. *The Case for Women's Ministry*. London: SPCK: 1989. Pp. 230.
       A study of biblical foundations together with historical and contemporary discussion of the issue.

980   Lampe, G. W. H. "Church Tradition and the Ordination of Women," *Expository Times* 76 (1964-65): 123-25.
       _____. *The Church's Tradition and the Question of the Ordination of Women*. London: Anglican Group, 1967. Pp. 10.
       _____. "Women and the Ministry of Priesthood," in *Explorations in Theology*. London: SCM, 1981. Pp. 89-102.
       Hodgson, Leonard. "Theological Objections to the Ordination of Women," *Expository Times* 77 (1965-66): 210-13.
       _____. *Theological Objections to the Admission of Women to Holy Orders*. London: Anglican Group, 1967. Pp. 11.
       Arguments from two of the leading proponents in the 1960s.

981   Craston, Colin, et al. *Evangelicals and the Ordination of Women*. Bramcote, Notts.: Grove, 1973. Pp. 30.
       Three essays that illustrate the differences among Evangelicals on the question.

982   Willis, Eirene. "Women Priests: A Risk Too Dangerous to Take?" *Theology* 78 (1975): 370-76.
       Considers two concerns: tensions in life that a priest is called

to carry, and the relation between continuity and change in doctrine. Willis assumes that women priests would exercise their vocation "through their feminine nature" (372); her answer to her question is "no, but . . . ."

983   Wilson, Harold, ed. *Women Priests? Yes—Now!* London: Denholm House, 1975. Pp. 96.

Montefiore, Hugh, ed. *Yes to Women Priests.* London: Mayhew McCrimmon, 1978. Pp. 88.

Eight essays in the first and six in the second, exploring a number of arguments and topics.

984   Hampson, Daphne. *Let Us Think about Women.* N.P.: Group for the Ministry of Women in the Scottish Episcopal Church, 1979. Pp. 18.

Speller, Lydia. *Theological Objections?* London: MOW, 1980. Pp. 12.

Howard, Christian. *Women in Society and the Church.* London: MOW, 1981. Pp. 15.

Sr. Teresa. *Anglican/Orthodox Relations and the Ordination of Women.* London: MOW, 1981. Pp. 14.

Phipps, Simon. *Priesthood and Humankind.* London: MOW, 1982. Pp. 12.

Carey, George. *Women and Authority in the Church—A Scriptural Perspective.* London: MOW, 1983. Pp. 10.

Short tracts with arguments supporting ordination of women.

985   Howard, Christian. *The Ordination of Women to the Priesthood: Further Report.* London: CIO, 1984. Pp. 122.

A guide to the debate in the years since the 1978 Lambeth Conference.

986   Thompson, Ross. "Male and Female in Christ's Priestly Dance," *Theology* 87 (1984): 95-101.

Newsom, G. H. "The Ordination of Women," *ibid.*: 180-85.

Badham, Linda. "The Irrationality of the Case against Ordaining Women," *Modern Churchman* n.s. 27 (1984): 13-22.

Baker, John Austin. "Eucharistic Presidency and Women's

Ordination," *Theology* 88 (1985): 350-57.

Craston, Colin. *Biblical Headship and the Ordination of Women*. Nottingham: Grove, 1986. Pp. 21.

Several perspectives from the mid-1980s, indicating increased confidence in the arguments in support of ordination.

987   McClatchey, Diana. "Take a Long and Steady Look: Reflections on the Consequences of Ordaining Women," in *The Reality of God*, ed. James Butterworth. London: Severn House, 1986. Pp. 139-47.

Considers three practical issues: ecumenical relations, repercussions in the Church of England, and the character of the priesthood itself.

988   "Women in the Ordained Ministry," *St. Mark's Review* 125 (March 1986): 1-58.

A single issue of the Australian journal, with seven articles.

989   Wilson, W. Gilbert. *Why No Women Priests?* Worthing: Churchman Publishing, 1988. Pp. 169.

Peberdy, Alyson, ed. *Women Priests?* Basingstoke: Marshall Pickering, 1988. Pp. 84.

Two engagements with the Roman Catholic position on the issue.

990   Langley, Myrtle S. "One Baptism, One Ministry: The Ordination of Women and the Unity in Christ," *Transformation* 6:2 (1989): 27-31.

Walker, David. "Are Opponents of Women Priests Sexists?" *Churchman* 105 (1991): 326-31.

Theological argumentation, this time from the nature of church and ministry.

C. Debates

Some examples of efforts at direct engagement of issues are:

991   Craston, Colin. "The Case for the Ordination of Women: Reasons for Acting Now," *Churchman* 92 (1978): 296-309.

Wenham, Gordon. "The Ordination of Women: Why Is It So

Divisive?" *ibid.*: 310-19.

992   Cressey, Martin. "The Ordination of Women: Theological
       and Biblical Issues," *Epworth Review* 10:3 (1983): 56-66.
       Leonard, Graham. "The Ordination of Women: Theological
       and Biblical Issues," *ibid.* 11:1 (1984): 42-49.
       Dyson, Anthony. "Dr. Leonard on the Ordination of Women:
       A Response," *Theology* 87 (March 1984): 87-95.

Anglican Religious Orders

993   *Guide to the Religious Communities of the Anglican Commu-
       nion.* 1951: London: Mowbray, 1955. Pp. 140.
       A Directory of the Religious Life. 1943; London: SPCK,
       1957.
       Resources issued by the Advisory Council of Religious Com-
       munities offer information on communities, discussion of the
       religious life, explanation of governance, and the like.

994   Individual biographical and autobiographical works include:
       *Fulfilled in Joy: The Order of the Holy Paraclete, Whitby, and
       Its Foundress Mother Margaret.* By a Foundation Member.
       London: Hodder and Stoughton, 1964. Pp. 158.
       Sister Janet. *Mother Maribel of Wantage.* London: SPCK,
       1973. Pp. 92.
       Howard-Bennett, Rosemary. *I Choose the Cloister.* London:
       Hodder and Stoughton, 1956. Pp. 125.
       Pinions. *Wind on the Sand: The Story of a 20th Century
       Anchoress.* London: SPCK, 1980. Pp. 80.

Anglican Deaconesses

995   The step prior to the approval of ordination of women to the
       priesthood was the dramatic change in the understanding and
       function of the office of deacon as it applied to women. The
       nineteenth-century recovery of the office of deaconess contin-
       ued into the twentieth century and was vigorously defended
       despite its limited appeal to Anglican women. The history and
       constitution of the office is recounted in:

Panton, Ethel and Batho, Dorothy. *The Order of Deaconesses Past and Present*. London: SCM, 1937. Pp. 62.

Deaconesses in the Church of England. London: Church Assembly, 1946. Pp. 8.

The Order of Deaconesses. London: Church Assembly, 1948. Pp. 32.

996   *Deacons in the Church*. London: CIO, 1974. Pp. 37.

The Ministry of Deacons and Deaconesses. London: CIO, 1977. Pp. 27.

Deacons in the Ministry of the Church. Report to the House of Bishops of the General Synod of the Church of England. London: Church House, 1988. Pp. 144.

Deacons Now. London: Church House, 1990. Pp. 97.

Several questions considered from the 1960s and leading to major change in the office can be seen in these documents. With renewed emphasis on lay ministry, does the church require deacons? If not, what would happen to deaconesses? The 1977 report rejects the negative judgment of the 1974 document and raises the possibilities of a "permanent diaconate," that is, an office that is not merely a step toward priesthood. After 1986 women were permitted to become deacons, and within three years there were some one thousand women in this office.

997   Childs, D. G. "Deaconesses in the Church in Wales," *Province* 12 (1961): 95-98.

A brief history of developments in Wales.

998   Swensson, Gerd, ed. *The Churches and the Diaconate in the Ecumenical and International Perspective*. Uppsala, 1985. Pp. 442.

A comprehensive collection, with six essays on the British situation.

999   Aldridge, Alan. "In the Absence of the Minister: Structures of Subordination in the Role of Deaconess in the Church of England," *Sociology* 21 (1987): 377-92.

_____. "Discourse on Women in the Clerical Profession:

The Diaconate and Language-Games in the Church of England," *Sociology* 26 (1992): 45-57.
These articles explore issues of frustration and subordination in this transitional decade.

1000   Autobiographical narratives by deaconesses include:
        Willetts, Phoebe. *Sharing a Vision*. Cambridge: J. Clarke, 1978. Pp. 116.
        Cundiff, Margaret. *Called to Be Me*. London: Triangle, 1982. Pp. 107.

Roman Catholicism

1001   Hornsby-Smith, Michael P. *Roman Catholics in England: Studies in Social Structure since the Second World War*. New York: Cambridge, 1987. Pp. 253.
        This broad study includes discussion of women's roles in the Church and the small but growing feminist critique in the 1980s.

1002   Ryan, Majorie. *Yesterday Recalled: A Jubilee History of the Catholic Women's League, 1906-81*. London, 1981. Pp. 34.
        Parnell, Nancy Stewart. *A Venture in Faith: A History of St. Joan's Social and Political Alliance, Formerly the Catholic Women's Suffrage Society, 1911-1961*. London, 1961. Pp. 18.
        Brief institutional histories of organizations that began in advocacy of women's suffrage.

1003   Hartley, Olga. *Women and the Catholic Church, Yesterday and To-Day*. London: Burns Oates & Washbourne, 1935. Pp. 262.
        Hartley's broad historical survey argues that the Catholic tradition has safeguarded and encouraged women.

1004   Anson, Peter F. *The Religious Orders and Congregations of Great Britain and Ireland*. Worcester: Stanbrook Abbey, 1949. Pp. 413.

Organized alphabetically; women's communities are presented in pp. 152-413.

1005   Benedictines of Stanbrook. *In a Great Tradition.* London: J. Murray, 1956. Pp. 313.
A history of the order, with special attention to the leadership of Dame Laurentia McLachlan (1866-1953), abbess from 1931 to her death.

1006   Corrigan, D. Felicitas. *The Nun, the Infidel, and the Superman.* London: J. Murray, 1985. Pp. 152.
On the relationships via correspondence of Dame Laurentia with Sydney Cockerell, Bernard Shaw, and others.

1007   Bernstein, Marcella. *Nuns.* London: Collins, 1976. Pp. 361.
A journalist surveys the religious life, with special interest in the changes occurring since the 1960s.

1008   Campbell-Jones, Suzanne. *In Habit: An Anthropological Study of Working Nuns.* London: Faber & Faber, 1979. Pp. 229.
A sympathetic investigation of two contemporary communities, a Franciscan and a teaching congregation, focusing on how each responded to the sweeping changes in religious life since 1960; the one that had to make the more limited break with its past made the easier transition to the more open post-Vatican II world, Campbell-Jones concludes.

1009   Williams, Drid. "The Brides of Christ," in *Perceiving Women*, ed. Shirley Ardener. London: Malaby, 1975. Pp. 105-25.
Studies a community of Discalced Carmelites in Britain, its daily life, space and time, and vows.

1010   *Why Can't a Woman Be More Like a Man?* London: Laity Commission, 1981. Pp. 30.
Pratt, Ianthe. "Women and the Church," in *The Church Now: An Inquiry into the Present State of the Catholic Church in Britain and Ireland*, ed. John Cumming and Paul Burns. Dublin: Gill and Macmillan, 1980. Pp. 135-45.
The Way 16:1 (1976): "Woman." Six essays, pp. 3-56.

The Way 26:2 (1986): "Woman." Five essays, pp. 91-144.
Contemporary discussions of the role of women in the Church,
issues for theology and spirituality, and other questions.

1011   Hannon, Sister Vincent Emmanuel, S.U.S.C. *The Question of*
Women and the Priesthood. London: Geoffrey Chapman,
1967. Pp. 141.
Wijngaards, John. *Did Christ Rule Out Women Priests?*
1977; Great Wakering: McCrimmon, 1986. Pp. 108.
Lakeland, Paul. *Can Women Be Priests?* Dublin: Mercier,
1975. Pp. 77.
Hill, Christopher. "The Ordination of Women in the Context
of Anglican/Roman Catholic Dialogue," *Month* 253 (1992):
6-13.
Some English Catholic considerations of this question.

1012   Biographical and autobiographical accounts include:
Segar, Mary G. T. *Margaret Fletcher, 1862-1943: Artist and*
Pioneer, Founder of the Catholic Women's League. Lon-
don: Catholic Truth Society, 1945. Pp. 20.
Corbishley, Thomas. *The Life of Reverend Mother M. Cecilia*
Marshall IBVM. London: St. George's, 1969. Pp. 160.
Baldwin, Monica. *I Leap over the Wall: A Return to the*
World after Twenty-eight Years in a Convent. London: H.
Hamilton, 1949. Pp. 308.

Roman Catholicism in Ireland

1013   Despite the significant role of the Church in Irish life, only a
limited number of studies have appeared on implications for
women of the Church's involvement in politics and culture;
some of these include:
O'Dowd, Liam. "Church, State, and Women: The Aftermath
of Partition," in *Gender in Irish Society*, pp. 3-36.
Rudd, Joy. "Invisible Exports: The Emigration of Irish Wom-
en This Century," *WSIF* 11 (1988): 307-11.
Porter, Mary Cornelia and Venning, Corey. "Catholicism and
Women's Role in Italy and Ireland," in *Women in the*
World, ed. Lynne B. Iglitzin and Ruth Ross. Santa Barba-

ra: Clio, 1976. Pp. 81-103.

Flanagan, Donal. "The More Subtle Discrimination," *Studies* 64 (1975): 231-42.

Randall, Vicky and Smith, Ailbhe. "Bishops and Bailiwicks: Obstacles to Women's Political Participation in Ireland," *Economic and Social Review* 18 (1987): 189-214.

_____. "The Politics of Abortion in Ireland," in *The New Politics of Abortion*, ed. Joni Lovenduski and Joyce Outshoorn. London: Sage, 1986. Pp. 67-85.

Compton, Paul A., et al. "Religion and Legal Abortion in Northern Ireland," *Journal of Biosocial Science* 6 (1974): 493-500.

1014 For explorations of religious issues, images, and competing spiritualities, see:

Beale, Jenny. *Women in Ireland: Voices of Change.* Bloomington: Indiana, 1987. Pp. 164-83.

Kolbenschlag, Madonna. "Women and the Future of Irish Catholicism," *Christian Century* (April 18, 1984): 401-404.

MacCurtain, Margaret. "Towards an Appraisal of the Religious Image of Women," *Crane Bag* 4:1 (1980): 26-30 [also in *The Crane Bag Book of Irish Studies (1977-1981)*, ed. Richard Kearney and Mark Hederman (Dublin, 1982), pp. 539-43].

_____. "Moving Statues and Irishwomen," *Studies* 76 (1987): 139-47.

_____. "Fullness of Life: Defining Female Spirituality in Twentieth-Century Ireland," in *Women Surviving*, pp. 232-63.

Suenens, L. J. *Edel Quinn, Envoy of the Legion of Mary to Africa.* Dublin: Fallon, 1954. Pp. 272.

1015 One journal, *Doctrine and Life*, has included a number of articles exploring feminist issues: see Joan Doyle Griffith, "When God Is Woman, Too," 39 (1989): 181-86; Kathleen Coyle, S.S.C., "Tradition, Theology, and Women," 40 (1990): 72-84; Vera Price, "A Feminist Looks at Catholic Social Teaching," 41 (1991): 123-29; Paul O'Leary, O.P., "The Church and Feminism," 41 (1991): 362-70; and Ruth

Harnett, C.P., "Collaborative Pastoral Ministry Today," 42 (1992): 84-91.

Free Churches

1016   National Free Church Women's Council. *Fifty Years: A Survey of the Work of the National Free Church Women's Council, 1907-1957.* London, 1957. Pp. 23.
A brief review.

1017   Brake, G. T. *Policy and Politics in British Methodism, 1932-1982.* London: Edsal, 1984. Pp. 314-28.
Davies, Rupert E. "The Ordination of Women in Methodism: A Personal Account," *PWHS* 48 (1992): 105-12.
The story of Methodist consideration of women in ministry, from the union in 1932 to final approval of women's ordination in 1974.

1018   *Towards Cooperation. A Record of the Service of the Women's Committee to the Congregational Union of England and Wales.* London: Independent, 1966. Pp. 24.
A summary of work from its founding in 1915 to dissolution in 1966.

1019   Kaye, Elaine. "Constance Coltman—A Forgotten Pioneer," *JURCHS* 4:2 (1988): 134-46.
_____. "A Turning-point in the Ministry of Women: The Ordination of the First Woman to the Christian Ministry in England in September 1917," in *Women in the Church*, pp. 505-12.
Coltman's life (1889-1969) and ministry prompt interest also in the work of other early twentieth-century pioneers of women's ministry.

1020   Ashton, Helen. "Women's Ministry in the United Reformed Church," *Modern Churchman* 32:3 (1990): 1-31.
Discusses a survey of Provincial Moderators, representative churches, and women ministers; regarding differences in ministries, Ashton suggests that marital status rather than gender is

more significant.

1021 Among English Baptists, issues related to women have been most visible in the *Baptist Quarterly*; see Violet Hedger, "Some Experiences of a Woman Minister," 10 (1940-41): 243-53; L. G. Champion, "The Ministerial Service of Women," 20 (1964): 201-205; Edward C. Lehman, Jr., "Reactions to Women in Ministry: A Survey of English Baptist Church Members," 31 (1986): 302-20; Shirley Dex, "The Church's Response to Sexism," 31 (1986): 320-25; Margaret Jarman, "Attitudes to Women in Baptist Churches in the Mid-1980s," 31 (1986): 326-30; Ruth Matthews, "God, Women, and Men: Language and Imagery," 31 (1986): 331-34; Carol McCarthy, "Ordained and Female," 31 (1986): 334-36; Diana Tidball, "Walking a Tightrope: Women Training for Baptist Ministry," 33 (1990): 388-95; Karen E. Smith, "Beyond Public and Private Spheres: Another Look at Women in Baptist History and Historiography," 34 (1991): 79-87; and Paul R. Dekar, "Muriel Lester, 1883-1968: A Baptist Saint?" 34 (1992): 337-45.

1022 Croft, Joy, et al., eds. *Growing Together*. London: Essex Hall, [1984]. Unpag.
A report of the Unitarian Party on Feminist Theology to the denomination's General Assembly; includes a history of the denomination in relation to women and a list of the thirty-eight women ministers who have served from 1905 to 1984.

1023 *The Place of Women in the Society of Friends*. London: Committee on Christian Relationships, 1950. Pp. 15.
Quaker Women's Group. *Bringing the Invisible into the Light: Some Quaker Feminists Speak of Their Experience*. London: Quaker Home Service, 1986. Pp. 103.
Considerations of the role of women in contemporary Quaker life.

1024 Hough, James, ed. *The Christian Life—Lived Experimentally: An Anthology of the Writings of Kathleen Lonsdale*. London: Friends Home Service Committee, 1976. Pp. 59.
Lonsdale (1903-71) was a scientist and prolific author, active

in the Quaker witness for peace.

Judaism

1025 Cantor, Aviva, ed. *The Jewish Woman, 1900-1985: A Bibli-
      ography*. Fresh Meadows, NY: Biblio, 1987. Pp. 193.
      Ruud, Inger Marie. *Women and Judaism: A Selected Anno-
      tated Bibliography*. New York: Garland, 1988. Pp. 232.
      Each bibliography has a much larger focus, but includes a few
      relevant entries.

1026 Loewe, Raphael. *The Position of Women in Judaism*. Lon-
      don: SPCK, 1966. Pp. 63.
      Originally produced in response to a request from the Anglican
      Commission considering the question of women and holy
      orders; Loewe reflects on the potential relevance of the view
      of women in Judaism in a secular age.

1027 Navé-Levinson, Pnina, et al. "Women and Judaism," *Euro-
      pean Judaism* 15:2 (1981): 25-35.
      Six brief reflections on the struggle for rights as full religious
      partners with men, three on their experiences as rabbis.

1028 Shulman, Sheila. "A Radical Feminist Perspective on Juda-
      ism," *European Judaism* 21:1 (1987): 10-18.
      On the experience of otherness as a Jewish woman.

1029 Neuberger, Julia. "Women in Judaism: The Fact and the
      Fiction," in *Women's Religious Experience*, pp. 132-42.
      Discusses the impact of tradition on the status of women,
      together with the responses of Reform and Liberal commu-
      nities to this question.

1030 Webber, Jonathan. "Between Law and Custom: Women's
      Experience of Judaism," in *Women's Religious Experience*, pp.
      143-62.
      Considers the interaction between tradition and social change.

1031 Cromer, Gerald. "Intermarriage and Communal Survival in a

London Suburb," *Jewish Journal of Sociology* 16 (1974): 155-69.
Argues that "the family, for better or worse, still holds the key to Jewish survival" (167).

1032   Cowan, Evelyn. *Spring Remembered: A Scottish-Jewish Child-hood*. Edinburgh: Southside, 1974. Pp. 160.
Reflections from childhood, to 1932.

Spiritualism

1033   Skultans, Vieda. "A Study of Women's Ideas Relating to Traditional Feminine Roles, Spiritualism, and Reproductive Functions." Ph.D., Swansea, 1971. Pp. 243.
_____. *Intimacy and Ritual: A Study of Spiritualism, Mediums, and Groups*. London: Routledge & Kegan Paul, 1974. Pp. 106.
Studies contemporary spiritualism in a Welsh city, where 80% of the members are women, but men make up 50% of the mediums and 90% of the healers; argues in the dissertation that ritual helps women to accept a traditional feminine role which they frequently find frustrating and difficult.

Missions

1034   Barr, Pat. *The Dust in the Balance: British Women in India, 1905-1945*. London: Hamish Hamilton, 1989. Pp. 186.
Chapter 5 considers medical missions and the work of women doctors and nurses.

1035   Webb, Pauline Mary. *Women of Our Company*. London: Cargate, 1958. Pp. 148.
_____. *Women of Our Time*. London: Cargate, 1963. Pp. 132.
Stories about Methodist women in overseas missions.

1036   Thompson, Phyllis. *Gladys Aylward: A London Sparrow*. 1971; Crowborough, E. Sussex: Highland, 1984. Pp. 190 [also published as *A Transparent Woman: The Compelling*

Story of Gladys Aylward (Grand Rapids: Zondervan, 1971)].

Burgess, Alan. *The Small Woman*. London: Evans, 1957. Pp. 221.

Aylward was missionary to China (1932-49) and Taiwan (1957-70).

1037   Ashley, Audrey. *Peace-Making in South Africa: The Life and Work of Dorothy Maud*. Bognor Regis: New Horizon, 1980. Pp. 141.
Maud (1894-1977) was a missionary and member of an Anglican religious community.

1038   Burgess, Alan. *Daylight Must Come: The Story of Dr. Helen Roseveare*. London: Michael Joseph, 1975. Pp. 279.
Roseveare worked as a medical missionary to the Congo from 1953.

1039   For some autobiographical accounts, see:
Stanfield, John and May. *From Manchu to Mao*. Ed. Margaret Thom. London: Epworth, 1980. Pp. 114.
Church, Elisabeth. *Jubilant My Feet*. Evesham: Arthur James, 1980. Pp. 153.
Goldsmith, Elizabeth. *God Can Be Trusted*. 1974; Eastbourne: STL, 1984. Pp. 202.

Wives of Ministers

1040   Keable, Gladys, ed. *Such As We Are: Parsons' Wives and Parsons' Families*. London: Darton, Longman & Todd, 1967. Pp. 160.
Several articles offer candid reflections on expectations, stereotypes, finances, and other topics.

1041   Thomson, D. P., ed. *The Minister's Wife—Her Life, Work & Problems*. Crieff: St. Ninian's, 1964. Pp. 52.
The report of a 1964 conference on the subject.

1042   Spedding, Janet V. "Wives of the Clergy: A Sociological

Analysis of Wives of Ministers of Religion in Four Denominations." Ph.D., Bradford, 1975. Pp. 635.

Finch, Janet. "Devising Conventional Performances: The Case of Clergymen's Wives," *Sociological Review* n.s. 28 (1980): 851-70.

_____. *Married to the Job: Incorporation in Men's Work.* London: Allen & Unwin, 1983. Pp. 182.

Data gathered from interviews across several denominations in Bradford; the latter work incorporates this material into a larger framework, considering constraints, identities, and options for career and other activities.

1043 Freestone, Dora. *An Ideal Minister's Wife.* London: Stockwell, 1932. Pp. 12.
Practical, period advice on how to be one.

1044 Arnott, Anne. *Wife to the Archbishop.* London: Mowbray, 1976. Pp. 161.
A biography of Jean Coggan.

1045 Autobiographical narratives include:
Hicks, Kathleen Nugent. *From Rock to Tower: Memories with Reflections.* London: Macdonald, 1947. Pp. 284.
Jarvis, Kathleen. *The Impressions of a Parson's Wife.* London: Mowbray, 1951. Pp. 95.
_____. *More Impressions of a Parson's Wife.* London: Mowbray, 1957. Pp. 85.
Williams, Cicely. *Bishop's Wife—But Still Myself.* London: Allen & Unwin, 1961. Pp. 226.
_____. *Diary of a Decade: More Memoirs of a Bishop's Wife.* London: Allen & Unwin, 1970. Pp. 256.

Sexuality, Marriage, and Divorce

1046 *Sex and Morality.* A Report to the British Council of Churches. London: SCM, 1966. Pp. 77.
Moss, Rachel, ed. *God's Yes to Sexuality.* Glasgow: Collins, 1981. Pp. 189.
Two reports for the BCC, with the second responding to a

broader range of issues than the first had done.

1047   *Putting Asunder: A Divorce Law for Contemporary Society.*
       London: SPCK, 1966. Pp. 172.
       Marriage, Divorce and the Church. London: SPCK, 1971.
       Pp. 166.
       Marriage and the Church's Task. London: CIO, 1978. Pp.
       183.
       Marriage and the Doctrine of the Church of England. Lon-
       don: House of Bishops' Marriage Education Panel, 1985.
       Pp. 109.
       An Honourable Estate. London: Church House, 1988. Pp.
       100.
       A series of reports, position papers, and proposals for the
       Church of England; issues considered include proposals for
       changes in the law, the question of remarriage of divorced
       persons in the church, and the impact of social change upon
       the church.

1048   Winnett, Arthur R. *Divorce and Remarriage in Anglicanism.*
       London: Macmillan, 1958. Pp. 284.
       _____. *The Church and Divorce.* London: Mowbray,
       1968. Pp. 110.
       The first is a history of the teaching and practice of the Church
       of England on the question of the indissolubility of marriage
       from the Reformation to the mid-twentieth century. Winnett
       notes that two themes have been present almost from the be-
       ginning, the principle of indissolubility and a view that permits
       divorce; although the Church adopted the former view, the
       latter has also had strong support over the centuries. The
       second volume deals with issues from the intervening decade
       and concludes with a call for reconsideration of the Church's
       position on divorce.

1049   Borrowdale, Anne. *Distorted Images: Christian Attitudes to
       Women, Men and Sex.* London: SPCK, 1991. Pp. 152.
       Some issues considered are sexual harassment, pornography,
       and sexual violence, with some proposals for the church in
       addressing these "distorted images."

1050 Wilkinson, Alan. "Three Sexual Issues," *Theology* 91 (1988): 122-31.
A review of issues facing the Church of England in the early twentieth century (participation of women in the government of Church and State, the marriage service in the 1928 Prayer Book, and contraception) to learn what criteria and authorities it uses in its process of consideration.

1051 Campbell, Flann. "Birth Control and the Christian Churches," *Population Studies* 14 (November 1960): 131-47.
Looks at the history of Christian attitudes to birth control, focusing on changes in the early twentieth century.

1052 Nash, Daphne. "Women's Liberation and Christian Marriage," *New Blackfriars* 53 (1972): 196-205.
Urges Christians to develop alternative forms of community beyond the nuclear family.

1053 *New Dimensions.* The Report of the Bishop of Willesden's Commission on the Objects and Policy of the Mothers' Union. London: SPCK, 1972. Pp. 303.
One issue receiving considerable attention in this report is the breadth of the organization's membership standards, specifically, whether divorced and re-married persons would be accepted.

1054 Williamson, Joseph. *In Honour Bound.* London: N.p., 1971. Pp. 95.
On the Church's continuing work with prostitutes, using the activities of Josephine Butler as model and inspiration.

Women, Ritual, and Symbol

1055 Hoch-Smith, Judith and Spring, Anita, eds. *Women in Ritual and Symbolic Roles.* New York: Plenum, 1978.
Two relevant essays in this collection: Ruth Borker's "To Honor Her Head: Hats as a Symbol of Women's Position in Three Evangelical Churches in Edinburgh, Scotland," pp. 55-73, investigates biblical core meanings emerging from mem-

bers' attitudes, such as subordination, modesty, and formality; and Daniel N. Maltz's "The Bride of Christ Is Filled with His Spirit," pp. 27-44, explores female imagery as interpreted in Pentecostal churches in Edinburgh, suggesting that church members are encouraged to view their spiritual bond to Christ from a female point of view.

1056   McDonald, Merryle. "Rituals of Motherhood among Gujarati Women in East London," in *Hinduism in Great Britain: The Perpetuation of Religion in an Alien Cultural Milieu*, ed. Richard Burghart. London: Tavistock, 1987. Pp. 50-66.
A consideration of rituals of pregnancy and childbirth, organized by women and performed in the home.

Women and War

1057   Where studies of this topic have religious dimensions, they are usually found in considerations of the pacifist movement; for some examples, see:
Mitchell, David. *Monstrous Regiment: The Story of the Women of the First World War*. New York: Macmillan, 1965. Pp. 400 [published in England as *Women on the Warpath*, 1966].
Ceadel, Martin. *Pacifism in Britain, 1914-1945: The Defining of a Faith*. Oxford: Oxford, 1980. Pp. 342.
Oldfield, Sybil. *Women Against the Iron Fist: Alternatives to Militarism, 1900-1989*. Oxford: Blackwell, 1989. Pp. 224.
Byles, Joan Montgomery. "Women's Experience of World War One: Suffragists, Pacifists, and Poets," *WSIF* 8 (1985): 473-87.
Hughes, William R. *Sophia Sturge: A Memoir*. London: Allen and Unwin, 1940. Pp. 188.

Individuals

1058   *Evangeline Booth (1865-1950)*
P. W. Wilson's *General Evangeline Booth of the Salvation Army* (New York: Scribner's, 1948) is the only biography of the Fourth General (1934-39).

1059   *Catherine Booth-Clibborn (1858-1955)*
On the Salvation Army's evangelist in France and Switzerland, see Carolyn Scott, *The Heavenly Witch: The Story of The Maréchale* (London: H. Hamilton, 1981); earlier and more heroic accounts include James A. Stewart, *The General's Daughter* (Lansdale, PA: Revival Literature, 1968) and James Strahan, *The Maréchale* (London: J. Clarke, 1914).

1060   *Catherine Bramwell-Booth (1883-1987)*
Mary Batchelor's *Catherine Bramwell-Booth* (Tring: Lion, 1986) is a recent biography of the first grandchild of the Salvation Army founders.

1061   *Vera Brittain (1893-1970)*
The religious interests of this important writer are usually explored through the development of her pacifist views; see especially Muriel Mellown, "One Woman's Way to Peace: The Development of Vera Brittain's Pacifism," *Frontiers* 8:2 (1985): 1-6; Yvonne A. Bennett, "Vera Brittain and the Peace Pledge Union: Women and Peace," in *Women and Peace: Theoretical, Historical, and Practical Perspectives*, ed. Ruth Roach Pierson (London: Croom Helm, 1987), pp. 192-213; and Lynne Layton, "Vera Brittain's Testament(s)," in *Behind the Lines: Gender and the Two World Wars*, ed. Margaret R. Higonnet, et al. (New Haven: Yale, 1987), pp. 70-83.

1062   *Mother Maria (Lydia Gysi) (1912-77)*
Founder of a small Orthodox religious community, her life is presented in Sister Thekla, *Mother Maria: Her Life in Letters* (London: Darton, Longman & Todd, 1979).

1063   *Emily Hobhouse (1860-1926)*
Pacifist and missionary, her visit to Germany during the First World War created considerable controversy. Two biographical studies are John Fisher, *That Miss Hobhouse* (London: Secker & Warburg, 1971) and Anna Ruth Fry, *Emily Hobhouse* (London: J. Cape, 1929). The article by John V. Crangle and Joseph O. Baylen, "Emily Hobhouse's Peace Mission, 1916," *Journal of Contemporary History* 14 (1979): 731-44,

takes up the critical event in the context of her sense of vocation as a humanitarian.

1064   *Lily H. Montagu (1873-1963)*
        Montagu was the founder of the Jewish Religious Union in
        England and a key figure in the establishment of the World
        Union for Progressive Judaism in 1926. Ellen M.
        Umansky's *Lily Montagu and the Advancement of Liberal Judaism: From
        Vision to Vocation* (New York: Edwin Mellen, 1983), "The
        Origins of Liberal Judaism in England: The Contribution of
        Lily H. Montagu," *Hebrew Union College Annual* 55 (1984):
        309-22, and "Women in Judaism: From the Reform Movement
        to Contemporary Jewish Religious Feminism," in *Women of
        Spirit*, pp. 333-54, provide insights into her work. See also
        Steven Bayme, "Claude Montefiore, Lily Montague, and the
        Origins of the Jewish Religious Union," *TJHSE* 27 (1978-80):
        61-71.

1065   *A. Maude Royden (1876-1956)*
        Royden was an active suffragist, a prominent preacher after
        World War I, and a prolific writer on issues relating to women
        and the church; the first extensive work on her is Sheila
        Fletcher's *Maude Royden: A Life* (Oxford: Blackwell, 1989).
        One dissertation is Beverly James Mosley, "Rhetorical Strategies
        for Women in the Church: A Study of the Rhetoric of
        Maude Royden" (Ph.D., Pittsburgh, 1990). Short portraits by
        contemporaries are included in Albert Clare, *The City Temple,
        1640-1940* (London: Independent, 1940), pp. 189-93; and
        Janet E. Courtney, *The Women of My Time* (London: Lovat
        Dickson, 1934), pp. 206-12.

1066   *Dorothy L. Sayers (1893-1957)*
        Best known as a mystery writer, Sayers was also a religious
        dramatist and theological apologist. Because of the many
        works by and about her, the following reference works will be
        helpful: Ruth Tanis Youngberg, ed., *Dorothy L. Sayers, A
        Reference Guide* (Boston: G. K. Hall, 1982); Colleen B. Gilbert,
        ed., *A Bibliography of the Works of Dorothy L. Sayers*
        (Hamden, CT: Archon, 1978); and Robert B. Harmon and

Margaret A. Burger, eds., *An Annotated Guide to the Works of Dorothy L. Sayers* (New York: Garland, 1977). Among the more recent literary studies and biographies, see Mitzi Brunsdale, *Dorothy L. Sayers: Solving the Mystery of Wickedness* (Oxford: Berg, 1990); Catherine Kenny, *The Remarkable Case of Dorothy L. Sayers* (Kent, OH: Kent State, 1990); James Brabazon, *Dorothy L. Sayers: A Biography* (New York: Scribner, 1981); Mary Brian Durkin, *Dorothy L. Sayers* (Boston: Twayne, 1980); Nancy M. Tischler, *Dorothy L. Sayers, A Pilgrim Soul* (Atlanta: John Knox, 1980); Ralph E. Hone, *Dorothy Sayers: A Literary Biography* (Kent, OH: Kent State, 1979); Alzina Stone Dale, *Maker and Craftsman: The Story of Dorothy L. Sayers* (Grand Rapids: Eerdmans, 1978); Janet Hitchman, *Such a Strange Lady: A Biography of Dorothy L. Sayers* (New York: Harper and Row, 1975); and Barbara Reynolds, *The Passionate Intellect: Dorothy L. Sayers' Encounter with Dante* (Kent, OH: Kent State, 1989). Several essays in Margaret P. Hannay's *As Her Whimsey Took Her: Critical Essays on the Work of Dorothy L. Sayers* (Kent, OH: Kent State, 1979), deal with religious and theological topics; see also Hannay's "'Through the World Like a Flame': Christology in the Dramas of Dorothy L. Sayers," *Vox Benedictina* 2 (1985): 148-66.

1067   *Margaret "Stevie" Smith (1902-71)*
Smith was a poet and novelist fascinated by the beauty of religion but disillusioned by Christianity. Some biographical and literary studies include Sanford Sternlicht, *Stevie Smith* (Boston: Twayne, 1990); Jack Barbera and William McBrien, *Stevie: A Biography of Stevie Smith* (London: Heinemann, 1985); Frances Spalding, *Stevie Smith: A Critical Biography* (London: Faber and Faber, 1988); and Michael Tatham, "That One Must Speak Lightly," in *In Search of Stevie Smith*, ed. Sanford Sternlicht (Syracuse: Syracuse, 1991), pp. 132-46 [an earlier version appeared in *New Blackfriars* 53 (1972): 318-27].

1068   *Muriel Spark (1918-)*
Religious themes are prominent in Spark's novels. Some

studies include Ruth Whittaker, *The Faith and Fiction of Muriel Spark* (New York: St. Martin's, 1982); Rodney Stenning Edgecombe, *Vocation and Identity in the Fiction of Muriel Spark* (Columbia: Missouri, 1990); Jennifer Lynn Randisi, *On Her Way Rejoicing: The Fiction of Muriel Spark* (Washington: Catholic Univ. of America, 1991); Peter Kemp, *Muriel Spark* (London: Elek, 1974); and Allan Massie, "Calvinism and Catholicism in Muriel Spark," in *Muriel Spark: An Odd Capacity for Vision*, ed. Alan Bold (London: Vision, 1984), pp. 94-107.

1069   *Evelyn Underhill (1875-1941)*
Underhill is best known for writings that explore the mystical tradition; attracted to Roman Catholicism as a young adult, she was deterred by the Modernist crisis in 1907 and later settled as an Anglican, with Anglo-Catholic sympathies, conducting numerous spiritual retreats.   For a reference work, see Dana Greene, "Bibliography of Works About and By Evelyn Underhill," *Bulletin of Bibliography* 45 (1988): 92-107; Greene has also written *Evelyn Underhill: Artist of the Infinite Life* (New York: Crossroad, 1990); "Evelyn Underhill and Her Response to War," *HMPEC* 55 (1986): 127-35; and "Toward an Evaluation of the Thought of Evelyn Underhill," *History of European Ideas* 8 (1987): 549-62.   Additional studies include Margaret Cropper, *Life of Evelyn Underhill* (New York: Harper, 1958); Christopher J. R. Armstrong, *Evelyn Underhill (1875-1941): An Introduction to Her Life and Writings* (Oxford: Mowbray, 1975); and Michael Ramsey and A. M. Allchin, *Evelyn Underhill: Two Centenary Essays* (Oxford: SLG, 1977).   For relevant articles, see Kevin Hogan, "The Experience of Reality: Evelyn Underhill and Religious Pluralism," *Anglican Theological Review* 74 (1992): 334-47; Terry Tastard, "Divine Presence and Human Freedom: The Spirituality of Evelyn Underhill Reconsidered," *Theology* 94 (1991): 426-32; A. Elizabeth Dalgaard, "The Churching of Evelyn Underhill," *Arc* 17:1 (1989): 43-54; and Henry Bodgener, "Evelyn Underhill: Spiritual Director to Her Generation," *London Quarterly and Holborn Review* 183 (1958): 45-50.

1070 *Maisie Ward (1889-1975)*
Widely influential as a religious publisher with her husband, Ward helped to introduce contemporary Catholic intellectuals to a wider audience; her *Unfinished Business* (London: Sheed and Ward, 1964), while an autobiography, contains reflections on Catholic life in the twentieth century from one of its most prominent lay members. Brief studies of her life and work include Debra Campbell, "The Gleanings of a Laywoman's Ministry: Maisie Ward as Preacher, Publisher, and Social Activist," *Month* (Aug/Sept 1987): 313-17 [also in *Records of the American Catholic Historical Society of Philadelphia* 98 (1987): 21-28]; and Moureen Coulter, "'A Terrific Bond': The Spiritual Friendship of Caryll Houselander and Maisie Ward," *Downside Review* 107 (1989): 106-18.

1071 *Beatrice Webb (1858-1943)*
Webb's presence in this listing is as one who rejected orthodox religion and became a convert to "the religion of socialism." Some studies that probe these dimensions of her life are Carole Seymour-Jones, *Beatrice Webb: A Life* (Chicago: Dee, 1992); Deborah Epstein Nord, *The Apprenticeship of Beatrice Webb* (Amherst: Massachusetts, 1985), and "Beatrice Webb and the Affirmation of Progress: The Writing of *My Apprenticeship*," *Prose Studies* 3 (1980): 254-70; Kitty Muggeridge and Ruth Adam, *Beatrice Webb: A Life, 1858-1943* (London: Secker and Warburg, 1967); Gertrude Himmelfarb, "The Webbs: The Religion of Socialism," in *Marriage and Morals Among the Victorians* (New York: Knopf, 1986), pp. 192-209; Barbara Caine, "Beatrice Webb and the 'Woman Question'," *History Workshop* 14 (Autumn 1982): 23-43; and Shirley R. Letwin, *The Pursuit of Certainty* (Cambridge: Cambridge, 1965), Part IV.

1072 *Mary Whitehouse (1910-)*
A contemporary moral reformer, Whitehouse began a campaign in the 1960s against what she perceived as the damage to morals in the media; her own work, *A Most Dangerous Woman?* (Tring: Lion, 1982), recounts this activity. Michael Tracey and David Morrison's *Whitehouse* (London: Macmillan, 1979) is the only biography.

INDEX OF AUTHORS AND EDITORS
(numbers refer to text entries)

INDEX OF COLLECTIONS
WITH MULTIPLE ENTRIES
(the number identifies the first entry)

ABOUT THE AUTHOR

Dale Johnson is professor of church history in the Divinity School of Vanderbilt University, Nashville, Tennessee. He is a graduate of Colgate University, Oxford University, the Lutheran School of Theology at Chicago, and Union Theological Seminary (New York). He has also published *Women in English Religion, 1700-1925* (Edwin Mellen Press, 1983), a collection of documents on the subject.

Johnson, Dale A., 1936-
Women and religion in
Britain and Ireland : an
annotated bibliography from
the Reformation to 1993

Dover Memorial Library
Gardner-Webb University
P.O. Box 836
Boiling Springs, N.C. 28017

FOR REFERENCE
Not to be taken from library
GARDNER-WEBB UNIVERSITY LIBRARY